Star Trek,
History and Us

Also by A.J. Black

*Myth-Building in Modern Media:
The Role of the Mytharc
in Imagined Worlds* (McFarland, 2020)

Star Trek, History and Us

Reflections of the Present and Past Throughout the Franchise

A. J. BLACK

McFarland & Company, Inc., Publishers
Jefferson, North Carolina

LIBRARY OF CONGRESS CATALOGUING-IN-PUBLICATION DATA

Names: Black, A. J., 1982– author.
Title: Star trek, history and us : reflections of the present and past throughout the franchise / A. J. Black.
Description: Jefferson, North Carolina : McFarland & Company, Inc., Publishers, 2021 | Includes bibliographical references and index.
Identifiers: LCCN 2021008595 | ISBN 9781476681696 (paperback : acid free paper) ∞
 ISBN 9781476643229 (ebook)
Subjects: LCSH: Roddenberry, Gene—Political and social views. | Star Trek television programs—History and criticism. | National characteristics, American, on television. | Exceptionalism—United States.
Classification: LCC PN1992.8.S74 B53 2021 | DDC 791.45/75—dc23
LC record available at https://lccn.loc.gov/2021008595

BRITISH LIBRARY CATALOGUING DATA ARE AVAILABLE

ISBN (print) 978-1-4766-8169-6
ISBN (ebook) 978-1-4766-4322-9

© 2021 A. J. Black. All rights reserved

No part of this book may be reproduced or transmitted in any form or by any means, electronic or mechanical, including photocopying or recording, or by any information storage and retrieval system, without permission in writing from the publisher.

Front cover images © 2021 Shutterstock

Printed in the United States of America

McFarland & Company, Inc., Publishers
 Box 611, Jefferson, North Carolina 28640
 www.mcfarlandpub.com

For Gene
Thank you for imagining a better future

Acknowledgments

Thank you to my ever-supportive wife, Steph, my friends, my family, and my mother, who never made me feel silly as a child watching *Star Trek*, science fiction and worlds of imagination.

My thanks to author Duncan Barrett, with whom I created a podcast in 2017 which served as the chief inspiration for this book. I also thank publisher C. Bryan Jones for supporting that podcast on his network, Trek FM.

And thank you to everyone involved in *Star Trek* since the beginning. It makes a difference.

Table of Contents

Acknowledgments vi

Preface: A Primitive Culture 1

1. The 1960s 5

2. The 1970s and 1980s 43

3. The 1990s 78

4. The 21st Century (So Far) 115

Epilogue: Getting from Here to There 155

Chapter Notes 161

Bibliography 181

Index 185

Preface:
A Primitive Culture

When *Star Trek* premiered on September 8, 1966, few truly understood the impact the show would have, not just on television or science-fiction storytelling, but on American society and culture as a whole.

Gene Roddenberry, the show's creator, famously envisaged what has become known as *The Original Series* as "Wagon Train to the Stars," a reference to the well-known and prolific Western TV series which had aired from 1957 to 1964.[1] Roddenberry's pitch, a crew made up of humans from nations that had put aside their cultural and social differences by the 23rd century and explored the galaxy in a starship named the *Enterprise*, was the ultimate frontier story. Only this time rather than trailblazing American pioneers panning for gold or oil, his was a humanistic vision of a unified Earth seeking out new life and new civilizations and, so goes the legend in the opening credits, to "boldly go where no man has gone before."

In this, *Star Trek* was revelatory.

Following "The Cage," a 1965 pilot episode which failed to quite nail the alchemy of the concept,[2] the episode that aired in the fall of 1966 featured a heroic, dashing white American troubadour in charge.[3] Surrounding William Shatner's Captain James T. Kirk, all working together without any hint of animus, were a Japanese-American helmsman in George Takei's Sulu, James Doohan's cantankerous but resourceful Scottish engineer Scotty, and Nichelle Nichols' beautiful and highly adept communications officer Uhura, a woman of African American descent. Perhaps most astonishingly, even more than a woman of color on the bridge, by the second season Walter Koenig joined the main ensemble as Chekov, a Russian security officer.

From a cultural perspective, between 1966 and 1969, when *Star Trek* was ignominiously cancelled after its third season, the representation of

Preface

both women and Black people as part of an intrepid crew in an idealized, peaceful, progressive future for mankind, not to mention the idea of Russians and Americans having torn down their historic ideological conflict that had raged for over two decades, was a powerful message for NBC to broadcast. It suggested that *Star Trek* was not going to be another throwaway piece of entertainment with a fanciful setting and concept. In truth, Roddenberry from the outset had envisaged *Star Trek* as a canvas on which to paint all kinds of allegory and reflect our world from a social, political and cultural perspective. He explained, "[By creating] a new world with new rules, I could make statements about sex, religion, Vietnam, politics, and intercontinental missiles. Indeed, we did make them on *Star Trek*: we were sending messages and fortunately they all got by the network."[4]

This was not the first-time science-fiction had endeavored to talk about our world through the lens of the fantastical. *The Twilight Zone* preceded *Star Trek* by half a decade, with Rod Serling's anthological series from 1959 telling a range of strange, terrifying and fascinating parables, morality plays, cautionary tales and allegorical, symbolic stories which have resonated through the decades with as much power as *Star Trek* itself. Roddenberry in many ways picked up Serling's baton, as did *The Outer Limits*, which concluded in 1965 just before *Star Trek*'s debut.

The reason *Star Trek* sparked such imagination and lingered so profoundly in the American, and ultimately global cultural consciousness, is that it managed to balance operating as a reflection of society while simultaneously performing as an adventure series with elements of comedy, romance, suspense and the colorful 1960s exuberance audiences were seeing at much the same time weekly in shows such as *Batman* or *Lost in Space*. The 1960s, at the height of Western counter-culture, may have been the spiritual birthplace of on-screen allegory, certainly on television, but it was equally the center of high-concept entertainment, which saw the creation of some of the small screen's most memorable characters.

Over five decades on, the Vulcan science officer and second in command, Spock, remains one of the singular iconic creations in not just the history of *Star Trek*, but the history of 20th century television. His most recent incarnation was a key part of the second season of *Star Trek: Discovery*, a show with an enormous level of nostalgia where the 1960s origin of the franchise is concerned. Spock has resonated through three different incarnations because he operates as the eternal "outsider"; half-human, half-alien (much like the Doctor in *Doctor Who*), Spock's journey to understanding human behavior and emotion has been replicated in almost every single *Star Trek* series to date through numerous characters of a similar disposition. Via his questioning and reflection, we, through *Star Trek*, are gifted the opportunity to understand ourselves and try to unpick the human experience.

It is quite apt that *Star Trek: The Motion Picture*, which ten years after the end of *The Original Series* brought the crew of the USS *Enterprise* to the big screen, ended with the legend "the human adventure is just beginning…." In that ensuing decade, *Star Trek* had developed the first true "fandom" of rabid supporters who attended conventions across the country and lobbied hard for the series to return. Viewers had become invested in the crew of the *Enterprise* beyond the initial (curtailed) five year mission, and while *The Original Series* films, starring the original TV cast, were designed more as big screen spectacle than to be the same morality plays of the increasingly distant 1960s, they nonetheless touched on subjects that spoke to where we were as a species: climate change and whale hunting in *The Voyage Home*; our relationship with religion in *The Final Frontier*; the end of the Cold War in *The Undiscovered Country*, and so on. *Star Trek* could shoot for spectacle and still entertain the masses on a broad canvas while reflecting who we were as people.

The fact that *Star Trek*'s cinematic success sparked arguably its most successful television generation, from 1987 through to 2005, added to the accepted truth that *Star Trek* remained, as a franchise, a powerful cultural mirror.

Before his death in 1991, Gene Roddenberry launched *The Next Generation*, set almost a century after the day of Kirk and Spock, with a new *Enterprise* and a new crew, only with the more progressive mission of boldly going where "no one," not just "no man," had gone before. *The Next Generation* did not just have a multi-ethnic, multi-gender, multi-national cast and crew, it further explored humanity's relationship with the alien, the Other, and more acutely attacked political and social issues which reflected modern America and beyond, while at the same time growing increasingly obsessed with the post-war paradigm of the Western world and particularly the legacy of that conflict. The same could be said for the subsequent 24th century spinoff series *Deep Space Nine* and *Voyager*, and later prequel *Enterprise*, set in the 22nd century.

Midway through the 2000s, it appeared that the need for *Star Trek*, however, was on the wane. *Enterprise* collapsed steadily in the ratings across four seasons, resulting in it being the first *Star Trek* show to be cancelled since *The Original Series*. It was cancelled at the point that many felt it had begun to hit its stride and, coincidentally, during a season marked

Preface

by tapping a groundswell of franchise nostalgia that worked to plug gaps within *Star Trek* canon and continuity. Did people need *Star Trek* as a tool of reflection anymore? Had we learned all we could from Gene Roddenberry's vision of the future?

When the franchise rebooted in 2009, it leaned heavily on nostalgia whilst propelling the saga forward. J.J. Abrams' *Star Trek*, the costliest cinematic entry for the franchise in its history, used time travel chicanery to reboot the adventures of *The Original Series* crew while remaining in line with the canon fans had held so dear for decades. Though angled heavily on the action adventure axis, Abrams' sequels *Into Darkness* and *Beyond*[5] attempted to find a balance between the escapism of the 1960s and the same awareness that *Star Trek* needed to speak to us about our world today. When CBS gained the rights to create a whole new TV series, which eventually became *Discovery*, that same balance was in evidence, as was the nostalgic gaze back to where the franchise first started. This continued with *Star Trek: Picard*, bringing back Sir Patrick Stewart as *The Next Generation*'s legendary *Enterprise* captain, and in doing so heavily exploiting fans' fond memories of the '80s and '90s era of the franchise.

Over the last half century, *Star Trek* has always maintained, throughout many iterations and incarnations, the same mission statement: to use the futuristic utopian ideal of the United Federation of Planets and *Star Trek*'s mission of discovery as a way for us to understand who we are, where we come from, and where we're going.

That is also the mission statement of this book: to explore the span of how *Star Trek* reflects the world we live in by examining how it has engaged with history and culture across the latter half of the 20th century; from how Roddenberry's experiences serving in World War II fuelled his aspirations as a storyteller and futurist, through to beyond his death and a post–9/11 world in which *Star Trek* is now re-defining itself in the early 21st century amid rapid social and political change. Can we reach the future promised by the Federation and Starfleet's mission to explore the universe, seeking out new life and new civilizations? Or are we destined never to learn from the messages *Star Trek* teaches us as human beings?

We are, as Deanna Troi opines under the influence in *First Contact*, a "primitive culture." We will explore in this book if, despite how *Star Trek* has mirrored our own development and progress over the latter half of the 20th century and into the 21st, we are likely to remain one.

1

The 1960s

Star Trek was born in a cauldron of uncertainty, battling on various fronts against the odds in the mid–1960s.

"The Cage" had not been embraced by NBC, the network allied with Desilu Studios to fund and broadcast *Star Trek*. They were less than enamored both with the cerebral concept in a TV landscape filled with both historical and present-day escapism, and of Jeffrey Hunter's restrained lead performance as Captain Christopher Pike.[1] At the time the show was created, science fiction was, as a genre, in a depression after an initial peak of schlocky interest during the 1950s. *Star Trek* committee founder Jacqueline Lichtenberg observes:

> At the time, the attitude of the general public in the U.S.A. prior to *Star Trek* was total rejection of science fiction as just for people who were completely out of touch with reality. Being in touch with reality was the litmus test for being trustworthy. Science-fiction readers were not respected, and the literature was viewed by English teachers as toxic to a student's development of good taste. The same was true on TV (and radio, for that matter). The writers, producers, and audience all agreed 'that' is nonsense. Of course, detective series, westerns, and others were admired even though they contained more fantasy than any science-fiction story.[2]

Gene Roddenberry, therefore, faced an uphill battle to convince the powers that be that *Star Trek* could be a hit with audiences and tell stories which went beyond the one-dimensional escapism of the adventure serial or the science-fiction B-picture, while reflecting the human condition and allowing audiences to understand the world around them and find context in their own experiences within the adventures of the USS *Enterprise*.

> I recalled that when Jonathan Swift was writing *Gulliver's Travels*, he wanted to write satire on his time and went to Lilliput in his story to do just that, and then he could talk about insane prime ministers and crooked kings and all of that. It was sort of this wonderful thing. Children could read it as a fairy tale, an adventure, and as they got older, they'd recognize it for what it really is. It seemed to me that perhaps if I wanted to talk about sex, religion, politics, make some comments against Vietnam, and so on, that if I had similar situations involving these subjects

Star Trek, History and Us

happening on other planets to little green people, indeed it might get by, and it did. It apparently went right over the censors' heads, but all the fourteen-year-olds in our audience knew exactly what we were talking about. The power you have is in a show like *Star Trek*, which is considered by many people to be a frothy little action-adventure; unimportant, unbelievable, and yet watched by a lot of people. You just slip ideas into it.[3]

It is fair to say that ideas, for all they sometimes worked and sometimes did not, were in no short supply on *Star Trek*. Roddenberry placated a jittery network with a fairly unprecedented second pilot episode, "Where No Man Has Gone Before," which introduced the primary cast of Captain James T. Kirk, Doctor Leonard McCoy, Sulu, Scotty and Uhura, all new to the series after "The Cage" bar the retained Leonard Nimoy as Spock,[4] and provided NBC with a story of God-like beings and galactic barriers which tilted as heavily on the action-adventure axis as it did the thought-provoking spectrum. Roddenberry was buoyed by a team of skilled writers, including script editor Gene L. Coon and writers boasting towering intellects such as Harlan Ellison and Theodore Sturgeon, to mold a series unlike anything that, frankly, had gone before.

Thomas Doherty considers *Star Trek* to be reflective of the defining aspect of American psychology: the frontier.

> It's not our Puritan past, but how the frontier is always rehabilitating and nurturing and re-establishing the American traits of individualism and freedom. It's the frontier which makes us Americans, and we have to have initiative and inventiveness and youth and strength and canniness to survive on the frontier—and also, we also have to kill the Indians. "Space, the final frontier" is really manifest destiny.[5]

This sense of American exceptionalism permeates *Star Trek*, which would become known in subsequent decades as *The Original Series*, with Kirk representing the idealized American commander leading a multi-ethnic crew into the unknown. Doherty adds how *Star Trek* very much establishes a confidence, even arrogance, about America's place in displaying to the rest of the world, nay the galaxy, this idealized model.

> The show is sort of both modest enough to respect the indigenous aliens of off-worlds, but at the same time, we know in the end we have to show them how to do things and our values are better. It has the arrogance of American exceptionalism, even though we say we have the non-interference prime directive, but basically we're going into these places and showing them "how to live right," which is very American, too.[6]

1. The 1960s

Yet while *Star Trek* became a television series and movie franchise synonymous with peace and scientific discovery, it was a progressive concept born of war. *Star Trek* emerged as a pioneer within a decade in which television had truly risen from the ashes of the biggest conflict in human history—World War II. America had rushed to the defense of Great Britain and Western democracy in the fight against Adolf Hitler's Axis war machine, curtailed one of the most heinous genocides of the last two millennia and defeated the forces of fascism, a conflict which cost millions of lives across the globe. The entire planet would be forever changed, physically and existentially, by a cataclysmic war that the surviving nations steadily worked hard to ensure would—could—never again come to pass. The name of Roddenberry's iconic Federation starship was born out of this conflict.[7]

A key part of this new world order, the post-war paradigm of United Nations and so-called "Cold War" between the last two dominant superpowers—the United States and the Soviet Union—was a capitalist boom across the recovering 1950s into a brighter, slicker, sexier 1960s. A post-war generation grew up in an America of renewed optimism, if under a figurative "Sword of Damocles" in the ever-present nuclear threat posed by a bullish Russian politburo, and by the 1960s the haunting specter of war began, slowly and surely, fading away. The so-called "nuclear family" could enjoy rising prosperity, new technological innovations, and entertainment which confronted many of their existential, post-war fears about their present and what the future could hold.

Key within this transformation, one which included the rise of science-fiction and horror at the movies chiefly in the form of the "B-movie," was the advent of television's first "Golden Age" across the late 1940s and 1950s.

This was a decade that saw the rise of Lucille Ball as the dominant queen of the sitcom in *I Love Lucy* and ended with the arrival of Rod Serling's *The Twilight Zone*. It opened the floodgates for a swath of colorful television shows that pushed boundaries, with Serling's seminal show in particular helping to define the 1960s. Dr. Richard Kimble's weekly struggle for justice in *The Fugitive*, the Smith family *Lost in Space*, the weird paranoia of Number 6 trapped in "the Village" in *The Prisoner*, or the Caped Crusader and the Boy Wonder battling camp threats to Gotham City in the adaptation of the popular *Batman* comic series from DC, all encapsulated the era. They opened the doorway for *Star Trek*.

Roddenberry's 1960s series was a show steeped in idealism about humanity's future yet powerfully obsessed with the nature of religion and a fascination with warfare, particularly the ever present, Cold War shadow of the bomb. "Balance of Terror" cemented the Romulans as a Russian/Chinese allegory as the *Enterprise* played a pitched game of chicken in the manner of nuclear submarines in a tense face-off. "A Taste of Armageddon" places the *Enterprise* crew in the middle of a simulated war between two alien nations. Much like how "Balance of Terror" cemented the Romulans as a key ideological proxy against the "American" United Federation of Planets, the equally seminal "Errand of Mercy" brings the Klingons to bear as an aggressive Russian antagonist, seeking subjugation and control of a satellite state in the midst of a sustained, post-war tentative peace between two superpowers.

This is only across the first season of *Star Trek*, between 1966 and 1967, an era following the Cuban Missile Crisis of 1962, which brought America and Russia closer to nuclear confrontation than they would ever face during the entire Cold War. Tensions would begin to subside during the 1970s. The political mechanism of *detente* would infiltrate geopolitics, however nuclear anxiety and the fear of a new era of conflict remained prevalent in *The Original Series* and into the subsequent generation of *Star Trek*, as the franchise crossed a depressed '70s into a brighter 1980s marked by the neoliberal economic project spearheaded by the Reagan administration.

Balanced, however, alongside the constant push/pull of Cold War anxiety came what would be termed "counter-culture." America's protracted, ugly war in Vietnam, alongside numerous flash-points between white and black communities triggering the Civil Rights movement, not to mention increasingly relaxed social attitudes to sex, drugs and rock 'n' roll, contributed to the '60s as a powder keg of social and political change in American society. Episodes such as "A Private Little War" brought home the cost of the unwinnable proxy war in the Asian peninsula, while "City on the Edge of Forever" was favorable to anti-war sentiment with its ethical dilemma of letting a woman die who might have brought about the peace that prevented World War II, the Cold War, Vietnam, and all of the conflict the 20th century would deliver.

For a franchise devoted to the idea of peaceful exploration of the galactic frontier, of a future unified Earth pushing beyond the boundaries of tribalism, *Star Trek* has spent over five decades attempting to come to terms with man's inhumanity to man, its perpetual, recurrent state of warfare, and whether or not we have the capacity to look beyond conflict and chart a new course.

One man believed it was possible.

Without Gene Roddenberry's experiences in the conflict that defined

1. The 1960s

the 20th century, *Star Trek*'s vision and what it inspired might never have come to pass.

A Recurring Pattern of Force

While the main character in *Star Trek* was the dashing Captain James T. Kirk, and not the helmsman of the USS *Enterprise*, Lieutenant Sulu, Gene Roddenberry doubtless recognized himself as a man who existed in the midway point between leader and pilot, thanks to his experiences during World War II and beyond.

Gene Roddenberry was an original "flyboy."

During his youth growing up in El Paso, Texas, Roddenberry dreamed of worlds beyond his own, reading classic science-fiction tales such as Edgar Rice Burroughs' *John Carter of Mars*, Tarzan and E.E. Smith's *Skylark* series, dreams he carried through into gaining a pilot's license with the United States Army Air Corps and signing up as a second lieutenant. He was eventually posted to the 394th Bomb Squadron, 5th Bombardment Group, of the Thirteenth Air Force, a squadron which flew the Boeing B-17 Flying Fortress that Roddenberry would later pilot flying bombing missions over Guadalcanal in the Pacific Theater in the latter years of the war, while only in his early twenties. He was driven, in no small part, by the Japanese attack on Pearl Harbor that pulled America into the raging, global conflict.[8]

Though embroiled in the continued devastation of the war, Roddenberry already imagined more of a hopeful, idealistic future. This is clear in precisely how Sulu came to bear, an Asian man who piloted a representation of humanity's unified future. Roddenberry had every reason to distrust or even despise the Asian peninsula following Pearl Harbor and his involvement in military action in the South China Sea, but he intentionally created Sulu as a sign of peace in the wake of such trauma. George Takei recalls this genesis:

> He said my character would be representative of Asia. But he said he had some difficult times coming up with a name for my character because all Asian names are nationally specific. And the name Kim is specifically Korean. Wong is Chinese. Tanaka is Japanese. So, he was trying to find something that would suggest all of that part of the map. And so, he found to the west of the Philippines a sea called the Sulu Sea. And he thought, ah, the waters of the sea touch all shores, and that's how he came up with the name Sulu.[9]

Tragedy very swiftly came knocking to challenge Roddenberry's idealistic dreaming during his days as a pilot, however. He suffered two distinct events that would mark both his life and career, not to mention influence several episodes of both *Star Trek* and *Star Trek: The Next Generation* during his lifetime.

As a bomber in 394th squadron, on August 2, 1943, in Guadalcanal, Roddenberry would be flying recon as a "first louie,"[10] an otherwise relatively dull 800-mile observation mission, when the B-17 he was piloting suffered a seized brake[11] and failed to pull up for takeoff, running off the runway into the jungle and crushing the bomber's front nose. Though Roddenberry was far from responsible, two fellow pilots died in the accident, and it was not his only brush with the death of fellow "flyboys."

After leaving the military following the end of World War II, Roddenberry became a commercial pilot for Pan Am, the trend-setting company for whom in June 1947 he co-piloted the launch of the Clipper America, the latest model Lockheed Constellation. Engine damage rattled them over the Middle East, but while flying across the Syrian desert, fire broke out on the left wing and the plane crashed violently in the dead of night. The captain and 14 others died tragic, horrific deaths as a result of the accident, and Roddenberry was, for the second time, lucky to escape with his life. Only his move to comfort a passenger as the plane plunged toward the ground ended up saving his life. The experience had a profound effect on his psychology, particularly from a theological perspective:

> As we were coming down, and death was absolutely certain, I was thinking all sorts of things—should I scratch a message to my wife on the metal side of the plane? What was I going to say—"I love you?" She already knew that. I thought maybe I just ought to pray. I remember thinking, "Wait a minute." I didn't ordinarily pray, and I wouldn't have much respect for a god that would accept prayers when I was in dire straits like this. He would be bound to judge you, if he's judging you, on what you did in ordinary times. He just wouldn't accept prayers at times like this. I remember making up my mind not to pray. I thought, "Ok, take me as I am."[12]

You can see root formations in statements such as this which speak to Roddenberry's profound distrust in organized religion, distrust that would influence his portrayal of gods on *Star Trek*, from the trickster faux-deities of the Q or Trelane, through to a false Christian God in *Star Trek V: The Final Frontier*. And while this experience came post-war, Roddenberry's instincts as not just a pilot but a commander, a leader of men responsible for crew and civilians, would bleed heavily into the characters of Captain Jean-Luc Picard and first, particularly, James T. Kirk.

While Roddenberry chose never to write directly about the experience of Pan Am Flight 121, believing he could never quite relay the visceral

1. The 1960s

life and death moment on screen,[13] he would begin to parlay aspects of the crashes he experienced both before and after the war into *Star Trek* some two decades later and beyond. One of the first, working alongside writer Don M. Mankiewicz, was *The Original Series*' twentieth broadcast episode, "Court Martial," in which Kirk finds himself court-martialed. During an ion storm, the *Enterprise* captain is forced to eject a research pod containing Starfleet Lieutenant Commander Benjamin Finney in order to save the ship from possible destruction, a decision questioned by the chain of command.

What becomes apparent very quickly in "Court Martial" is the exceptionalism of Kirk's position as captain of a starship. The Starfleet arbiter who questions Kirk initially, Commodore Stone, remarks, "Not one man in a million could do what you and I have done. Command a starship. A hundred decisions a day, hundreds of lives staked on you making every one of them right."[14] This is an extension of the responsibility Roddenberry felt flying military and civilian airlines, of having to make split second decisions that could save or cost lives. Areel Shaw, Kirk's old flame who ends up prosecuting the case against him for Finney's death, suggests, "You're not an ordinary human. You're a Starship captain, and you've stepped into scandal."[15] In the role of captain of the *Enterprise,* Kirk is expected, indeed required, to be a better example of humanity and leadership than those around him. "Court Martial" suggests he has failed in that respect and must be punished. Roddenberry, conversely, may have latently felt some anxiety and guilt about his own failure, however brave his actions, to save the crew and passengers who perished on Flight 121 that day and the B-17 bomber before it.

"Court Martial" is also deeply suspicious of the reliability of technological testimony, with Roddenberry constantly questioning the veracity of anything but the human, personal experience. Stone cannot fathom this: "It's in the transcript, and computer transcripts don't lie!"[16] He assures Kirk about the fact that he jettisoned Finney, it appears, before the ion storm hit, thereby invalidating his claim it was about saving the ship, and more due to personal animus between them going back to a previous relationship. Kirk's defense attorney, Samuel Cogley, refuses to rely on the computer he has containing all the historical precedents of law at his fingertips, instead choosing physical written texts: "This is where the law is. Not in that homogenised, pasteurised synthesiser. Do you want to know the law, the ancient concepts in their own language? Learn the intent of the men who wrote them, from Moses to the tribunal of Alpha 3? Books."[17]

This is crucial because in this story, Roddenberry seems anxious about human infallibility, at the idea Kirk may have willfully, or indeed accidentally, caused Finney's death because he was psychologically incapable of the exceptional role put before him. Stone accuses him of being exhausted and played out. "A physical breakdown. Possibly even mental collapse,"[18] Kirk speculates. It is a deep-seated fear of not living up to the gold standard needed to cross the final frontier as a beacon of humanity. In the end, in "Court Martial," Kirk is vindicated in this role, saved as Finney is revealed to be the flawed and bitter example of a fellow crewman unable to attain Kirk's natural ability. Yet Roddenberry often across Season One of *The Original Series* appears unsure about whether men such as Kirk, men who have survived conflicts, accidents and trials, are capable of maintaining such human, and in this case, American exceptionalism.

Take "The Menagerie," a two-part episode which stands as one of *Star Trek*'s more fascinating production decisions; it was created in order to both resolve hanging story threads and utilize footage as a cost-cutting measure from "The Cage," from which only Leonard Nimoy's Mr. Spock survived a complete cast change before the show went to series.[19] "The Menagerie" reintroduces the character of Captain Pike as a broken shell of a man, horribly maimed and crippled, able only to communicate through a series of light transmissions—far from the strong, able captain we briefly got to know in "The Cage." Spock is prepared to sabotage his entire career by stealing the *Enterprise* to return Pike to Talos IV, a world which promises him the illusion of a normal life with Vina, a woman he fell in love with.

Though we do come to learn more specific details of Pike's history with Spock and Talos IV decades later in the second season of *Star Trek: Discovery*, Roddenberry uses the cast change of Jeffrey Hunter to William Shatner to depict, following a terrible accident on a training vessel following the rescue of several cadets, a Pike who is incapable of living up to the accepted standard of military leadership. Spock also compromises his own moral code, not to mention his logical Vulcan position, to help his troubled former captain find a sense of peace. He is exonerated by the fact the court-martial proceedings of the second part of "The Menagerie" are another Talosian illusion to further Spock's plan to save Pike. Kirk cannot understand why he acted alone, why he refused to bring his current captain in on the scheme: "Ask you to face the death penalty, too? One of us was enough, Captain."[20]

In this, one feels Roddenberry's continued grappling with self-sacrifice in the face of possible death. Pike's end is tragic, the victim of a random terrible accident, but "The Menagerie" focuses more on Spock's attempt to

1. The 1960s

save him from further pain. *Discovery* gilds the lily somewhat by suggesting Pike gained foreknowledge that he would end up scarred and crippled in the future,[21] consigned to a terrible fate. While the end of Pike's career is not a result of war, Roddenberry's post-war mission to understand leadership and heroism through the allegorical lens of *Star Trek*'s symbols of command filters through into these kinds of stories in *The Original Series*, not to mention the movie continuations and *The Next Generation*.

Captains Kirk and Picard, though separated by almost a century, end up sharing a common tragedy: they both witness the destruction of their own commands. Kirk is forced to self-destruct the *Enterprise,* having stolen it from Starfleet shipyards, in *Star Trek III: The Search for Spock*, after the vessel is boarded by murderous, renegade Klingons under the command of the vicious Commander Kruge. "My God, Bones … what have I done?"[22] Kirk remarks to McCoy on planet Genesis as he watches the ship burn up in the atmosphere, clearly aware of the drastic import of what he had to do for the greater good. This results in a court-martial in the subsequent film, *Star Trek IV: The Voyage Home*, and Kirk's punishment is a token demotion to captain and a brand-new *Enterprise* only after he and his crew save the Earth from atmospheric collapse. Even this late in the voyages of *The Original Series* crew, Roddenberry is exploring the costs of losing the ship you serve on; indeed, Kirk's actions in *The Search for Spock* very nearly trigger war with the Klingon Empire. "There shall be no peace, as long as Kirk lives!"[23] the Klingon Ambassador to the Federation haughtily barks in *The Voyage Home*, and while this doesn't entirely come to pass, it is a thread Nicholas Meyer pulls on for Kirk's swan song as captain in *Star Trek VI: The Undiscovered Country*.

Picard loses two vessels in the course of his career. Aside from the *Enterprise*-D crashing on Veridian III during *Star Trek Generations*,[24] Picard also loses his first command, the *Stargazer*, during the so-called Battle of Maxia against the Ferengi,[25] for which Picard ends up facing court-martial proceedings. Though the Ferengi are never directly presented as the antagonists the Federation went to war with and subsequently in *Star Trek: Deep Space Nine* are transformed into a comedic alien species, "The Battle" in the first season of *The Next Generation* attempts to question Picard's moral fortitude as a leader, with logs that suggest he fired on Ferengi targets that triggered the battle in which the *Stargazer* was eventually lost.[26] Again, Roddenberry is haunted by the idea that Picard may have experienced issues in judgment when it came to his command. Though fuelled by his role in an insidious conspiracy to infiltrate Starfleet, Commander Remick in "Coming of Age" openly questions this in relation

Star Trek, History and Us

to the *Stargazer* incident: "Do you believe the captain is emotionally and psychologically fit for command of this starship? There is nothing in his history or his personality that would suggest mental lapses?"[27]

This is remarkably similar to Kirk questioning in "Court Martial" if Starfleet believe that he may have suffered a "mental collapse" and speaks to the ongoing uncertainty during Roddenberry's stewardship of the franchise that leaders, even men as strong and resolute as Kirk and Picard, are protected from compromise. Fate can often have other plans. This is a mindset fuelled by the experiences of war and positions of authority, of command, during extraordinary circumstances. It perhaps speaks to why Roddenberry could never square the crash experiences of the 1940s with any kind of certain religious belief, and why he was never able in *Star Trek* to square a scientific, technologically advanced future with a theological one. Life was just too random. People died without rhyme or reason, no matter sometimes what exceptional leaders could do.

Gene Roddenberry may have subsequently created one of the defining, hopeful, forward-thinking and progressive examples of science-fiction of the 20th century, but the echoes and scars of war never left him. David Alexander chronicles how, toward the end of his life, Roddenberry ended up watching a documentary about B-17 bombers flying over Germany from World War II:

> As we watched the grainy black and white footage of hundreds of B-17 bombers flying missions over Germany, I watched him. After a few moments it was clear he wasn't watching the broadcast, he was back almost fifty years, remembering. After about ten minutes, I stood up and asked, "Have you seen enough, Gene?"
>
> Sitting in his wheelchair, tired, his body betraying the force of the intellect inside, he looked directly at me and said in a voice firm with conviction. "Yes, quite enough."[28]

Beyond Roddenberry's personal experiences as a flyboy, *Star Trek* remained somewhat obsessed over the original three seasons with the legacy of World War II, and frequently attempted to try and reconcile the global conflict with the utopian ideas of its aspirational future. "Patterns of Force," the twenty-first episode of the second season of *The Original Series*, is a rather striking entry which attempts to reconcile the horror of Nazism with a post-war healing process, reconceptualizing their methods and structure through the prism of an alien society.

In the episode, written by John Meredyth Lucas, the *Enterprise* is dispatched to the planet Ekos in search of John Gill, a Federation historian who was sent to observe the species on the planet but with whom communication has been lost. Kirk and Spock beam down to discover the

1. The 1960s

inhabitants, believed to be a pre-warp civilization,[29] not only have thermonuclear power but somehow have evolved into an identical parallel of Nazi Germany from 20th century Earth, with Gill installed as their Fuhrer. In order to reach the reclusive Gill, Kirk and Spock pose as Nazi officers, suffer torture, and have to join forces with a resistance movement, all in an attempt to correct Gill's interference and understand why the Ekosian people have adopted this culture, and why they are persecuting citizens of the neighboring planet Zeon as the Nazis persecuted the Jewish people.

Ostensibly, "Patterns of Force" appears a strange aberration within *The Original Series*, but *Star Trek*'s fascination with existing human culture through an alien microscope can be seen in everything from Season Two's "A Piece of the Action," recreating 1920s Chicago and a world of gangsters and prohibition on an alien planet, to Season Three's "Bread and Circuses," which transplants the Roman Empire to a far-flung world in a far more direct, and less allegorical, context than the Romulan Empire in *Star Trek* mythology. Lucas himself wanted to examine the pure technocratic mindset behind Nazism himself in his idea for the episode:

> It was fun to write a well-meaning Nazi, a guy who for the right cause completely fucked everything up. Y'know, we started with the question, "How the hell did Nazism get past the shits and the street gangs and take root among the basically decent people? How did sane, reasonable adults come to buy into this bullshit?" The answer seemed to be because it was efficient and because, in a society beset by all kinds of problems, it may have seemed like a feasible necessity. So, it becomes feasible, and the people take that leap.[30]

The episode takes on a personal dimension in that both William Shatner and Leonard Nimoy were children of Jewish immigrants. Shatner was raised in Montreal to second generation Jewish immigrants from the Russian and former Austro-Hungarian Empires, while Nimoy was the product of Jewish-Ukrainian immigrants who raised him in Boston during the Great Depression and the outbreak of war. Nimoy remained actively involved in the Jewish community throughout his life.[31] His Jewish roots were so important to him that Nimoy refused to wear the Nazi uniform sported by Spock during the episode for promotional photo shoots while filming the episode, perhaps underscoring the difficulty in filming a story which attempts to revise and reconcile Nazism as a theoretical concept, free of a literal Holocaust to ground the ideology in horror. Yet Lucas' script nevertheless relies on particular names and reference points that directly resemble Jewish life. Zeon is not far away from Zion, after all, while characters in the Zeon resistance are given names such as Isak, Abrom and Davod. "Patterns of Force" in this regard is indicative of how, despite remembering *Star Trek* principally as a cultural reflection, *The Original Series* could be deliberately literal in transmitting a defiantly "anti-war" message.

Bodie Ashton argues that the idea of Nazi efficiency is itself a myth:

> Nazi Germany, contrary to popular belief, was actually startlingly inefficient. While it did enjoy economic recovery from the Great Depression, this recovery had already been set in motion by the preceding Weimar governments. In terms of bureaucracy the National Socialist regime had a profoundly chaotic impact. The once-powerful German civil service was treated as a bastard child of the Party administration, though the Party could not afford to totally dissolve it. The idea of National Socialism as being a reasonable political alternative, had the brutality of the regime been avoided, is nothing more than fiction. Furthermore, since racial "purity" and the vileness of Untermenschen was at the heart of Nazi ideology, it is impossible to strip it from that ideology. If we were to be clinical, it can be argued that the Holocaust itself, launched in 1942, is the ultimate, terrible expression of Nazi economic inefficiency; with a huge, captive population of potential slave labour, the Nazis resorted to extermination instead.[32]

"Patterns of Force," consequently, feels particularly tone deaf in how it approaches subject matter, a mere two decades on, which remained real and raw for the many survivors of the Nazi war machine. It also only pays lip service to an aspect of the Nazi experiment, through Spock's notable difference due to his genetics, that would be dealt with in one of the series' more celebrated episodes: Season One's "Space Seed."

Written by Gene L. Coon and Carey Wilber, from the latter's story, the *Enterprise* encounters in deep space the S.S. *Botany Bay*, a sleeper ship from the 20th century containing a group of exiled humans in cryo-sleep led by Khan Noonien Singh, a former prince and one of numerous genetically enhanced "superhumans" created in the late 20th century in eugenic experiments. Khan went on to become a warlord who, as Spock puts it, was "from 1992 through 1996, absolute ruler of more than a quarter of your world. From Asia through the Middle East."[33] Following the so-called Eugenics Wars, Khan and his band of "supermen" were exiled from Earth, sealed within the nuclear-powered *Botany Bay*, and have been drifting in space ever since. Once thawed out, Khan falls in love with *Enterprise* lieutenant Marla McGivers and attempts to steal the *Enterprise*, forcing Kirk to exile him and his people once again to the seemingly idyllic, uninhabited world of Ceti Alpha V.

In part thanks to Khan's memorable return on the big screen in 1982's *The Wrath of Khan*, "Space Seed" has been immortalized as one of *The Original Series'* most successful episodes, but it is easy to forget how Khan and his band of supermen are products of eugenics, and a

1. The 1960s

particular scientific ethic within the Third Reich to appropriate the Nietzschian idea of the "Übermensch." This philosophical idea of human betterment was corrupted by Nazi ideology into a racial purity for a destined Aryan or Germanic, biologically superior master race. Nietzsche expert Brian Leiter is keen to point out that the philosopher himself did not share these Aryan views, but he did perhaps lean toward more extreme ideas about human worth:

> I think it's always worth saying that Nietzsche was no Nazi. To start with, he hated Germans. This created a lot of problems for the Nazis. They had to edit the texts quite selectively because he hated German nationalists, he hated anti–Semites, he hated militarists. He wouldn't have fitted in too easily at Nuremberg! On the other hand, it is absolutely true that Nietzsche has quite shocking views about traditional Christian morality. Nietzsche is deeply illiberal. He does not believe in the equal worth of every person. Nietzsche thinks there are higher human beings. His favourite three examples are Goethe, Beethoven and Nietzsche himself. And that higher human beings, through their creative genius, can actually make life worth living—that Beethoven's 9th Symphony is enough to justify all the suffering the world includes.[34]

Khan is, in some sense, a combination of Nietzsche's concept of the higher human being and the corrupted, biologically superior notion of a Nazi master race. David Greven suggests similar:

> Given that the most well-known fusion of ideologies of eugenics and a bid for global power occurred in World War II German fascism, the indirect Trek suggestion is that Khan is a kind of Nazi. Along these lines, the "Indian" Khan also represents both the colonial subject and the coloniser. Perplexingly and fascinatingly, Khan represents both the racial Other and a figure who attempts to destroy racial otherness.[35]

Spock, perhaps aware of humanity's historical propensity to disparage the "Other" that his Vulcan lineage would correspond to, is concerned when Kirk and Scotty actively discuss the romanticism of Khan's past. "He was the best of the tyrants and the most dangerous. They were supermen, in a sense. Stronger, braver, certainly more ambitious, more daring," Kirk claims.[36] Scotty defends him as a dictator who, unlike the Nazi analog, committed no massacres, but Spock still classes him as a dangerous tyrant. Kirk defends his response: "Mister Spock, you misunderstand us. We can be against him and admire him all at the same time." Spock's one-word response? "Illogical."[37] It's hard not to side with Spock on this one, as Kirk and Scotty defend a man described as an "Alexander" or a "Napoleon."

This speaks perhaps to the 1960s unwillingness to face the horror of eugenic experimentation in the same way *Star Trek* will explore in future decades. Khan may end up a vengeful psychopath touched by madness when he *does* manage to steal a starship in *The Wrath of Khan*, but here he is urbane and charming enough to convince Marla to give up her life in utopia to join him on Ceti Alpha V, which is likened to Milton's *Paradise Lost*, as Kirk comments, "The statement Lucifer made when he fell into the pit. 'It is better to rule in hell than serve in heaven.'"[38] Khan is considered less a Nazi, more of a Devil, thrown out of *Star Trek*'s Edenic utopia. Later series will unpick the dark legacy of eugenic experimentation, and *Star Trek* would do a better job in the 1960s—indeed it does a better job earlier in the first season—in framing how the Nazi, as an entity, is considered by survivors in the post-war, idealized future of the Federation.

Erin K. Horakova believes the post-war Jewish experience, particularly among Jewish Americans, has been reflected in *Star Trek* in the context of the show's aspirational approach to the so-called "final frontier." She suggests that the 1958 book *Exodus*, and its 1960 film adaptation, sowed the seeds for the existential ideas Roddenberry's series would explore about the experience of survivors:

> *Exodus*'s narrative of settlement relied somewhat on the already familiar and popular framework of the Western (paralleling the "new" nation of Israel with early America-the Jews are just like us!) for its American appeal. *Exodus* also presented a heroic and current narrative of "the frontier" that was then coded as socially progressive. (Though all three frontiers in play—the West, Israel and space—were of course already peopled with culturally, racially Other inhabitants). Thus, to an extent not now readily accessible to us, TOS was being read in light of this slightly antecedent Jewish political story that, like TOS, "adapted" the Western framework. This gave TOS a sort of implied, structural Jewish association.[39]

Can we therefore read James T. Kirk as a Jewish character, in essence? If Shatner brought his own associations to the role, as did Nimoy in Spock, from their shared cultural experience as Jews who came of adolescence amid witnessing a Holocaust upon their people, then perhaps Kirk himself embodies some of these definable Jewish characteristics in this futuristic paradigm, even if the character himself does not share such ancestry.[40] Could this be why Shatner brings such performative brio to "The Conscience of the King," an episode in Season One which more elegantly deals with the lingering specter of Nazism than "Patterns of Force" through the character of Kodos the Executioner?

"The Conscience of the King," written by Barry Trivers, sees the *Enterprise* called to Planet Q by an old friend of Kirk's, Dr. Thomas Leighton, ostensibly to investigate a new synthetic food source. On arrival, witnessing a performance of *Hamlet* by celebrated actor Anton Karidian leading a Shakespearian acting troupe, Kirk is told by Leighton that Karidian is,

1. The 1960s

in fact, "Kodos the Executioner." Kodos was the former governor of Earth colony Tarsus IV who presided over a mass holocaust of half the population when a lack of food supply threatened the entire colony with starvation. Kirk and Leighton were witnesses, one of a small few who survived the massacre. Kirk subsequently becomes obsessed with proving Karidian is Kodos and bringing him to justice for his previous crimes.

This is, of course, one of the most overt references to Nazism in *The Original Series* without having to resort to a literal exploration such as in "Patterns of Force." Kirk's drive to expose Kodos is pure allegory and very clearly recalls the public pursuit, trial and ultimate execution of Nazi war criminal Adolf Eichmann in 1962, which would have still resounded in the public consciousness when *Star Trek* first came on the air. Horakova states that these crusades created a clear moral ambiguity that "Conscience" would explore:

> Mossad also killed Herberts Cukurs, the "Butcher of Riga" (note the appellation's similarity to "Kodos the Executioner") in 1965. Mossad's work has long provoked moral debates about justice, punishment, personal guilt and communal memory (especially as Mossad's targets aged).[41]

Kirk can be likened in "Conscience" to the figure of Simon Wiesenthal, a Jewish survivor of multiple Nazi concentration camps during the war who subsequently became the prominent post-war hunter of Nazi officers who had escaped justice, in particular the highly popularized Nuremburg trials in the late 1940s which prosecuted many perpetrators of war crimes. Wiesenthal, despite his involvement in exposing Eichmann and many other prominent escaped Nazi criminals such as Franz Stangl, was accused of exaggerations, fabrications and inconsistencies, perhaps proving the difficulty in trying to definitively identify Holocaust perpetrators years, sometimes decades, later, after they had substantially changed their appearances and lived for many years in different countries under assumed aliases. This is a problem Kirk faces as he, by his own admission, places his command and career in jeopardy by pursuing his quest against Karidian, and remains uncertain about the veracity of his beliefs, even when Spock believes he has proven the issue thanks to his own research. "I saw him once, twenty years ago. Men change. Memory changes. Look at him now, he's an actor. He can change his appearance. No. Logic is not enough. I've got to feel my way, make absolutely sure."[42]

"The Conscience of the King" presents this idea of an escaped war criminal in dramatic, theatrical overtones with Karidian in the guise of an actor, a Shakespearian one no less.[43] Kirk ends up surrounded by victims of a man who never once says the words Kirk wants to hear: "I am Kodos." His daughter Lenore murders men who could have exposed him in order to protect his future. Riley, the damaged *Enterprise* lieutenant who lost his parents to Kodos' massacre, is ready to become a murderer to avenge them. Leighton is just one of those killed to protect the secret. And Kirk's anger is righteous and furious, and often feels a transmogrification of the latent Jewish fury, extemporized through survivors like Wiesenthal in his life's crusade, in Shatner's own cultural experience. Kirk is as haunted and marked by what he witnessed, and crucially *survived*, on Tarsus IV as a Jewish Holocaust survivor might well be. Yet, importantly, Kirk seems capable of amnesty, if not forgiveness. He won't become that avenger, taking blood for blood. "If he is Kodos, then I've shown him more mercy than he deserves."[44]

The episode never absolves Karidian of the horror he perpetrated but it does suggest that, perhaps, the guilt that Kodos subsequently experienced in the wake of the massacre, and never facing punishment for it, has haunted him in the years he escaped into a persona where he became an actor. As he puts it, he plays many parts. Karidian actively is encouraging the gradual loss of Kodos in his mind, perhaps as some way of ameliorating his guilt. "Blood thins. The body fails. One is finally grateful for a failing memory. I no longer treasure life, not even my own. I am tired! And the past is a blank."[45] Karidian later seems genuinely disturbed at Lenore's actions. "Oh, my child, my child. You've left me nothing! You were the one thing in my life untouched by what I'd done."[46] He sees Lenore as his purity, his hope, and once that is taken away, he gives his life to save Kirk's. In one sense, the Nazi, on some level of redemption, saves the Jewish survivor.

This is a simplistic reading, to some extent, and *Star Trek* never seems to be suggesting that the horrors of Nazism should be forgiven, or indeed forgotten, but "The Conscience of the King" perhaps wants to believe that survivors like Kirk can move on from such trauma, and that the optimism of humanity's future can provide a salve against the darkness of our own past. Kirk is not ready yet to talk about the events on Planet Q by the end of the episode, and that is perhaps fitting. He might have been able to throw off Khan as the romantic ideal of a historical tyrant, disconnected as he was to the horror of the Eugenics Wars by centuries, but he cannot be so blithe with the events he witnessed in his lifetime. The 1960s remained a time of healing, searching for answers and truths about how the horror of World War II could have happened. It would not be until the 1990s that *Star Trek* began to reconcile that horror and allow those survivors to truly come to terms with their experience and grow, as we will particularly witness in *Deep Space Nine*.

1. *The 1960s*

As *Star Trek* reconciles the shadows of war, it embraces the new social and cultural constructs of the '60s, fashioning a utopian vision out of a rapidly changing world, both on the ground and in orbit.

Ways to Eden

In November of 1960, as if to seal the transformation of the decade from post-war austerity to a revolution in progressive counterculture, John F. Kennedy was elected president, defeating Republican nominee Richard Nixon (more on him later) and ascending to the White House on a largely liberal, optimistic ticket.

Just a year later, following the Soviet Union's launch of their satellite Sputnik and Yuri Gagarin's historic mission in 1961 that made him the first man to orbit the Earth, Kennedy committed all American efforts in winning the so-called "Space Race." His goal was to produce a singularly American achievement, a form of manifest destiny that would define the decade, and undoubtedly aid the conditions under which Gene Roddenberry brought *Star Trek* to the screen: putting a man on the Moon.

Kennedy, in a 1962 speech, distilled the reasoning behind this great experiment.

> There is no strife, no prejudice, no national conflict in outer space as yet. Its hazards are hostile to us all. Its conquest deserves the best of all mankind, and its opportunity for peaceful cooperation may never come again. But why, some say, the Moon? Why choose this as our goal? And they may well ask, why climb the highest mountain? Why, 35 years ago, fly the Atlantic? Why does Rice play Texas? We choose to go to the Moon! We choose to go to the Moon.... We choose to go to the Moon in this decade and do the other things, not because they are easy, but because they are hard; because that goal will serve to organize and measure the best of our energies and skills, because that challenge is one that we are willing to accept, one we are unwilling to postpone, and one we intend to win.[47]

If the previous decade was marked by the psychological recovery from world war and the tense geopolitical realities of mutually assured destruction between the superpowers, the 1960s worked to live up to Kennedy-era optimism, even despite his assassination in 1963 and the challenges that America faced both nationally and internationally across the decade as a result. Establishment thinking was challenged by countercultural social, sexual and political mores: the rise of the Civil Rights movement in tandem with black revolutions in music and politics, led by figureheads such as Malcolm X and Martin Luther King, Jr.; and the

Star Trek, **History and Us**

anti–Vietnam peace movement; the birth of the "hippie;" and the mantra of "Make love, not war." This innate clash of liberalism and conservatism *Star Trek* would project outward, while using science-fiction as a platform to explore a great many of these issues facing America and the world beyond at this point in history.

It is easy to romanticize the 1960s in retrospect as a decade filled with color and prosperity: socialist and democratic movements improving the lives of the less fortunate to the tune of iconic, century-defining music from The Beatles and The Rolling Stones; movie houses screening epics from *Lawrence of Arabia* to the deliberately anti-establishment, drug-fuelled *Easy Rider* and so on. However, *Star Trek* came to bear in a decade riven with cultural, social and political unrest which entirely up-ended the status quo, and as a result was forced to balance the dueling forces of conservative pragmatism with progressive liberal values. On the whole, Roddenberry's own personal liberalism tends to win through in *The Original Series*, with the futuristic canvas able to convey a progressive ideology on matters of civil liberties and racial integration.

Mike O'Connor believes the show is quite clear in terms of its openness and tolerance of racial cohesion:

> Beyond the racial characteristics of the cast and the characters they played, the specific plots of many episodes, and comments from characters within them, expressed in a direct way that the show strongly supported racial integration. The show's heroes consistently invoked an ideal of what might be called liberal color blindness. Their comments and actions suggested that there is something deeply unjust about holding a person's physical characteristics against him/her, and many episodes presented characters offhandedly mentioning the fact that bigotry has been eradicated from twenty-third-century Earth and is frowned upon throughout the galaxy.[48]

Season Three's "Plato's Stepchildren" is not, in truth, a stand-out episode of *Star Trek*, but it has passed into legend for depicting what has been described as the first interracial kiss on American television, between James T. Kirk and his Black communications officer Uhura. While this is not strictly true,[49] it does remain one of the more signature examples of changing cultural realities among American society, the depiction of a white man and black woman openly kissing on prime-time network television. This comes within an episode built around the representation of an ancient Earth civilization which is based purely on a eugenic, bigoted ideal.

Responding to a distress call from an unknown planet, Kirk, Spock and McCoy beam down to an identical replication of Ancient Greece,

1. The 1960s

where they find a powerful psychokinetic being needing medical treatment. He is part of an alien race who came to Earth during the age of Plato and subsequently departed following the end of Greek civilization, re-creating the architecture and society on an alien world, except along the way they eugenically developed their Platonian culture into what they consider a "perfect," immortal ideal. The crew meet a kindly dwarf, Alexander, who epitomizes both the fallacy of the Platonian power, which they eventually and inevitably turn on the *Enterprise* crew, and the liberal, equal rationale of the series as espoused by Kirk when Alexander doesn't understand why they don't discriminate against him based on his size. "Where I come from, size, shape or color make no difference."[50]

While the Platonians believe they have created a utopia on their world, fashioned out of eugenic experimentation and the psychic, God-like power bestowed upon them by the natural chemicals on the planet, the episode consistently reinforces the idea that the truly utopian figures are the *Enterprise* crew, forced into serving as the controlled playthings of twisted aliens. One might question how the infamous Kirk and Uhura kiss is represented, of course. Their lips barely touch, the camera half obscures the view of it, and the circumstances are in no way a truly romantic gesture, with both of the characters under alien duress. However, Uhura's assertion, "I am not afraid," ostensibly trying to combat her fear of being controlled, seems fitting in the context of a major interracial landmark in the public sphere. *Star Trek* itself, as an entity, was showing no fear of responding to the undulating realities of the civil rights movement.

Nichelle Nichols, the actor who played Uhura, has herself discussed how Dr. Martin Luther King, Jr., himself encouraged her to remain in the series when she considered quitting, before the kiss in "Plato's Stepchildren" would have been filmed. In her biography *Beyond Uhura* she claims he said to her,

> "Don't you realize this gift this man [Roddenberry] has given the world? Men and women of all races going forth in peaceful exploration, living as equals. For the first time, the world sees us as we should be seen, as equals, as intelligent people—as we should be."[51]

This suggests that *Star Trek* was providing an important service in terms of race relations in the late 1960s, with "Plato's Stepchildren" airing in late 1968, not long before the cancellation of the series, and in the same season as "Let That Be Your Last Battlefield," which directly challenges and openly mocks racial difference and segregation. Mike O'Connor believes, however, that *Star Trek* across its run didn't go far enough in clarifying issues being raised in American society about race relations.

Star Trek, History and Us

> The show's strong and even moralistic stand against overt racism and legalized segregation was not conceptually equipped to address the more subtle and nuanced issues raised by the racial situation of the late 1960s. Are whites who move away from integrating neighbourhoods actually doing something wrong? Is violence justifiable as a tool against oppression? Might innocent members of a dominant group be hurt by policies intended to bring about racial equality? To what extent should victims of racism be held responsible for destructive behaviours that might stem from frustration or the lack of opportunity? Should society bear the responsibility for the unequal economic opportunities that are rooted in the racial inequality of the past? *Star Trek* did not have answers to these questions. In its television universe of liberal colour-blindness, bigotry was a personal or social flaw akin to a mistake in judgment. Once corrected by the good people of the starship *Enterprise*, the scales fell from the offenders' eyes, the social policies were appropriately changed, and the formerly subjugated group emerged, none the worse for wear, to take its rightful place in society.[52]

You can arguably suggest this is what happens by the end of "Plato's Stepchildren," as Platonian leader Parmen admits the folly of their actions, after Kirk—the supposed lesser being—spares his life. "None of us can be trusted. Uncontrolled, power will turn even saints into savages, and we can all be counted upon to live down to our lowest impulses." The Platonians realize their mistake, corrected by the "perfect" beings from the Federation, and Parmen is suitably admonished enough to welcome future "interstellar visits," which Kirk suggests would be unlikely. It posits that the answer, in this example, is simply that the *Enterprise*'s galactic voyagers are more advanced and innately utopian than many of the races—filled as they are with tricksters and revolutionaries and savages—they often encounter. *The Original Series* establishes that Earth has many of the conditions of utopia in the 23rd century, and Roddenberry will double down on the idea of perfected future Federation humans in *The Next Generation*, but *Star Trek*'s answer to civil inequality and institutional racism is simply that the enlightened humans of the future have the answer we do not!

This is also reflected in the other significant episode in Season Three to tackle, directly, the countercultural revolution of the 1960s: "The Way to Eden." Pursuing the *Aurora*, a stolen space cruiser which subsequently explodes, the *Enterprise* beams aboard what have subsequently been described in popular culture as "Space Hippies," a motley band of people dressed in flowing gowns who, under their leader Sevrin, espouse a rejection of Federation and humanistic technological values and are searching for their own spiritual utopia, Eden. Kirk finds himself in a difficult position of balance when one of the group turns out to be the son of the Catullan ambassador, during treaty negotiations between the Federation and

1. The 1960s

Catulla, and is determined to ensure the boy is safely retrieved, despite Sevrin's plan that he and his followers to reach their mythical Eden.

Once again, much like "Plato's Stepchildren," "The Way to Eden" is not a good episode of *Star Trek*, but it directly confronts the cultural confluence between conservative values and established systems with the "Hippie" movement which raged across the '60s. Indeed, Peter Braunstein's assertions about the late-'60s decay of this movement suggest *Star Trek* tackled this subject too little, too late.

> By late summer 1967, the Flower Child charade of the hippies had begun to wilt, overheated by the media hype it had generated. The advertised lifestyle of communalism, free love, and abundant drugs had enticed young people from across America to the two largest urban hippie enclaves, San Francisco's Haight-Ashbury and New York's East Village, and the crescendo of immigrants soon overwhelmed the hippies' meagre resources and ad hoc organisations assembled to aid the newcomers. As a result, the "Summer of Love '67" featured scores of young would-be hippies, many of them confused runaways, victimised by unscrupulous drug dealers, crammed in overpopulated hippie "communes," harassed by police and municipal authorities, and objectified by commercialisation and tourism meant to capitalise on the hippie phenomenon. By summer's end, two well-publicised murders in both coastal meccas redirected media scrutiny, which now focused on the 'dark underside' of the hippie dream.[53]

"The Way to Eden" arrived, early in 1969, on the back of this disintegration over the hippie movement lifestyle, and this is perhaps reflected in the authoritarian reaction to Sevrin and his group by Kirk in particular, representing the traditional values of a futuristic version of the American establishment in the Federation. Compare this to Spock, who is far more open to the possibilities of their spiritual quest for a utopia that Kirk believes fanciful, understanding the deeper rationale behind their search. "There are many who are uncomfortable with what we have created," Spock tells Kirk. "It is almost a biological rebellion. A profound revulsion against the planned communities, the programming, the sterilized, artfully balanced atmospheres."[54] All Kirk can really understand is, "They seek the primitive."[55]

It is key that Sevrin and his followers are all examples of people who fell away from the established systems and realities of the Federation future. Irina was a paramour of Pavel Chekov while in Starfleet, and Chekov cannot understand why she would give all that up. Irina is the one, however, who considers herself free. "Oh, Pavel, you have always been like this. So correct. And inside, the struggle not to be. Give in to yourself. You will be happier."[56] Chekov is considered the buttoned up, repressed example that Federation and Starfleet structures foster, yet "The Way to Eden" still considers Irina to have been corrupted by naive, foolish values of utopia. Sevrin was a brilliant scientist and engineer from the planet Tiburon who is in fact the "Typhoid Mary"[57] of a disease McCoy believes would decimate his planned, Edenic colony, while he remained immune. Sevrin knows this but remains driven by his belief in the purity of his belief. "This is poison to me. This stuff you breathe, this stuff you live in, the shields of artificial atmosphere that we have layered about every planet. The programs in those computers that run your ship and your lives for you, they bred what my body carries. That's what your science have done to me. You've infected me. Only the primitives can cleanse me. I cannot purge myself until I am among them. Only their way of living is right."[58]

Star Trek remains subscribed here to the idea that any kind of countercultural movement devoted to a pure, cleansed existence, free of technological development and scientific advancement, is anathema to modern institutionalized values. Sean Munger considers this an example of how the *Star Trek* writing staff fail to truly understand the ebbing hippie philosophy, while at the same time being acutely aware of the reactive conservatism toward it.

> The creatures in Sevrin's crew, which includes some aliens, seem shallow and childlike, idealistic to a fault and not really in tune with how the universe really works. Their quest for Eden, which Spock says at the end of the show he admires, is portrayed as worthy, but the hippies' motives are very reductionist, defined solely in terms of what they're against rather than what they really believe in. Consequently, the group comes off as a bunch of buffoons, as much as characters like Chekov and Kirk seem like rigid authoritarians who are incapable of 'reaching' the hippies' motivations. The two groups seem to be talking past one another. That is real. That's the way it really was in America in 1969, especially within families where middle-class suburban parents couldn't quite understand why their son now had long hair or why their daughter started calling herself Moonbeam. This is what "The Way to Eden" gets right, albeit unwittingly.[59]

Ultimately, Sevrin's quest is deemed unworthy. His Eden turns out to be across the Neutral Zone in Romulan space, and while we never see the aliens play a role in the episode, the threat of Sevrin instigating an interstellar war is keenly voiced by Kirk in his pursuit when Sevrin steals the *Galileo II* shuttlecraft. Once the planet is reached, the episode doesn't even attempt to involve metaphor in invoking the Biblical story of temptation, as Sevrin's follower Adam is killed in the "garden" by eating poisoned fruit, and Sevrin himself, before he can unleash the plague he holds within, also takes a bite of an "apple" and collapses dead. *Star Trek* makes the point that such endeavors are ultimately folly, that Sevrin and his group were

1. The 1960s

not so much brilliant visionaries seeking paradise as reckless fools who were punished for their lack of adherence to Federation norms.

Only Spock sees value in their quest for paradise, telling Irina, "It is my sincere wish that you do not give up your search for Eden. I have no doubt but that you will find it or make it yourselves."[60] While this may seem uncharacteristic, it tracks with Spock's experience in the late Season One episode, "This Side of Paradise," which deals with similar themes of utopian idealism.

"This Side of Paradise" sees the *Enterprise* travel to the beautiful world of Omicron Ceti III, where they expect to find an agricultural colony of humans led by Elias Sandoval dead from the radiation emitted by Berthold rays, a newly discovered phenomenon. They find Sandoval alive but thriving in a utopian colony where Spock, soon under the possession of alien spores littering the planet, falls in love with an old flame, a human botanist called Leila Kalomi. When the rest of the crew begin to fall prey to these toxins, which draw them to the paradise of the world around them, Kirk—as the only one unaffected—has to find a way to save Spock and his crew.

While undoubtedly "The Way to Eden" more directly disparages the colorful, musical and spaced-out notions of the hippie movement, "This Side of Paradise" prefigures it when it comes to doubting the veracity of a utopian ideal. None of the *Enterprise* crew give up their technological lives of scientific exploration willingly; they are all under a malign influence which affects their brain chemistry. *Star Trek* produces plenty of "possession" episodes over the many television series it develops within the franchise but "This Side of Paradise" more directly positions utopian desire as a corrupting, dangerous influence steering the enlightened future humans away from their traditional lives, as opposed to embracing Sandoval's philosophy for his world. "Our philosophy is a simple one, that men should return to a less complicated life. We have few mechanical things here. No vehicles, no weapons. We have harmony here. Complete peace."[61]

Jon Wagner and Jan Lundeen consider Kirk, operating in a similar vein to how he will in "The Way to Eden," as representing the authoritarian example of a progressive paradigm against utopian stagnation:

> Kirk angrily counters Sandoval's claim of a "perfect world," saying that "man stagnates if he has no wants, no ambitions, no desire to be more than he is." Against the arrested cultural development of the Feeders of Vaal, or the deliberate primitivism of a return to a "simpler: life in "The Return of the Archons" and "This Side of Paradise," Trek suggests that people have a responsibility to their species' collective project of growth and change. Perfection, insofar as it is conceived of as

a state of being rather than a project of becoming, is detrimental to the health of the individual, the society, and the species. By a cruel irony, utopians are doomed to live eternally in their constricted situation unless someone else intervenes, for utopia enervates people and deprives them of the drives that, in the usual course of things, would lead to growth and change.[62]

It is telling that D.C. Fontana, writing from a story by Jerry Sohl, suggests this kind of enforced, corrupted utopia is the only mechanism for Spock to find true happiness. He is almost diametrically opposed to Kirk in this fashion here, with Kirk having to ultimately goad his first officer with insulting, racial epithets and personal taunts, and quite literally fight him in the *Enterprise*'s transporter room to shake him out of his brainwashing and rid him of the infecting spores. "You said they were benevolent and peaceful. Violent emotions overwhelm them, destroy them. I had to make you angry enough to shake off their influence," Kirk claims.[63] Far from representing an idealized future human free of conflict, Kirk turns quite monstrous in order to "free" Spock of his utopian desire, the happiness with Leila that frees him from his Vulcan, emotionless restraint, and cures him of the "disease" of the pure, Omicron Ceti III life, getting him back "to normal."

Jerry Sohl, who developed the story with Fontana under the pseudonym Nathan Butler, explains the rationale behind this.

> I had the idea that ... spores, as you know, are inanimate up until the point when they are mixed with water or with anything else, then they come alive. Like yeast. So, I had the idea that these things could be consumed by someone and as a result the whole character chemistry of that person could change to a nice, peaceful and loving person. In other words, it was a psychedelic kind of thing. A lot of that was going on at the time. The premise of the thing was that everyone on the *Enterprise* takes LSD. What would happen? In effect, that's what this was. They go down to the planet and they all get the spores in them and turn into different people. That was the basis of the whole thing, and I thought it was an interesting premise. It was the only time that Spock was allowed to be a loving, caring, cherishing human being. That was my idea. Worked out just swell, I think.[64]

It's almost heart-breaking reading this that Spock admits it was the only time he was truly happy at the end, even more so that his Vulcan restraint means he could not be angrier at Kirk for robbing him of it.

One aspect of *Star Trek*'s liberal utopia that has been retroactively questioned is the sexualization of the female crew members in Starfleet and on the *Enterprise*, popularized most keenly in the cultural mindset with Nichelle Nichols' Lieutenant Uhura's extremely short skirt in *The Original Series*, replicated equally by Majel Barrett's Dr. Christine Chapel and many other female crew members, even just in walk-in roles, over

1. The 1960s

the course of the three seasons. Does this, combined with Kirk's regular dalliances with female guest characters who would swoon at the idea of romancing the *Enterprise*'s intrepid captain, suggest *Star Trek* is ultimately sexist in how it approaches gender politics in the 23rd century? Or, conversely, does it rather offer a counterpoint in providing these multicultural, highly skilled women of the future serving in Starfleet with agency over their bodies, and how they present themselves, which they were unable to exert in ages past?

Patricia Vettel-Becker suggests that Starfleet's female officers are the future incarnation of Helen Gurley Brown's "Single Girls":

> They do not cook, clean, raise offspring, or get married. They are professional women devoted to their careers who also delight in their femininity, the very model of single womanhood promoted by Brown in her internationally best-selling books *Sex and the Single Girl* (1962) and *Sex and the Office* (1964) and as editor of *Cosmopolitan* magazine for over thirty years. Brown claimed that women did not have to marry to have fulfilling lives, extolling instead the satisfaction gained through career success, the personal pleasure to be experienced in sex outside of matrimony, and the delight to be taken in fashioning one's own appearance and individual surroundings.[65]

This certainly tracks with Nichols' personal viewpoint on how Uhura herself dressed, and how it did not reflect a sexist, lascivious approach to gender politics, rather the reverse.

> In later years, especially as the women's movement took hold in the seventies, people began to ask me about my costume. Some thought it "demeaning" for a woman in the command crew to be dressed so sexily. It always surprised me because I never saw it that way. After all, the show was created in the age of the miniskirt, and the crew women's uniforms were very comfortable. Contrary to what many may think today, no one really saw it as demeaning back then. In fact, the miniskirt was a symbol of sexual liberation. More to the point, though, in the twenty-third century, you are respected for your abilities regardless of what you do or do not wear.[66]

Sexual liberation is therefore only retroactively framed by modern commentators as a negative, and *Star Trek* guilty of the "male gaze"[67] in how women are presented, forgetting that Roddenberry first envisaged Barrett particularly in "The Cage" as Number One, the mysterious first officer[68] second only to Captain Pike. Executives may have displayed sexist views in balking at a female character in such a key professional role, but the intent was there, and Barrett went on to play an experienced and highly capable doctor, albeit semi-regularly. *Star Trek* may have presented these female characters as a response to countercultural sexual mores, but the show never denigrated them as professionals or suggested women like Uhura or Chapel were unqualified to serve in the positions they do. In that, *Star Trek* is certainly pushing against the conservative grain that would cause it anxiety in other areas of cultural revolution.

What is *Star Trek* saying, then, about countercultural evolution, based on these examples? On the one hand, *Star Trek* is clearly a liberal series, with one eye on paralleling the Kennedy-era vision of a space-bound future given the multicultural nature of the *Enterprise* crew. Mike O'Connor points out this happened at a key, temperamental time in American society.

> Segregation and racial equality were still very live issues during the period in which *Star Trek* was on the air. *Star Trek* took a strong stand on these matters. The crew of the *Enterprise* presented a glimpse of what the idealized future Earth might look like: on the ship's bridge were not only a Russian navigator, but also an ethnically Asian helmsman and a black female communications officer. Considering the racial tumult in the United States during the period in which *Star Trek* aired, its cast alone made a progressive statement on race and gender relations that few in the late 1960s would have missed.[69]

It is, as a result, arguably progressive on matters of race and integration. Many episodes revolve around Starfleet and the *Enterprise* looking past color or creed to try to unite species lacking the progressive viewpoint of a 23rd century humanity who have reached some level of technological and spiritual utopia, having entirely devoted themselves to a secular, scientific creed.

Yet, on the other hand, *The Original Series* appears fundamentally suspicious of the countercultural reaction to modern American politics and society in the wake of the Kennedy assassination: the proliferation of free love and open sexual mores (its only concession to this being the sexualization without professional condemnation of its female crew), visible acceptance of recreational drug taking, and a youthful embrace of suggestive music by rebellious, youthful bands and performers, not to mention toward the end of the decade, the "American New Wave" launching in cinema with violent, challenging films such as *Bonnie & Clyde*, or sexually controversial pictures like *The Graduate*. *Star Trek* struggles to embrace, and even understand, the place of these new cultural practices and belief systems in the '60s, and questions them in its far future setting.

There is perhaps a reason for this uncertainty, and it ties directly into a broad, political, social and cultural, all-encompassing reality of American and Western democratic life that underpins everything *Star Trek* touches in the 1960s: the specter of the Vietnam War and behind it the billowing shadow of the Iron Curtain.

1. The 1960s

Tasting Armageddon

The height of *Star Trek* during the 1960s, the singular most potent icon of progressive, hopeful futurism conveyed on screen, paralleled the height of the conflict that would define that same decade: the Vietnam War.

If *Star Trek* was forged as a response to the horror of World War II, and as a direct antidote to the dystopian science-fiction of the 1950s which worried anxiously about extra-terrestrial invaders and beings from other worlds enslaving and destroying a humanity fretful of the atomic bomb and nuclear Armageddon, then the series is defiant in the face of Vietnam—the key, American proxy micro-conflict of the broader Cold War, and one which begins the transformation of the American psyche from a prosperous, forward-thinking and open society in the 1960s to one mired in uncertainty, austerity and existential angst come the 1970s.

Vietnam was born in the shadow of the assassination of President John F. Kennedy, the signature cultural and political marker of the 1960s for the American people. It took place just a year after the Cuban Missile Crisis that brought the Cold War superpowers of America and Russia closer to a Third World War than ever before or since and served as the trigger for the South East Asian conflict which escalated following another assassination—that of Ngo Dinh Diem, the U.S. installed proxy leader of South Vietnam, in a coup by his own generals, one sponsored indeed by the United States government. The result was a choice, made in the end by Kennedy's unexpected replacement as president: Lyndon B. Johnson. The choice was simple—withdraw the several thousand U.S. troops already in Vietnam or begin a full-scale invasion against North Vietnam. The hawkish Johnson chose the latter. Whether Kennedy's assassination was the result of his less aggressive political choices has remained open to debate, and conspiracy theory, for over half a century.

In any event, *Star Trek* emerged in the slipstream of these events. "The Cage" was delivered in February 1965, the same month an elected Johnson—having won his first official term in office—began a bombing campaign against North Vietnam as the conflict officially began. It was well underway by the time Season One began airing in September of 1966 and the reverberations were already being felt, both within and without the series, and would continue to do so. As H. Bruce Franklin observes:

> By the time the first *Star Trek* episode was broadcast in September 1966, the United States was fully engaged in a war that was devastating Indochina and beginning to tear America apart. By the time the final *Star Trek* episode was aired

in June 1969, the war seemed endless, hopeless, and catastrophic. Four episodes that were broadcast between the spring of 1967 and January 1969, the most crucial period in the war and for America, relate directly to the war. Taken as a sequence, these four episodes dramatize a startling and painful transformation in the war's impact on both the series and the nation.[70]

The four episodes Franklin mentions are those we will study to understand the impact Vietnam had on *Star Trek* over the course of *The Original Series*: "The City on the Edge of Forever," "A Private Little War," "The Omega Glory" and finally "Let That Be Your Last Battlefield."

"The City on the Edge of Forever" is the best-known episode on this list, and indeed remains one of the most iconic and well-remembered *Star Trek* episodes of the 1960s, inspiring and being honored (and even lampooned) by examples as diverse as adult animated comedy *South Park* and British sitcom *Men Behaving Badly*.[71]

Written by esteemed science-fiction author Harlan Ellison initially,[72] the plot sees the *Enterprise* struck by a series of time displacement waves which result in Bones injecting himself with a dangerous dose of a drug named "cordrazine," triggering a psychotic break that leads him to change history by stepping through the source of the waves—the ancient, mysterious being known as the Guardian of Forever. The result? He changes Earth's history to the degree that the *Enterprise,* Starfleet and the crew's entire future cease to exist. Kirk and Spock are forced to go through the Guardian in order to repair the damage McCoy has wrought. That damage, it turns out, is saving the life of Edith Keeler, the headstrong leader of a New York mission during the Great Depression of the 1930s who goes on to be a leading pacifist. She delays the United States' entry into World War II, therefore changing history forever by allowing Nazi Germany to develop the A-Bomb ahead of the Allies and, perversely, directly preventing the utopian *Star Trek* future in which the crew of the *Enterprise* exist. Kirk has to make the terrible choice to ensure Keeler's tragic death in a car accident to restore their future.

It is, surprisingly when laid out, quite a deep and unraveling narrative built on a series of relatively complicated temporal mechanics, but the core of Ellison's story holds a moral imperative which, while narratively relating to the course of World War II, allegorically corresponds to the direction of the Vietnam War. In short, *Star Trek* places itself in a contradictory position considering its liberal, progressive politics. "The City on the Edge of Forever" is deliberately anti-pacifist and pro-war. Or that, at least, is the argument.

Franklin expands on this.

1. The 1960s

As broadcast in the spring of 1967, "The City on the Edge of Forever" was clearly a parable suggesting that the peace movement directed against the U.S. war in Vietnam, no matter how noble, alluring, and idealistic in its motivation, might pose a danger to the progressive course of history. The episode projected the view that sometimes it is necessary to engage in ugly, distasteful action, such as waging remorseless warfare against evil expansionist forces like Nazi Germany or the Communist empire attempting to take over Indochina, even doing away with well-intentioned, attractive people who stand in the way of such historical necessity.[73]

It is hard to disagree with this analysis even if *Star Trek* certainly anguishes over its necessary conservative stance. Albeit rather quickly and without a level of emotional depth, Kirk falls in love with Edith as she espouses wisdom which makes her sound beyond a prophet, and more akin to a time-traveller herself. "One day, soon, man is going to be able to harness incredible energies, maybe even the atom, energies that could ultimately hurl us to other worlds, maybe in some sort of space ship. And the men who reach out into space will be able to find ways to feed the hungry millions of the world and to cure their diseases."[74] Edith is a radiating beacon of goodness, centuries ahead of her time (Joseph Pevney's direction even lights her with an ethereal glow in close up), and someone you can understand being a pivot in the fabric of time. She is the utopian ideal in an age described as desperate. "I've seen old photographs of this period. An economic upheaval had occurred," Kirk states. "It was called Depression, circa 1930. Quite barbaric,"[75] Spock adds. The point is clear: Edith *is* the future.

Kirk's devastation at having to ensure her death to restore the established timeline, and Bones' subsequent fury when Kirk reflexively stops him from saving her life, is at least an acknowledgment that *Star Trek* is compromised by these ethics. At the same time, it reinforces the notion that the ends of war often justify the means.

Bruce Isaacs believes that *Star Trek* uses this story to promulgate the linear aspect of its utopian myth.

> The central conflict in "The City on the Edge of Forever" is perhaps the clearest expression of the classical utopian impulse in *Star Trek*. In constructing (American) history as linear, the episode prohibits a reading of history that runs alternate to the orthodoxy. History is utopian in its essential progress from a point of mythic origin to the utopian future of the Federated universe. The promulgation of Keeler's pacifist politics will not only lead to defeat in the Second World War but will evolve into a swelling pacifist movement that can potentially oppose the military establishment of the democratic ideal. While Spock acknowledges that Keeler's pacifism is in some sense "right," he suggests that it was simply not propitious in 1941, when America was considering intervening in the Second World War. Here

Star Trek, History and Us

history is accorded the status of always already existing and establishing in the evidence of its existence a "correct" interpretation. What was meant to unfold in the passage of time was in essence right. An unchangeable history is equated with a utopian belief in the natural, preordained progress of the humanist self and society.[76]

Where does the Vietnam War sit in this interpretation of *Star Trek*'s relentless march toward utopia? The peace movement was in full flow in April 1967 when "The City on the Edge of Forever" was broadcast. In January 20,000–30,000 people had organized a "Human Be-In" protest in San Francisco's Golden Gate Park (just a stone's throw from the future location of Starfleet Headquarters)[77]; Martin Luther King, Jr., was giving rousing anti-war speeches to crowds of thousands in Chicago and New York City, and in June, President Johnson would be met by an enormous and significant anti-war rally in Los Angeles, the first in which protestors and riot police clashed.[78] Yet at the same time, Operation Junction City was being undertaken in North Vietnam, an 82-day airborne operation which was the largest by the U.S. military since Operation Market Garden during World War II. The contradiction is clear, and, in this episode, *Star Trek* unexpectedly falls on the side of the pro-war argument.

Had Edith lived, Spock asserts that she would have changed history for, from our perspective, the worse. "While peace negotiations dragged on, Germany had time to complete its heavy-water experiments. With the A-bomb, and with their V2 rockets to carry them, Germany captured the world."[79] This is, of course, the nightmare possible future Shatner and Nimoy, as children of Jewish families as we have discussed, were raised as children to fear, and the one Roddenberry flew missions, along with thousands of other, to prevent. "The City on the Edge of Forever" posits that Edith's peaceful idealism would not have worked in the 1930s and 1940s and plays on the heroic myth that American intervention in World War II "saved the world." We don't know for sure if that would have been the case, though it is likely that Germany, perhaps in concert with the Soviet Union (maybe also Japan), would have conquered Europe without American assistance, and the joint Nazi/Soviet machine might eventually have taken the conflict to American shores. Nevertheless, *Star Trek* here asserts American military dominance as the key path to the utopian Federation future and suggests their efforts in Vietnam, against the cries of the peace movement, are buoyed by a similar "manifest destiny."

Star Trek does seem conflicted about this, to its credit. Spock's logical assertion, "Edith Keeler must die," may seem tough and orthodox, but he also points out Kirk's subsequent melancholy. Kirk equally has zero desire

1. The 1960s

to explore the Guardian as it declares, "Many such journeys are possible. Let me be your gateway."[80] There is no pleasure in the acceptance of the tides of history; great suffering and death are the only direct route to utopian peace for mankind. Yet surrounded by conflict over the very moral necessity of the Vietnam War, *Star Trek* here chooses to uphold it.

Franklin's second example, "A Private Little War," serves as the most direct Vietnam allegory *The Original Series* ever dabbles in. If "The City on the Edge of Forever" questioned the long-term impact of activism, and how it could threaten American geopolitical dominance, then "A Private Little War" openly questions the futility of constant warfare in the looming shadow of geopolitical superpowers.

Taking place on the planet Neural, where a younger Lieutenant Kirk undertook his first planetary survey and befriended a young man named Tyree, the *Enterprise* crew are observing a primitive species who brandish only bows and arrows at their pre-civilization point of development. They witness a rival village armed with flintlock pistols centuries ahead of where their civilization would be technologically, as a Klingon vessel is spotted in orbit. Kirk and McCoy return to Neural undercover in order to expose what they believe is a Klingon plot to seize control of Neural's population and territory by proxy through arming one side unfairly over the other. Since Spock was injured at the beginning of the episode and is in recovery, McCoy joins Kirk and takes serious issue when Kirk attempts to arm Tyree's people so they can fight on equal terms when the time comes. He challenges Kirk's decision despite the fact that Tyree is a pacifist under the spell of Nona, a beguiling healer and local witch sought by tribal men to gain power over their enemies.

Written by Roddenberry,[81] who was for reasons we have explored known to be very much the pacifist, "A Private Little War" aired in February 1968. Influenced presumably by the strong anti-war rhetoric against Vietnam, it is concerned with exploring the broader influences behind the conflict, which at this point defined American foreign policy and its place on the post–World War II stage under the Johnson administration. Just days earlier, as Thomas Doherty noted, the Tet Offensive would have impacted how viewers examined this episode.

> For twentieth-century viewers, the telecast date of *Star Trek*'s A Private Little War—Friday, February 2, 1968, at 8:30–9:30 pm EST—must have been more resonant than the star date entered in the captain's log. Three days earlier, the Viet Cong launched the Tet Offensive, the high-stakes semi-suicidal assault that turned allegedly pacified regions of South Vietnam into raging combat zones. Beamed by satellite from Japan, the first news images of the carnage and chaos in the cities of

Star Trek, History and Us

Hue and Saigon, thought to be citadels of American control, hit the nightly news shows of the three major networks just hours before the didactic episode of NBC's short-lived but eternally syndicated series.[82]

Tyree's people are the "good guys," the South Vietnamese under threat of invasion by the villagers led by Apella, a man in league with Krell, a representative of the Klingons providing them with the advanced weaponry. "You will be rich one day, Apella, beyond your dreams. The leader of a whole world. A governor in the Klingon Empire."[83] Apella's people are the North Vietnamese, the "enemy" under the influence and control of the Soviet Union, attempting to advance their interests by arming the invaders, who are classically in *Star Trek* terms seen as the allegorical influence for the Klingon Empire, in the 1960s and beyond.

Franklin explains this is an example of the bigger forces at play behind this episode:

> Thus "A Private Little War" promoted the official Administration version of the history of the Vietnam War—that it had begun as an intervention by an outside evil empire—the Soviet Union and/or Communist China. In fact, as millions of Americans were then discovering, the war had begun as a defense of an existing empire (France) against an indigenous movement for national liberation, and then transformed into a war of conquest by another nation attempting to advance its own imperial interests in Southeast Asia—the United States of America.[84]

This suggests an inherent contradiction in Roddenberry's script, if we are to assume that "A Private Little War" wants us to see Apella as the corrupted enemy looking to sell his soul to a greater power at the cost of slaughtering the rival tribes people on the planet. Kirk, of course, later does precisely the same as the Klingon Krell—he steals a flintlock and arms for Tyree's men, encouraging them to learn how to wield the weapon. McCoy provides our, and perhaps Roddenberry's, conscience in how appalled he is by Kirk's actions. "You're condemning this whole planet to a war that may never end. It could go on for year after year, massacre after massacre."[85] The inference is clear—Neural is Vietnam, which by this point was being seen by the American public as a curse rather than a blessing as thousands of drafted soldiers were fighting and dying in a war that had no direct benefit on American domestic interests. Kirk even obliquely references the conflict in his justifications: "Bones, do you remember the twentieth-century brush wars on the Asian continent? Two giant powers involved, much like the Klingons and ourselves. Neither side felt that they could pull out?" McCoy remembers it being a war seemingly without end. "But what would you have suggested? That one side arm its friends with an overpowering weapon? Mankind would never have lived

1. The 1960s

to travel space if they had. No—the only solution is what happened, back then, balance of power,"[86] Kirk adds, believing that the only way to preserve the future is through a deliberate, constant state of geopolitical detente. Franklin explains:

> At the time, the growing impatience of the American people with a seemingly endless war was producing an increasingly bitter conflict between advocates of total war, such as Barry Goldwater (who had suggested using tactical nuclear weapons) and Ronald Reagan (who asserted that "we could pave Vietnam over and bring our troops home by Christmas"), and the now huge peace movement, which was more and more demanding that the United States withdraw from Vietnam and let the Vietnamese settle their own affairs. With the logical Spock absent, McCoy is unable to articulate any coherent alternative to the Captain's analysis and is reduced to mere moral outrage. Kirk's own moral anguish in making his choice precisely mirrors that being projected by Lyndon Johnson, who presented himself as a realistic moderate, torn by his rejection of seductive but illusory extremes.[87]

Kirk, by the end of the episode, realizes he has made an incendiary situation even worse.

In that sense, Roddenberry's script has similarities to "The City on the Edge of Forever," in that they both are apologetic about the necessity of the Vietnam War in the larger scope and conflict of the broader Cold War being fought between the superpowers. "City" believes that pacifism would have made an already devastating future even worse. "A Private Little War" suggests that only by equaling the scales, by America supporting South Vietnam as a proxy against the Soviet manipulation of the North Vietnamese, can they prevent the entire South East Asian peninsula falling under Communist control and threatening, more broadly, the global post-war nuclear deterrent and *detente*. The difference is that "A Private Little War" is less overtly conservative about the rationale and crusading reasons to continue Vietnam, and its message is perhaps directly more contradictory.

Franklin sums this up best.

> Even as it was being produced, "A Private Little War" was anachronistic in its view of the Vietnam War, referring more clearly to the period of covert U.S. involvement prior to the assassination of Ngo Dinh Diem in 1963 than to the open U.S. war of 1968. Kirk even points out early in the episode that "keeping our presence here secret is an enormous tactical advantage" over the Klingons. The leader of the hill people has a wife clearly modeled on President Diem's wife, Madame Nhu, the infamous "dragon lady," and each wicked woman helps precipitate the event that triggers escalation by the good outside power. In late 1967 and the first month of 1968, despite all official and media reassurances, Kirk's policy of measured escalation had certainly not led to any resolution, and McCoy's warnings about "a war that may never end" could not be easily dismissed.[88]

Star Trek, History and Us

Only a few episodes later, during Season Two of *The Original Series*, Franklin's third example comes into play in "The Omega Glory," in which Roddenberry doubles down on his anxieties regarding American involvement in Vietnam by casting an identical alien race as savages reduced to barbarism after centuries of conflict.

The *Enterprise* arrives at Omega IV, finding the near-abandoned USS *Exeter* under the command of Captain Ron Tracey, who is missing on the surface while his entire crew have been killed by some kind of biological disease that has reduced them to crystalline chemicals. On Omega IV, Kirk, Spock and McCoy find Tracey in league with the Kohns, the Asian tribe who have subjugated the Yangs, a white, fair-skinned barbaric people, following a devastating biological war. During this war Tracey—having violated Starfleet's sacred Prime Directive not to interfere in other cultures—has interfered due to his belief that the long-life physiology of the Kohns is the key to extended life or immortality. Ultimately captured by the Yangs, Kirk and his crew realize that a duplicate form of the United States has developed here with the American Constitution as their holy text, and he encourages them to follow the words in that text with the Kohns in mind too, as a way of suggesting peaceful co-existence with their fellow tribe.

"The Omega Glory" is, arguably, a sign of how *Star Trek* began losing its way as the show headed into Season Three. *The Original Series* was considerably fascinated with the phenomenon of planetary duplication, as we discussed while looking at "Patterns of Force," but Roddenberry here takes the direct reference to Vietnam in "A Private Little War" one step further by actively recasting the American societal, cultural and quasi-religious experience as a manifest narrative on an alien world. "Yangs? Yanks. Yankees!" realizes Kirk, as Spock figures out, "Kohms. Communists!"[89] while the audience resists a heavy groan, one shared by Franklin in his analysis:

> "The Omega Glory" implies that the war in Southeast Asia, which no longer held any promise of victory or even suggestion of an end, could evolve into an interminable, mutually destructive conflict between the "Yankees" and the "Communists" capable of destroying civilization and humanity. True Americanism is shown as antithetical to mindless militarism and anti–Communism, and the episode rather paradoxically uses ultrapatriotic images of a tattered Old Glory and strains of the Star-Spangled Banner to preach a message of globalism. Kirk's emphasis on "We the People" might even be a suggestion to the American people that they must reassert their own role in the nation's affairs.[90]

"The City on the Edge of Forever" remains uncertain as to whether calls for peace could ultimately serve the long-term greater good in

1. The 1960s

Vietnam, while "A Private Little War" understands that the best needs to be made in engaging in the ideological conflict as a way of providing equanimity against the Soviet forces of Communism, concerned about the destructive nature of this territorial proxy war but accepting it must be fought. "The Omega Glory," only a few episodes later, seems determined to suggest that Vietnam in no way, shape or form can end well for the American people, and perhaps serves as a reaction to the growing protests and concerns among the American public over the nature and scale of the war, as well as the increasingly raised voices of a society angry at what they are witnessing.

Franklin goes on to describe the unrest.

> Most of the countryside of South Vietnam was lost to the insurgent forces, and the 1.4 million troops under U.S. command were locked into a defensive posture around their bases and the cities and towns of the south. General Westmoreland was dismissed from his command. The President of the United States was forced to withdraw from the election campaign, and anti-war forces swept every Democratic primary. Massive uprisings erupted in 125 cities within a single week after the assassination of Dr. Martin Luther King, Jr. More than 55,000 troops had to join police to suppress these uprisings. Washington itself had to be defended by combat troops, while towering above the Capitol rose columns of black smoke from burning buildings. Police and sometimes soldiers battled demonstrators on college campuses across the country. The international finance system reeled from blows to the U.S. economy and its credibility, and the Johnson Administration was forced into negotiations with Hanoi and the National Liberation Front of South Vietnam. Robert Kennedy, running as an anti-war candidate for president, was assassinated on the evening when he had virtually clinched the Democratic nomination. Forty-three GIs, mainly Vietnam veterans, were arrested for refusing to join the 12,000 soldiers, 12,000 Chicago police, and a thousand Secret Service agents who battled anti-war demonstrators outside the Democratic convention in August. Earlier that month, outside the Republican convention in Miami Beach, a line of tanks had sealed off the entire peninsula from Miami itself, where police and National Guard units fought rebelling African-Americans in what a Miami police spokesman called "firefights like in Vietnam."[91]

"The Omega Glory" also presents the allegorical example of a utopian future America in Starfleet as, for the first time, a malign and corrupted figure in the form of Captain Tracey[92] breaks Starfleet's key credo for his own prosperity. He is a forerunner of Admiral Dougherty in 1998's *Star Trek: Insurrection*, a man willing to forcibly relocate thousands of innocent civilians to access life-extending technology, in league with a race looking to exploit those advantages for their own ends. If the Yangs are a fallen, barbaric American civilization brought low by their own use of biological warfare in a conflict against their Asian fellows, Captain Tracey

39

is an example of how Earth's own utopia may not have necessarily fared better. Kirk exemplifies American futuristic values, particularly in his overwrought final speech, but Tracey's devilish corruption—as the episode mixes into American myth the underlying fear of Satanic influence—throws that all into question. "We merely showed them the meaning of what they were fighting for," Kirk claims, when asked if they too have violated the Prime Directive. "Liberty and freedom have to be more than just words."[93]

Allan Austin suggests that "The Omega Glory" establishes the Yangs—the Americans—as the "Other" as opposed to the more civilized Kohms.

> Ultimately, in fact, the "yellow" and "white" civilisations that Kirk identifies on Omega IV seem to live in a world where the white Yangs have become the Asian "other" of Roddenberry's own earth. Cloud William later explains succinctly—if unintelligently—that he did not initially talk because Yangs do not "speak to Kohms. They only for killing." The Yangs, it would seem, have literally become the "yellow horde" of the twentieth-century world. Tracy describes his battle with them with horror. In one bloody showdown, he relates, the Yangs "came and came," sacrificing lives to draw the Kohms into the open, not giving up even as their losses mounted into the thousands.[94]

We are left by the end of "The Omega Glory," therefore, with an American dream torn asunder. Roddenberry presents a vision of a future in which Vietnam was fought, where the peace activists were ignored, where the equal stage of conflict was set, and American imperialist dominance still faltered. Omega IV is a Vietnam in which, Soviets or not, the North Vietnamese won, dominated, and began to erode the South Vietnamese way of life, reducing them to a regressive history. In microcosm, it is a world in which the Soviets win their proxy war, and what could even come to pass should they win the Cold War—the American story being rendered as just that: myth, legend, and Biblical reverence passed down generation to generation without any true meaning of what life, liberty and the pursuit of happiness truly means, certainly until a "God" such as Kirk comes down to teach them. For all we remember Gene Roddenberry as a man resolved to *Star Trek* being an idealized, utopian success story for humanity, in 1968 at least, he was concerned that Vietnam might indicate such a story was not necessarily guaranteed a happy ending.

In Franklin's fourth and final example of Vietnam's direct influence on *Star Trek* in the 1960s, we turn our attention to Season Three's "Let That Be Your Last Battlefield."

While heading to Ariannus, a planet which has been ravaged by a bacterial infection, the *Enterprise* unexpectedly takes aboard a stolen

1. The 1960s

Starfleet shuttlecraft containing Lokai, of the planet Charon, who is being hunted by Bele, a Charon official who considers him a dangerous, murderous political revolutionary. Lokai, in return, believes Bele to represent a fascistic society who kept his people as slaves and committed genocide. What follows is a battle of wills between these two men aboard the *Enterprise* as Bele attempts to bargain for Lokai's release from Starfleet charges of theft, and Lokai seeks political asylum with the Federation. Ultimately, as they connive to steer the *Enterprise* back to their home world come what may, Charon is found to be a ruin, its entire society having been wiped out in bitter, destructive conflict, into which Bele and Lokai simply escape while hunting each other from diametric, ideological sides—their last battlefield.

While perhaps the least overt *Star Trek* episode to discuss the Vietnam conflict, "Let That Be Your Last Battlefield," certainly reflects the increased disquiet among the American people for a war that would rage well into the ultimately disgraced Nixon administration, the episode airing just ten days before Richard Nixon's inauguration. Nixon won partly on a ticket promise he could never deliver on, to "bring an honourable end to the war in Vietnam,"[95] and Oliver Crawford's teleplay is one riven with fatigue, sadness and desperation at the idea of ongoing conflict.

Lokai, seemingly named as a derivation of Loki the trickster, and Bele are denoted by their unusual skin pigmentation. Lokai is black on the right, white on the left, while Bele is white on the right, and black on the left. The racial connotations of their struggle, framed around Lokai attempting to free millions of his people from the yoke of slavery, represents another example of *Star Trek* lacking faith in the just American ideal already compromised by the war in Vietnam. America's bloody history is built on the back of a dark and complicated history of slavery, and "Let That Be Your Last Battlefield" strongly suggests that such a racial dichotomy is far from resolved. The suggestion is even more pointed given that this episode aired in 1969, at the end of a decade marked by, as we have discussed, the birth of the Civil Rights movement and the rise and fall of Martin Luther King, Malcolm X and other champions of racial equality.

James Maycock suggests that Vietnam strongly exacerbated racial tensions among black America as a result:

> Although President Johnson predicted that the Vietnam war would create a political nightmare, he neglected to foresee the racial one. The ongoing domestic conflicts between black and white Americans were reflected and exacerbated over in Vietnam, principally because the very apex of this increasingly unpopular war, between 1968 and 1969, coincided explosively with the rise of the Black Power era

in America. In these years, there was a surge of inter-racial violence within the U.S. forces in Vietnam. Discrimination thrived and, as in America, a racial polarisation arose out of this tension. Black soldiers embraced their culture as well as the emerging Black Power politics and its external symbols.[96]

"Let That Be Your Last Battlefield" can therefore be read not just as a comment on the futile "total war" policy of Vietnam, one already shown in "The Omega Glory," but also as a theoretical collapse of the American ideal, one here expanded to complete and total annihilation: a zero sum game in which neither side conquers. It also serves to frame rising racial concerns at the conclusion of a decade fuelled by rapid social and cultural change.

Franklin considers this episode a summation of the series of *Star Trek* episodes that concern, directly, the cultural and psychological effect of Vietnam:

> The first of these two episodes, "The City on the Edge of Forever" and "A Private Little War," had suggested that the Vietnam War was merely an unpleasant necessity on the way to the future dramatized by *Star Trek*. But the last two, "The Omega Glory" and "Let That Be Your Last Battlefield," broadcast in the period between March 1968 and January 1969, are so thoroughly infused with the desperation of the period that they openly call for a radical change of historic course, including an end to the Vietnam War and to the war at home. Only this new course presumably would take us to the universe of the USS *Enterprise*.[97]

The lack of resolution to the existential trauma of Vietnam, and the broader Cold War behind it, would not end with *Star Trek* in 1969. It would carry through into a decade filled with difficult questions and even more troubling answers as the vanguard to a supposedly brighter future, and the next era of the *Star Trek* franchise.

2

The 1970s and 1980s

Despite being the only decade lacking a live-action *Star Trek* television series, the franchise was nevertheless alive and well in the 1970s, a decade from which there is an argument the American national psyche has never entirely escaped.

The Original Series was, of course, infamously cancelled following "Turnabout Intruder," the final episode of Season Three. That story, which saw Kirk fall victim to a body swap by villainous physician Dr. Janice Lester, cannot be considered a series finale in any traditional sense by which we understand television today.[1] *The Prisoner*, which aired for one season between 1967 and 1968 and became one of the defining cultural artifacts of the decade, ended in supremely nebulous terms with its finale "Fall Out," but there was a deliberate approach by writer and star Patrick McGoohan where that was concerned.[2] Similarly, other defining 1960s series such as *The Twilight Zone*, which was an anthology and unconcerned about narrative continuity, and *The Fugitive*—in which the One-Armed Man was indeed found by the end[3]—almost all had some semblance of an ending that *Star Trek* was not afforded.

It would be difficult to attest that *Star Trek* was cut off in its prime, given Season Three is arguably the weakest year of the show, but not until prequel series *Enterprise* in 2005 would *Star Trek* again be subject to cancellation, and even *Enterprise* was able to cobble together a finale of sorts in the controversial "These Are the Voyages…."[4] "Turnabout Intruder" was no way to bring down the curtain on the *Enterprise*'s five-year mission to explore strange new worlds.

The question therefore turns to why *Star Trek* was cancelled so ignominiously. In truth, *The Original Series* had from day one been fighting against the odds. After getting a second chance with its second pilot, audience figures during the first run failed to ever reach levels NBC would have wanted. There was constant infighting between cast and crew—William Shatner frustrated by Leonard Nimoy's popularity, with the latter playing on that to a degree; Roddenberry operating like an absentee father, leaving

Star Trek, History and Us

much of the best work of the show to producer Gene L. Coon, after losing original script editor John F.W. Black over rewriting scripts; subsequent producers John Meredyth Lucas and especially Fred Freiberger failing to improve a downward trend in the storytelling; and the decision by NBC, not seeing the potential in the series, to cancel the show after Season Two.

This triggered a furious letter writing campaign from the already strong fanbase demanding *Star Trek* avoid cancellation, which in part contributed to keeping the show on air for a patchy Season Three hampered by less money for ambitious storylines and the so-called "Friday night death-slot." Such a flurry of written support would do little to save *Star Trek* come 1969, when the axe finally fell amid falling ratings within an awful time slot. Nichelle Nichols is of the firm belief that these decisions were intentional on behalf of a network who wanted *Star Trek* to fail.

> While NBC paid lip service to expanding *Star Trek*'s audience, it [now] slashed our production budget until it was actually 10% lower than it had been in our first season.... This is why in the third season you saw fewer outdoor location shots, for example. Top writers, top guest stars, top anything you needed was harder to come by. Thus, *Star Trek*'s demise became a self-fulfilling prophecy. And I can assure you, that is exactly as it was meant to be.[5]

You can see the effect of these significant budget cuts on Season Three of *The Original Series*. Darren Mooney suggests it lends the season something of a funereal tone.

> It seems almost as though *Star Trek* is anxious about what will happen to it in death, as if worried that it might become trapped in amber through reruns and syndication. Budget cuts meant that fewer extras were available to play crowd scenes on the *Enterprise,* so the ship frequently looks understaffed and empty. In fact, Kirk finds himself wandering through mostly empty versions of the *Enterprise* in "Wink of an Eye" and "The Way to Eden." The penultimate episode of the season, "All Our Yesterdays," is the only episode of the show to feature no scenes on the *Enterprise* and no appearance from any of the show's regular cast other than the three leads.[6]

Was *Star Trek* dying at the end of the 1960s? Had it reached the end of the idealistic journey, battered by the winds of social, cultural and political change which had rendered the final years of one of the 20th century's most climactic decades in trauma? The Manson Family murders would occur just three months after *Star Trek* departed from screens—a fitting, bloody capstone on *Star Trek*'s era.[7]

And yet, almost impossibly, *Star Trek* survived. Not its cancellation, as we were never gifted the fourth or fifth live action years of the

2. The 1970s and 1980s

Enterprise's five year mission, but it did consistently air in syndicated re-runs across the 1970s and remained in the public consciousness as more than a show that lasted a few seasons and then faded away. *Star Trek* had captured something within the American psyche and, remarkably, began to achieve greater viewing figures and a deeper popularity among the public than it did when it was actually on air. Gene Roddenberry, in a 1972 interview, reflected on perhaps the reason his series struck such a lingering chord:

> I think the thing people dug was that *Star Trek* was one show that was optimistic about the future. Kids today are growing up at a time when people are saying there is no tomorrow, that it may all be over in 20 years. *Star Trek* said there is a tomorrow and that it can be as challenging and as exciting as the past. It said there are things to be done, places to be explored, that things are not at a standstill.[8]

This cultural anxiety about the future was to be expected in the 1970s. Within five years of "Turnabout Intruder" airing, the Vietnam War—so all-pervasive on the American consciousness across the 1960s—was approaching an ignominious, inconclusive end, while President Richard Nixon's term in office would come crashing down following the infamous Watergate scandal which saw him resign rather than be impeached and removed from office. The optimism of the previous decade was giving way, generally, to an ingrained cynicism about the future. Thousands of American boys had died for little or nothing in South East Asia. The Cold War was stagnating, but the threat of nuclear holocaust remained in the atmosphere. And the commander-in-chief was a crooked liar, compromising the sanctity of the vaunted American Constitution. The future of *Star Trek*, on the face of it, could not have appeared further away.

Nonetheless, appetite for the series remained. While fan gatherings and promotions of the show had existed during the '60s when the show was on air,[9] 1972 saw the first recognized *Star Trek* fan convention held in New York. The moniker of "Trekkie" (or indeed "Trekker") began to permeate fan consciousness to describe fans who watched the series, attended conventions, dressed up as crew members and aliens, swapped trivia and facts about the show, and even lived their lives by the ideas and creeds of the future humans of *The Original Series*. For the first time, fan culture responded to the cancellation of its favorite television series by building an entire community around it in response, breathing life into what was fast becoming an artifact of a very different decade.

David A. Goodman, consulting producer on *Enterprise* decades later, believes it was indicative of how the show endured across this decade:

Star Trek, History and Us

> *Star Trek* wasn't a big hit in the sixties when it came out, but it hit in the seventies when there was this malaise and lack of trust in government and you had this iconic American hero at the center of it, and he's surrounded by an international group. It really spoke to America as this great thing. For the British, James Bond is sort of patriotic. The British are still at the center of the world, even though historically they're not. There's a way in which *Star Trek* is the same thing for America.[10]

This no doubt contributed to the inevitable: *Star Trek*'s return, which unfurled steadily across the 1970s with *The Animated Series*, the aborted "Phase II" sequel series, and the subsequent 1979 feature film, *Star Trek: The Motion Picture*, which sent the *Enterprise* and her crew into the 1980s on impulse power. It triggered a rebirth which would be neatly paralleled by the spiritual and emotional journey now Admiral James. T. Kirk undertakes in *Star Trek II: The Wrath of Khan*, as the six movies spanning that decade into the very early 1990s focused on the familial, platonic love story between Kirk and his best friend Spock, via his death, resurrection and rebirth, through to the natural retirement of the crew who had defined the very essence of *Star Trek*.

If the movies were far more about our love of those characters, and their love for each other, than our modern day world reflected through their adventures, Roddenberry sought to redress that balance with the bold new step of *The Next Generation* which, in 1987, would relaunch the franchise with the first live action television series in 18 years, this time with an all-new crew and a futuristic *Enterprise*, set over 80 years after the adventures of Kirk, Spock et al.

The Next Generation was a series born in the embers of the Cold War, working to place the crew under new Captain Jean-Luc Picard on a vibrant, modern, 24th century *Enterprise* within a utopian ideal Roddenberry worked to try and recapture. Interpersonal drama would be sacrificed for a group of advanced humans, close to moral and spiritual perfection, who would push at the frontier *Star Trek* imagined, only to approach an ordered level of exploration, and a confluence of chaos when the Borg are introduced as a major existential threat to *Star Trek*'s emerging battle between individualist gain vs. collective endeavor. This would all take place at the end of the Reagan era and the "success" of the United States, ideologically, over the Soviet Union.[11]

Long before *Star Trek* began the journey to its peak as the 1990s beckoned, however, a long journey lay ahead across a depressed decade where the franchise fought to stay alive against the odds. That fight would begin with what might be described, appropriately, as a rather "animated" enterprise.

2. *The 1970s and 1980s*

The Second Phase

Just before the cancellation of *The Original Series*, NBC proposed the creation of an animated series to run alongside the live-action show, one that would be deliberately aimed at the child market. The proposition included characters from *The Original Series* mentoring a collection of youthful Starfleet officers on a ship called the USS *Excalibur*,[12] who would then go off and enjoy youthful adventures in the *Star Trek* universe.[13]

Ultimately, Roddenberry made the decision that any animated series should be accessible for all ages, particularly given that the active, post–*Original Series* fan base was comprised of as many adults enjoying the show in re-runs as children.

> I just didn't want space cadets running all over the *Enterprise* saying things like, "Golly gee whiz, Captain Kirk!" You know, like Archie and Jughead going to the moon. There are enough limitations just being on Saturday morning.[14]

Hence, in the 1973–1974 network schedule, *Star Trek: The Animated Series* was born. Hiring *Original Series* series writers including David Gerrold, Marc Daniels & D.C. Fontana, not to mention including the voice talent of almost the entire cast of the live action series,[15] *The Animated Series* was approached by those involved as an unofficial fourth season of *The Original Series*, even if its place as "canon" within the universe remains hotly debated even today.[16]

One might ask why, if there remained a clamor for *Star Trek* into the 1970s, *The Original Series* was simply not revived after a few years off air so the five-year-mission could continue. Putting aside the reality of the cast going off to work on different projects following the cancellation, the reasons were primarily financial. The cost of animating the series was far lower than a live-action staging, and the budget wasn't even there for the inclusion of the entirety of the cast as voice-actors. *The Animated Series* serves, therefore, as something of a placating move, a way of capitalizing on the continued fandom of the series while avoiding the prohibitive costs, in a decade of economic downturn, that reviving the series proper would involve.[17]

As William Shatner himself has noted, however, *The Animated Series* allowed Roddenberry the best of both worlds in keeping *Star Trek* fandom and interest alive.

> Story editor Dorothy Fontana would assign scripts, shepherd them through a rewrite or two, and pass the completed manuscripts along to Gene, who had assumed the title of executive consultant. Gene would then read each script, perhaps make a suggestion or two, and sign off. It was that simple. Roddenberry had

Star Trek, History and Us

found the perfect vehicle. The animated *Star Trek* required almost none of his time, it kept his most durable brand name alive, and it served as a lightning rod, rallying the forces to cry, "Bring back *Star Trek!*" In their minds, and this was carefully groomed by Gene at countless conventions, they won their first battle. The animated *Star Trek* should be seen not as a reward in and of itself, but as the first step back toward new and improved live-action Treks, be they on television or the silver screen. Over and over again, fans were urged to keep fighting.[18]

In this sense, *The Animated Series* can be seen as a temporary measure, a torchbearer, but it would be unfair to categorize the twenty-two produced, under half-hour episodes as of little artistic merit. While lacking the depth or craft of the best episodes of *The Original Series*, *The Animated Series* is packed with ideas and concepts that would not have gone amiss during the original three live-action seasons, while having the scope and platform to place the *Enterprise* crew in stories they never would have had the budget, time or special effects to pull off in the latter half of the 1960s.

Take "The Ambergris Experiment," in which Kirk and Spock are transformed into sea-dwelling creatures with the ability to breathe underwater, which leads to their exploring sunken, Atlantean-esque cities and escaping towering sea monsters. Or "Yesteryear," the D.C. Fontana–written half-sequel to "City on the Edge of Forever," in which Spock ends up via the Guardian of Forever in his own past on Vulcan, caught in a temporal paradox whereby he ends up befriending and saving the life of his child self. Fontana discusses how the animated template allowed her to call back to *The Original Series* and the Guardian she had created:

> I thought we could use that for a legitimate trip, but then have something happen so that Spock has to return to Vulcan to his childhood. We could probe into these characters and see the beginning of some of the trouble with Spock and Sarek, Amanda's problems back then, and part of what made Spock Spock. I had wanted to see Vulcan in "Journey to Babel" with a matte shot, but it got cut out. So, with the script for "Yesteryear," I went back to the description from that script and said, "Let's do this now." I wanted to see a city with parkways and trees with growing things, and with unique spires. And we achieved that with animation.[19]

This underscores the point that *The Animated Series* was not simply a less nuanced version of *Star Trek* designed specifically for children, but rather an alternate canvas on which to play out stories that aimed for the same balance of character exploration and social or cultural commentary that had been so beloved of *The Original Series*. It succeeded as frequently as it failed, and the animation to modern eyes is often dated to say the least, but Roddenberry insisted that it not be cheapened for the sake of a different medium:

2. The 1970s and 1980s

The animated series was not a compromise. NBC wanted a strong show in their morning cartoon time slot, and they were willing to go along with my demand that it not be written down to the kiddie level. I believe children are much more intelligent than people give them credit for, so we used *Star Trek* writers and had standard stories. It wasn't a pacifier; it was just an effort to do something a little better on Saturday mornings.[20]

The Animated Series would even try and push the boundaries of what it could get away with, such as in the (admittedly quite ludicrous) "The Magicks of Megas-Tu," which sees the *Enterprise* sucked into a different dimension where magic is the order of the day, and Kirk has to defend the existence of the human race during the trial of the, quite literal, Lucifer. There was meant to be ambiguity as to whether they were encountering the *actual* Devil, but the inference is clear. You sometimes feel *The Animated Series* pushing what it can get away with, tackling Lovecraftian space monsters and shapeshifting beings that the live-action series simply would have been unable to characterize effectively, while holding to a deliberately 1970s aesthetic. Gone, for instance, is Alexander Courage's legendary theme, replaced with Ray Ellis's funkier, brass-filled strings mixed with echoing, haunting interstellar refrains.

Nevertheless, this remains distinctly, in many ways, the same show as *The Original Series*. It has an identical mission statement, a very similar tone, and attempts to pull the same trick as the live-action series—blending wonder, drama and theme into one futuristic, meaningful package. It is by necessity more throwaway, but it extends the aesthetic of *Star Trek* into a decade where, outside of fan circles, it was sorely missed.

Gene's son, Rod Roddenberry, firmly believes it deserves similar appreciation.

> The caliber of the stories was on par and even better than a number of TOS episodes. The animation, of course, was terrible. But storywise, for what they had to work with, it was phenomenal. I like to think of it as the fourth and fifth year of the voyage.[21]

Of course, had Roddenberry's plans in the late 1970s panned out, while we would not have returned directly to the initial five-year mission, we would have experienced a rebirth of the *Enterprise* and her crew in a vibrant, unforgettable way. *Star Trek* would have evolved far differently had *Phase II* ended up a reality, and the first cinematic adventure, *The Motion Picture*, had not come into being.

Star Trek: Phase II was designed as the intended rebirth of *Star Trek* on television, announced by Paramount and scheduled to air in the fall of 1977, almost a decade after the cancellation of *The Original Series*.

Phase II would have been a vindication of the continued fandom and interest in the franchise, kept alive during the aforementioned conventions and thanks in part to *The Animated Series*. It was designed to retain the services of many writing alumni from *The Original Series* to ensure a form of continuity, despite how the *Enterprise* and her sets were due for a significant redesign and update from where they were in 1969, as a way of reflecting the changing aesthetic of the 1970s. *The Motion Picture* would carry this over, with the color and verve of the original *Enterprise* bridge, particularly, replaced by pastels and greys, a sleeker yet emptier design.

The reasons why *Phase II* ultimately failed have been well-documented elsewhere,[22] being a combination of Leonard Nimoy's reluctance to return to the character of Spock on a weekly television basis, escalating costs, and Paramount's inability to fund the network that the series would have ended up on. It became the more legendary "lost" *Star Trek* project in the lore of the franchise—what would have been, after all, a second five-year-mission. Nevertheless, many of the proposed ideas for *Phase II*'s pilot episode and early scripts made it into Alan Dean Foster's draft for *The Motion Picture*. Harold Livingston, who served as chief writer on the intended series, wanted to bring a fresh approach to what audiences understood televised *Star Trek* at the time to be:

> I wanted to make *Star Trek* more universal. I felt that success notwithstanding, the show had a restrictive audience. There was a greater audience for this. I felt that almost all of the stories seemed to be allegorical, and I wanted to make them a little harder and a little more realistic. My broad intention was to create a series that would attract a larger audience by offering more. We would still offer the same elements that *Star Trek* did—i.e., science fiction and hope for the future—and do realistic stories.[23]

Some of the intended concepts for *Phase II* also serve to reflect how *Star Trek*, had it surfaced again as a series in the '70s in the manner *The Next Generation* later did in the '80s, would have reflected the decade in which it existed and perhaps captured some level of that harder realism. Larry Alexander's "Tomorrow and the Stars" would have seen Kirk, as the *Enterprise* was under attack by Klingons, transported in an emergency beam-up accidentally through time to Pearl Harbor, a day before the infamous Japanese attack in 1941. There he would have fallen in love with Elsa Kelly, wife of U.S. Naval Officer Richard Kelly, and wrestled with whether to warn Elsa and her husband while he is suspected by Naval Intelligence of being a spy. The plot is similar to the Don Taylor 1980 film *The Final*

2. The 1970s and 1980s

Countdown, starring Kirk Douglas,[24] and in *Star Trek* terms bests the tragic fatalism of Harlan Ellison's "City on the Edge of Forever," which it could well have been accused of too closely imitating.

"Tomorrow and the Stars" does hang on Kirk debating whether to change history, and warn the U.S. Navy of the attack, much like the question of letting Edith Keeler die to ensure history runs as planned. However, Alexander's story feels just as angled on whether Kirk can be trusted by an intelligence organization spooked at the possibility of impending war for America. Written in the midst of the Cold War, at the end of a decade where Soviet and Communist espionage was a continued American anxiety in the face of developing technology, the idealism of "City" in the '60s—and how it believes Edith dies to protect a better future—is replaced by the mournful sadness of not helping Elsa prevent an attack that kills thousands of people. It is a story with far more direct consequences than "City's" long-term analysis. In that tale, one woman dies. In this version, Pearl Harbor happens. It would potentially have been quite powerful to see *Star Trek* grapple with the lingering trauma of what brought America into World War II.

"The Child," eventually re-written for the character of Deanna Troi in *The Next Generation*,[25] would have focused on one of the new main characters developed for *Phase II*, Lieutenant Ilia (as played by Persis Khambatta, who would go on to play the role in *The Motion Picture*), impregnated by an alien entity and bringing to term a daughter with the *Enterprise* serving as a "womb" of sorts before the child ascends to a higher state of being. Authors Jon Povill and Jaron Summers' choice to focus on Ilia could perhaps have explored *Star Trek*'s approach to *The Original Series*' conflicted sexual liberalism in the 1960s. Ilia was a Deltan, a race with a heightened sexual pheromones and empathic and telepathic abilities, a slick bald pate, and a calm appearance, deeply attractive to another lifeforms.

Roddenberry would later tone down the Deltan idea for the Troi's Betazoid race in the conservative era of *The Next Generation*, but Ilia represented a far more open *Star Trek* approach to overt, post–'60s sexuality. Where Troi looked attractive but was fashioned by her age to be fairly inert as an empath, when we see Ilia in *The Motion Picture*, she is both sexual and compassionate, serving as a key linchpin to the story. "The Child," a failure when it eventually appeared in *The Next Generation*'s second season, could well have been a far more successful tale through the '70s prism of latent sexual openness, although Alan Dean Foster doesn't believe the movie went far enough:

Star Trek, History and Us

> One aspect of Ilia that didn't get utilized when she did show up in the first movie was the sexuality aspect of her. It barely got touched on. Deltans are sexually irresistible people and they cause a lot of trouble wherever they go. They unsettle guys.[26]

If *The Animated Series* had first posited the idea of the holodeck in an early form,[27] and it became one of the key constructs of *The Next Generation* era, then "Practice in Waking," from one of the newer writers intended for the series in Richard Bach, prefigures what would become termed the "holodeck episode" in *The Next Generation*–era. Scotty, Sulu and another of the new main characters for *Phase II*, first officer Commander Will Decker[28] (played eventually by Stephen Collins in *The Motion Picture*), find themselves in a "directed dreaming" scenario after beaming aboard the Long Chance, a drifting sleeper ship from 2004. They wake in a "dream" in 16th century Scotland where they are all, alongside one of the sleeper ship passengers (a woman named Deborah McClintock) suspected of witchcraft and face being burned at the stake. Only dreaming of something they love, something important to them, can bring them back to the real world, and the 23rd century and the *Enterprise* itself become a totem for them all, respectively, to hang onto.

"Practice in Waking" feels like a story that exists as a natural advancement from *The Original Series*' propensity to place the *Enterprise* crew amid historical scenarios and situations from Earth's history that have inexplicably been recreated on alien worlds. While not as simplistically elegant as a virtual reality arena like the holodeck, Bach seems keen to ground the characters inside a historical scenario within science-fiction parameters, hence the "directed dreaming" of the sleeper ship. Casting back to an era of witch trials and a rejection of scientific advancements or heretical ideas feels keenly observed some two decades after America's own political version of such repressive history in the McCarthy Communist hearings. Bach's deliberate point of our future characters holding onto the idealism of the 23rd century as a way to escape the darkness of our own past feels acutely *Star Trek*, particularly during a decade of depressed economic prosperity and political uncertainty. As Scotty remarks to Kirk at the end of the script, "The *Enterprise,* if she is a dream I meet one time only, I'll not want to be waking early."[29]

"Deadlock" taps into a river of particularly 1970s conspiratorial paranoia as David Ambrose's script presents a Starfleet corrupted by alien forces who subject Kirk and his crew to psychological testing and mind-control techniques when the *Enterprise* is falsely recalled to a starbase in order to take part in a simulated war game. "Deadlock" feels designed as a story to reflect the profligacy of successful cinematic outings

2. The 1970s and 1980s

which suggested that dark, insidious forces within the American political system were actively working against the best interests of citizens. Films such as Alan J. Pakula's *All the President's Men* or his earlier *The Parallax View*, and John Frankenheimer's earlier 1962 Cold War tale *The Manchurian Candidate*, directly concern mind-control techniques to dictate political assassination on home soil. *Star Trek* would later return to these ideas with Geordi La Forge in *The Next Generation* Season 4's "The Mind's Eye"[30] and via the work of Nicholas Meyer in *The Undiscovered Country*.

Phase II does also feel inclined to borrow from *Star Trek*'s own history, recycling certain concepts and character templates for the sequel series which may or may not have played as well in the late 1970s as they did in the 1960s. "Are Unheard Melodies Sweet?" by Wesley Thorne plays once again into the overtly sexualized role of women on *Star Trek* in the '70s paradigm. Decker is corrupted by a race of women who use projected fantasy images to entice men to their planet in a mesh of previous ideas utilized in "The Cage" and *The Animated Series*' episode "The Lorelai Signal," a story which would have called for nudity and sexual imagery that almost certainly would never have made it to air. Shimon Wincelberg's "Lord Bobby's Obsession" fused together the character of Trelane from "The Squire of Gothos" with the roguish instincts of a Harry Mudd with a story about a cryogenically-frozen 19th century English nobleman who was abducted by Klingons in the year 1900. It also prefigures the 1990s' resurgent interest in alien abduction and UFO culture, which episodes such as "Tomorrow Is Yesterday" in *The Original Series* tapped into at points.

The script from *Phase II*'s development that arguably had the biggest impact on the future of *Star Trek* was "In Thy Image," from Harold Livingston, which served as the story Paramount eventually decided to level up and turn into *The Motion Picture*—that of the alien entity V'Ger returning to Earth looking for its "creator." The majority of the plot beats instigated by Livingston would eventually make it into the script Alan Dean Foster and Gene Roddenberry were credited for in the final movie. There were shades of the first big-screen treatment Roddenberry had written in the mid–1970s called "The God Thing,"[31] though none of Roddenberry's original idea of a Starfleet Academy-prequel story revolving around Kirk and Spock's friendship, nor perhaps the most fascinating unrealized *Star Trek* cinematic endeavor, "Planet of the Titans,"[32] planned to be helmed by one of the signature purveyors of science-fiction '70s paranoia in his remake of *Invasion of the Body Snatchers*,[33] Philip Kaufman, made their way onto the screen.

The Motion Picture, though having achieved a greater appreciation among *Star Trek* fandom in recent years, is perhaps now best remembered and beloved for triggering the rebirth of the franchise and setting the conditions in place for the celebrated, successful journey of *Star Trek* in the 1980s.

Directed by Robert Wise, known for celebrated previous efforts such as *The Day the Earth Stood Still* and *The Andromeda Strain* among many other works, *The Motion Picture* is considered an elegiac and visually impressive but emotionally distant *Star Trek* movie. It fails to capture the spirit of *The Original Series* or the characters of the *Enterprise* crew, aged and updated a decade on. Critics and professionals today still debate the merits and drawbacks of the film.[34]

Thematically, *The Motion Picture* is tuned into a consistent idea Roddenberry, and numerous writers during *The Original Series*, would explore: that of the confluence between religion and technology, and Roddenberry's keen mistrust of organized religion, which he was only able to convey in the science-fiction scope of his futuristic stories.

Michele and Duncan Barrett have talked about how *The Original Series* established Roddenberry as a keen atheist who, in many of the 1960s episodes, and in the 1970s with *The Animated Series*, considered gods more like humans in their behavior.

> "Who Mourns for Adonais?" takes things a step further by representing Apollo as a petulant megalomaniac—a bad god, in other words. This anti-religious stance is taken further, in the disclosure that Apollo was "really" an alien who visited Earth thousands of years ago and not a divine being at all. (In *The Animated Series* this revelation is reprised in relation first to Lucifer and then the ancient Mayan deity Kukulkan, in the episodes "The Magicks of Megas-Tu" and "How Sharp a Serpent's Tooth?," respectively). While Kirk is willing to acknowledge that Apollo and the other Olympians "gave us so much ... much of our culture and philosophy came from the worship of those beings," nonetheless, the verdict of the episode is clear: by the 23rd century, "mankind has no need for gods.... We've outgrown you."[35]

If Roddenberry's vision had no need for gods, he seemed keen to reinterpret a combination of alien and machine intelligence as a way of exploring humanity as "God," stemming from his original idea for the aforementioned "The God Thing" script, as Richard Colla explains:

> Really, what Gene had written was that this "thing" was sent forth to lay down the law, to communicate the law of the universe, and that as time went on, the law was meant to be reinterpreted. And at that time two thousand years earlier, the law was interpreted by the carpenter image. As time went on, the law was meant to be reinterpreted and the Christ figure was meant to reappear in different forms. But this machine malfunctioned, and it was like a phonograph record that got caught in a groove and kept grooving back, grooving back, grooving back. It's important to understand the essence of all this and reinterpret it as time goes on. That was a

2. The 1970s and 1980s

little heavy for Paramount. It was meant to be strong and moving, and I'm sorry it never got made.[36]

The genesis of what would become *The Motion Picture*, in the human dispatched probe Voyager returning centuries later as V'Ger, a highly advanced machine intelligence inside a living, spaceborne cloud, searching for its "Creator," is clear in Roddenberry's desire to explain the Judeo-Christian tradition away as a greater intelligence, a form of alien life, as opposed to a mythic human construct. He codes the more direct atheism of "The God Thing," which as Colla says would have been a hard pill for studios to swallow even before the imminent return of political conservatism in the Reaganite project, inside V'Ger's less monotheistical *Christian* search for God. In fact, V'Ger is searching as much for meaning within the construct and idea of a creator. As Spock relays, after mind-melding with the consciousness, V'Ger's thoughts are asking questions such as "Is this all I am? Is there nothing more?"[37]

The Motion Picture seems, on some level, a rebuke of the growing rise of the religious right in '70s America, as Derek Thompson describes.

> Alarmed by the spread of secular culture—including but not limited to the sexual revolution, the *Roe v. Wade* decision, the nationalization of no-fault divorce laws, and Bob Jones University losing its tax-exempt status over its ban on interracial dating—Christians became more politically active. The GOP welcomed them with open arms. The party, which was becoming more dependent on its exurban-white base, needed a grassroots strategy and a policy platform. Within the next decade, the religious right—including Ralph Reed's Christian Coalition, James Dobson's Focus on the Family, and Jerry Falwell's Moral Majority—had become fundraising and organizing juggernauts for the Republican Party.[38]

The solution to the problem of V'Ger, to save humanity, is literally for Decker—in a Christ-like maneuver—to sacrifice his corporeal existence in order to join with the entity as a way of evolving beyond its form and programming. "What V'Ger needs in order to evolve is a human quality. Our capacity to leap beyond logic," Kirk surmises.[39] Humanity, encapsulated by Decker, *becomes* God. V'Ger blends with its creator in order to ascend to an unknown state of higher consciousness or being, or "Heaven" if you borrow from Christian parlance. Is this why Roddenberry was so fascinated by the fusion of religion and advanced intelligence? Did he secretly wish he *was* Decker, evolving to learn the answers to the universe beyond corporeal existence? Either way, V'Ger is represented less as God than a disciple seeking its own spiritual awakening.

While these themes made for many an entertaining and thought-provoking episode of *The Original Series*,[40] they struggled to translate at the time for audiences who had, two years earlier, been exposed to the swashbuckling romanticism and fantasy of George Lucas's *Star Wars*, which embraced a nostalgic reverie for 1930s adventure serials and collided their sense of derring-do with state of the art special effects. *The Motion Picture*, by contrast, even with a hefty budget, excellent production design and a magisterial score by Jerry Goldsmith, already by 1979 felt staid in comparison. The film was rushed into completion, and while the global box office more than tripled what the film had cost, Paramount had already spent, on this and *Phase II* before it, millions more than they would have intended at close to $50 million. To them, it was a commercial and, for the most part, critical failure.

David Gerrold believes, ultimately, even the fans themselves didn't truly embrace *Star Trek* of the late 1970s.

> The fans had come off this two-year high with *Star Wars*, and the audience wanted more *Star Wars*, but there wasn't any more. So, they went to see *Star Trek* and they were hungering for more, so *Star Trek* benefitted from the *Star Wars* phenomenon. They went and they saw it over and over again, but it was embarrassing to watch the fans because they were all apologists for this picture: "Well, it's not that bad. It's a different kind of *Star Trek*." Instead of really just acknowledging that it was a bad movie, they tried to explain that it was wonderful, and you were an idiot for not understanding it. It was wonderful to watch them fuck their minds over to explain away a bad movie. The truth was that there was this movie that they wanted to love, and they were so disappointed, but they wouldn't dare say that they were disappointed.[41]

Yet nobody quite realized the 1980s would be a renaissance for *Star Trek*, both as entertainment and in terms of its relevance, thanks to a continuing franchise first of motion pictures which captured far more of the enterprising spirit of the 1960s, a spirit which *Star Trek* fans had loved in the first place.

Undiscovered Countries

The arrival of the 1980s coincides with what many would consider the "savior" of the *Star Trek* franchise in *The Wrath of Khan*. It would kickstart a cinematic renewal that saw *Star Trek* take a prominent place in the cultural and cinematic lexicon of that decade, and arguably helped pave the way for the franchise's return to television with *The Next Generation*.

Following the lukewarm critical response to *The Motion Picture*, plus the financial and production difficulties therein, Paramount Pictures subsequently did two things. They sidelined Gene Roddenberry, pushing him

2. The 1970s and 1980s

upstairs to the role of "Executive Consultant," which gave him no power beyond that of the veto.[42] Secondly, they hired veteran TV producer Harve Bennett to substantially revise the budget and bring home a *Star Trek* sequel for, as it turned out, a quarter of the ballooned costs *The Motion Picture* experienced.

What resulted was a series of pictures across the 1980s which attempted, in varying ways, to recapture the spirit of *The Original Series*, something many of the cast believed had been lost during *The Motion Picture*'s valiant but flawed attempts to transform the franchise, on the big screen, into a *2001: A Space Odyssey*–style cerebral experience. DeForest Kelley believed a major reason that film didn't connect with audiences was because it lost that sense of characterization:

> I was worried when I saw the script, because the characterizations were not there, and the relationships were not there. I was disturbed, and so were Bill and Leonard. We had to put up a great fight. I think anyone will tell you that if the actors hadn't fought like hell to re-establish those relationships, they never would have been there. We would have had a special-effects war. So, there was a great deal of difficulty with the script, which was finally resolved to a certain extent. I still don't think there's enough of the interpersonal relationships in there, and I regret that some of them were lost.[43]

Gradually, the focus on those dynamics, particularly between Kirk, Spock and McCoy, would come to dominate the films which drove the franchise before and during the early days of *The Next Generation*, at times to the chagrin of the supporting cast and the detriment of their own character development.[44]

The Wrath of Khan almost immediately reintroduces the familial. Writer-director Nicholas Meyer, hired after pulling together ideas from five very different drafts while writing on fumes for two solid weeks, builds the entire story around the death of Spock being contrasted with the personal and psychological rebirth of a worn out, middle-aged Kirk, as the series finally embraces the aging reality of the seasoned main cast. He directly connects back to the 1960s by reintroducing the character of Khan Noonien Singh from "Space Seed," transforming the thawed out, princely, swashbuckling eugenicist into a shabby, nomadic, vengeance-seeking cauldron of insanity. Everything in *The Wrath of Khan* is personal for Kirk, in direct opposition to the distant, scientific coolness of *The Motion Picture*.

Yet we see changes in *The Wrath of Khan* that contradict the edict of returning to the vibrancy and adventure of the 1960s. Meyer transforms Starfleet into much more of a naval institution. The costumes morph from the sleek "space pyjamas" of *The Motion Picture* and away from the

Star Trek, History and Us

bouncy kitsch of *The Original Series* to a formal, buttoned up tunic with clear rank insignia. Characters are buried with traditional military honors. Kirk conducts company inspections of the crew. Cadets are put through their paces. *The Original Series* certainly had this structure, but it was less rigorously enforced, and *The Motion Picture* feels less like a military hierarchy than a liberal, scientific assortment of individuals. Meyer considered this returning to the innate realities of *Star Trek* that had always been a contradiction in Roddenberry's approach:

> Roddenberry definitely averred or opined that *Star Trek* was not a naval operation, not a military operation, it was a sort of a Coast Guard, is how he put it. And I thought watching these episodes that that didn't seem to be the case. This was definitely a form of gunboat diplomacy, in which the Federation was a yardstick of correctness. And it doesn't seem, aside from certain technological advancements, the world has substantially changed. People are still making fists and cutting off each other's heads. And, in that sense, my version of *Star Trek* was a gloomier, darker version. But the people were still the same people. They were just having to confront a less optimistic reality.[45]

This perhaps explains why Roddenberry, on regaining creative control to produce the early seasons of *The Next Generation*, heavily relies on the concept of a futuristic utopia for the 24th century with more overt rigor than he ever did on *The Original Series*. It believed in the idea that 23rd century humanity had overcome war and strife as an allied human culture but rarely averred when the series challenged ideas of the Prime Directive or placed the main characters in contradictory positions of personal conflict. Meyer, with *The Wrath of Khan*, seeks out the historical links inherent in Roddenberry's initial mission statement, the vision of Kirk as a "Hornblower in space." However, by middle-age, and by the time of *The Wrath of Khan*, some fifteen years after the end of the five-year mission, Kirk has lost his *joie de vivre*, his lust for life. "You're sitting here in your apartment when you want to be out there hopping galaxies,"[46] as McCoy puts it. Meyer's film is a return to those same values introduced in the 1960s, shot through with the weariness that the previous decade or more has brought.

You can see this in how Khan is depicted. Early drafts had him much more of a powerful being, a mind-controlling revolutionary capable of inflicting mass hallucinations, with the aim of stealing a Federation starship to conquer the galaxy[47]—an idea which later would work its way back around, in some form, into *The Final Frontier*. Meyer chooses to present Khan as an opportunist, a forgotten ancient warrior and the victim of powerful cosmic misfortune, who luckily takes advantage of the crew of

2. The 1970s and 1980s

the USS *Reliant* when they beam down to the sandstorm hell of what they believe is Ceti Alpha VI. The film never plays on his genetic superiority, except to have it mocked by Kirk and Spock's consistent outmaneuvering of him, such as in the prefix code. "He is intelligent, but not perfect. His methods suggest … two-dimensional thinking,"[48] Spock comments. Khan's followers do not even share his thirst for personal revenge against Kirk, considering stealing the Reliant enough for them to have a better life, perhaps themselves weary of more suffering and strife. Meyer's eugenic revolutionaries are as tired and exhausted of life as Kirk, and it contributes to their eventual downfall.

These are signs, perhaps, of the cumulative effect of the 1970s on *Star Trek* as a property. The failed attempt to recapture the optimistic '60s spirit of the show in *The Animated Series*, the difficulties of relaunching the original crew with a sequel TV show, the problematic approach of *The Motion Picture*—all reflect how America dragged itself through a political, cultural and economic malaise in the 1970s, before coming face to face with Ronald Reagan's optimistic conservatism upon his election in the 1980s. In the dying days of the Cold War, and the arrival of neoliberalist economic global policy, Reagan's America transformed American culture, reintroduced a nostalgic fervor for a brighter, more wholesome United States, and *The Wrath of Khan*—while creatively perhaps still the pinnacle of *Star Trek* in cinematic terms in how it balances story and character—serves as the bridge between these two Americas. It has the foreboding, tired sadness of a difficult 1970s and the hopeful conservatism of a brighter 1980s. "Young…. I feel young…,"[49] Kirk remarks, tinged with melancholy. He wants to believe we can all go back to how it used to be.

And what better example of striving for that than *The Search for Spock*, a film built entirely around being unable to let go of what has been lost.

Following the profound conclusion to *The Wrath of Khan*, in which Meyer intended to definitively kill Spock off as a way of lending a powerful weight to Kirk's rebirth in destroying Khan, Leonard Nimoy had discovered through the making of that film a renewed desire to continue playing a character he had grappled with across the 1970s, doing his best to craft a legacy beyond Spock himself. Paramount offered him the opportunity to direct a sequel, and both he and Harve Bennett agreed that the driving force behind the follow up to *The Wrath of Khan* should be Kirk's determination to save the life of his best friend. It leads him on a prohibited mission—against the wishes of Starfleet—back to planet Genesis, created by Khan's megalomaniacal actions and where Spock's body was sent. His

Star Trek, History and Us

goal is to bring Spock to Vulcan where his regenerated self, undergoing a swift biological evolution from child back to adult on the self-destructing Genesis, can be reunited with his "katra," his "living spirit," which Spock had deposited in Dr. McCoy's mind before his sacrifice to save the *Enterprise* and her crew.

The Search for Spock, as a result, is the film most openly indebted to *The Original Series*, certainly up to that point in *Star Trek* history. It has a roguish Kirk taking matters into his own hands. It re-introduces the Klingons for the first time as antagonists, in the form of Christopher Lloyd's quite savage Commander Kruge, looking to steal Genesis for his people. It brings back Spock's father, Sarek, last seen in *The Original Series* episode "Journey to Babel," and reintroduces aspects of Vulcan culture and mysticism not seen since episodes such as "Amok Time." And, most crucially, it focuses on the three most important characters from *The Original Series*—Kirk, Spock and McCoy. Everything about *The Search for Spock* is designed to tap into an internal nostalgia among audiences who did not want to see Spock as no longer part of the series, and equally hoped to see the spirit of the 1960s reflected in the films of the 1980s.

While a film like *The Search for Spock* might as a result be more directly entertaining, with bold and fun sequences such as stealing and then destroying the *Enterprise,* or having Kirk in an *Original Series*–style fistfight with villain Kruge, it is also arguably a step backward from how *Star Trek* was attempting, in cinematic terms, to assert its own style and not simply repeat the past. *The Motion Picture* had Kubrickian-scale. *The Wrath of Khan* had a classical scope and a familial, yet militaristic structure. *The Search for Spock* is, in every sense of the word, a sequel and indicative of how Hollywood entering the mid–1980s was truly embracing the blockbuster format. That same year, Indiana Jones would return in *The Temple of Doom*. A year earlier, the *Star Wars* trilogy concluded with *Return of the Jedi*, and we saw *Superman III* threaten to push that comic-book series too far. *The Search for Spock* fits neatly amid a collection of films which represent those conservative cultural changes in 1980s America. It is designed, soup to nuts, to pull *Star Trek* back rather than push it forward.

In doing so, *The Search for Spock* eschews any kind of broader societal or cultural message and would have existed as a pure-blood romp in the era of *The Original Series*, a film designed to represent action and adventure over an exploration of the human condition. It explores the biology of Spock, being physically reborn amid a dying and collapsing "Eden," but it never truly informs us of anything about who we are as human beings. The

2. The 1970s and 1980s

most it aspires to is a Descartian duality in the mystical nature of Spock's "katra" and the idea that he was able to download his "eternal soul" into McCoy before physical death. "Only his body was in death, Kirk, and you denied him his future,"[50] Sarek rails, unfairly, given Spock seems to have given no indication he had the power for such a mystical transformation. Mahesh Ananth suggests *Star Trek* here embraces the idea that the mind can exist distinct of the body, for a period of time at least:

> Within the philosophy of mind, the mind's ability to exist independently of the body can be explained by the view called dualism. On this view, the mind and the body are radically different kinds of entities; the body is extended physical matter, while the mind is thought to be a certain kind of non-physical entity. Decartes claims that the mind is very different from the body, because the mind can't be carved-up or separated into parts like the body can; the mind, on Descartes' account, is non-physical. This kind of argument supports Spock's mind-transfer event.[51]

Culturally, as a result of this, *The Search for Spock* works harder to inform us of Vulcan culture than our own human experience. We understand that the Vulcans, long able to communicate telepathically thanks to the "mind meld," can physically transfer consciousness. McCoy doesn't directly become Spock as a result, but his behavior changes, innate Vulcan logic conflicting with his own liberal rationalism, to the point it sends him spiraling close to madness. If anything, this plot choice, the manner of bringing Spock back, is designed more to reassert Spock's importance to *Star Trek* as a whole. Not even death can defeat Spock. His is a Christ-like resurrection, born again in a fallen paradise, and returning "cleansed." Post-*The Motion Picture*, after his encounter with the V'Ger entity unlocked the human emotion he was attempting to purge, Spock had grown warmer and more convivial in his Vulcan logic. Upon his return at the end of *The Search for Spock*, that development is stripped away. The character is, in a sense, reset, much like *Star Trek* as a whole. "I have been ... and ever shall be ... your friend,"[52] Spock recounts, as if his dying words were spoken by another man.

The Voyage Home is, therefore, in continuing the story and transforming this era into, essentially, a trilogy within the broader series, bringing *Star Trek* home. With Spock now once again part of the crew, the fourth film's voyage is back to the beginning: Kirk as captain, a united crew, and a brand-new *Enterprise*-A. It just takes them the long way around to get there.

In what might be a fairly unprecedented move, *The Voyage Home* begins with a television-style recap covering the key events of the previous two movies, given how it picks up directly after Spock's resurrection on Vulcan, with the crew of the destroyed *Enterprise* piloting a stolen Klingon Bird of Prey to face the consequences of Kirk's defiance of Starfleet orders. On their return, they discover an alien probe which is vaporizing Earth's oceans and causing fatal ecological damage to the atmosphere, a probe attempting to contact now-extinct humpback whales. Cue Kirk, via a slingshot around the sun, taking the Bird of Prey back in time to the year 1986 to find a pair of whales to transport back to the 23rd century, in order to save their future Earth and by default the Federation.

While on paper a patently ludicrous concept, it both manages to harken back to the spirit of *The Original Series* and at the same time pointedly comment on the growing calls for ecological conservation of the planet that Nimoy was particularly interested in. *The Original Series*, with episodes such as "City on the Edge of Forever," "Tomorrow Is Yesterday" or "Assignment: Earth," memorably used time travel to take the *Enterprise* crew back to the 20th century as a means of exploring various thematic ideas, and *The Voyage Home* serves as a deliberate throwback to those kind of stories.

Nimoy admits he was inspired by the ideas of Edward O. Wilson in considering the thematic possibilities of a conservation story.

> In his book *Biophilia*, he tells us we could be losing as many as ten thousand species off this planet per year—many of them having gone unrecorded. We won't even have known what they were, and they will be gone. He touches on the concept of a keystone species. If you set up a house of cards you may be able to pull away one card successfully … and another card successfully. But at some point, you are going to get a card that is a keystone card. When that one is pulled away, the whole thing will collapse.[53]

While *The Voyage Home* remains, principally, a time-travel romp designed to accentuate the comedic adventure aspects *of Star Trek*,[54] it stands as perhaps the most thematically relevant of *The Original Series* films in our modern day, early 21st century context, given the growing anxieties around climate change, species depopulation, and the developing role of corporations in exploiting our natural resources under a ticking clock of undoable global damage.

The Voyage Home depicts the Federation's future utopia, or Starfleet with its military might and powerfully advanced starships, as entirely neutered by the presence of the monolithic alien probe. Ships that come close are neutralized of power, with the captain of the U.S.S. *Yorktown*[55] forced into drastic measures: "Our systems engineers are trying to deploy a makeshift solar-sail. We have high hopes that this will, if successful,

2. The 1970s and 1980s

generate power to keep us alive."[56] Starfleet Headquarters in San Francisco is decimated by violent electrical storms, forcing the kindly, aged Federation president to broadcast the most fatalistic of subspace warnings: "All power sources have failed. All orbiting starships are powerless. The Probe is vaporising our oceans. Save your energy. Save yourselves. Avoid the Planet Earth at all costs ... farewell."[57] There is little doubt that were it not for Admiral Kirk and his intrepid crew, in their stolen Bird of Prey undertaking their daring mission, the Earth would have been punished with complete destruction for its hubris against nature in exterminating its own marine population. Nature, in that sense, returns to strike a blow against the Federation's futuristic utopia.

It feels the kind of script and story Roddenberry would have approved of. *The Voyage Home* sees 23rd century humanity, filled with enlightened humans who have solved the world's problems, being punished by the specter of 20th century savages, the humans of 1986 that the *Enterprise* crew encounter with all their crudeness, greed and technological lack of sophistication. "What is this? The Dark Ages?"[58] Bones comments at the medical techniques being used on the comatose Chekov, before applying a 23rd century gadget that immediately cures him. It feels akin to one of Arthur C. Clarke's famous three laws governing the future: "Any sufficiently advanced technology is indistinguishable from magic."[59] Bones and Scotty tap into the avarice of a manufacturer by promising him the formula for a futuristic technology, "transparent aluminium."[60] Nicholas Meyer's script plays with the comic possibilities of Spock adopting 20th century profanity in his speech. "It's a miracle these people got out of the twentieth century,"[61] Bones suggests, and the inference is clear: if we continue on the path we are on right now, we may not survive the next hundred years, let alone reach the Federation's utopian future.

In what also feels like a forerunner to *Star Trek*'s eventual exploration of the end of the Cold War in 1991's *The Undiscovered Country*, from Nicholas Meyer indeed, Chekov is even arrested by the FBI after breaking into a "nuclear wessel" in order to extract the uranium needed to help re-crystallize the dilithium in the Bird of Prey's engines following travelling through time. Spock comments, "There was a dubious flirtation with nuclear fission reactors resulting in toxic side effects. By the beginning of the fusion era, these reactors had been replaced, but at this time, we may be able to find some,"[62] again commenting on the 20th century's dangerous exploitation of natural resources for financial and political gain. The FBI consider Chekov to be "a Russkie," but for someone interested in Russian history, Chekov seems oblivious to the fact that government operatives in

Star Trek, History and Us

1986 may consider a Russian man, claiming to be a military officer (even for Starfleet), breaking into an American nuclear submarine something to be concerned about! Meyer plays the interaction for comedy, which perhaps tracks with the steady thaw of hostilities between the two superpowers in the latter half of the decade, but it remains part of *Star Trek*'s cultural history even within a fluffy adventure like *The Voyage Home*.

The hope that humanity may rise above all of these negative, regressive tendencies lies in the character of Dr. Gillian Taylor, played by Catherine Hicks,[63] a biologist at the Cetacean Institute who cares for the two whales, George and Gracie.[64] Kirk ends up taking her back with him after revealing who he and his crew truly are. Immensely compassionate about nature, angry at man's exploitation of it and the environment, and gifted of a photographic memory ("I see words," she claims),[65] Gillian ends up rewarded for her progressive, advanced mindset by being brought forward to the 23rd century for a whole new life in a utopian world she is considered worthy of. "I have three hundred years of catch up learning to do,"[66] she tells Kirk, forgoing the hint of attraction to him to jump aboard a science vessel and explore the galaxy, with the kind of romantic, adventuresome spring in her step that Kirk had pre–*The Wrath of Khan*. Gillian might end up gifted with entrance into utopia, but she affirms *Star Trek*'s hope in *The Voyage Home* that we might reach our potential and become the enlightened beings in Roddenberry's vision.

The fact modern *Star Trek* is now convulsing at this idea, and deconstructing that vision with every new project, suggests how little progress we have made over three decades on from Leonard Nimoy's film.

The final motion picture of the 1980s is, appropriately, the most far reaching in terms of thematic scope in terms of vision and, perhaps indicative of Icarus flying too close to the Sun, *Star Trek*'s biggest singular failure since *The Motion Picture*, both critically and commercially: William Shatner's *The Final Frontier*.

The one and only film directed by Shatner, thanks to a contractual clause that if Leonard Nimoy was allowed to direct a *Star Trek* film then so was he, *The Final Frontier* places now-Captain Kirk and his crew back on a new *Enterprise* as they are directed to Nimbus III, the so-called "Planet of Galactic Peace," which has been taken over by Vulcan revolutionary Sybok (also Spock's half-brother). He entraps the *Enterprise* via a form of mind-control induced by the relief of a person's inner turmoil, steering the ship toward the Great Barrier, an energy field which conceals, at the center of the galaxy, what he believes to be Sha'Ka'Ree or Eden—the physical home of God himself.

2. The 1970s and 1980s

The Final Frontier is the cinematic adventure perhaps most inspired by the conceptual hubris of *The Original Series*, combining pulpy adventure storytelling alongside big thematic ideas, while serving as a particularly conservative advancement on the religious concepts introduced in *The Motion Picture*. In Robert Wise's film and Gene Roddenberry's story, humanity was "the God thing" a superior intelligence looked to join with. In Shatner's script, written with David Loughery, a joint quest between humans, Vulcans, Klingons and Romulans—all believing in the same quasi-religious, mystical concept—push into the so-called "final frontier" to find a literal supreme being. Robert Asa describes *The Final Frontier* (and *The Motion Picture* before it) as films that "implicitly protest[s] against classical theism."[67] Shatner's film has Kirk face the traditional visage of Judeo-Christian Old Testament worship, the old man with a white beard, and question him with the infamous line, "What does God need with a starship?"[68] It is perhaps *Star Trek*'s ultimate example of monotheistic hubris, and while it lines up with Roddenberry's idea of gods as falsehoods and tricksters, it nevertheless prescribes to a conservative outlook. God, in the mind's eye of humanity, remains the Christian vision.

There is a sense that Shatner believes *Star Trek*, while ostensibly running away from religion, has always been looking for God.

> I took the TV evangelist persona and created a holy man who thought God had spoken to him. He believed God had told him, "I need many followers, and I need a vehicle to spread my word through the universe." The vehicle he needed became a starship, which the holy man would captain when it came to rescue some hostages he had taken. Finally, the *Enterprise* arrives at the planet where God supposedly resides, in the center of the universe. Kirk, Spock, McCoy, and the holy man are beamed down to the planet. It's like drawings of Dante's inferno, like a flaming hell. When God appears, he seems like God ... but gradually, in a conversation between God and the holy man, Kirk perceives that something is wrong and begins to challenge God. God gets angrier and angrier and begins to show his true colors, which are those of the Devil. So essentially that was my story: that man conceives of God in his own image, but those images change from generation to generation, therefore he appears in all these different guises as man-made gods. But in essence, if the Devil exists, God exists by inference. This is the lesson that the *Star Trek* group learns. The lesson being that God is within our hearts, not something we conjure up, invent, and worship.[69]

The title of Shatner's film corresponds to the idea of the "frontier," which is tied closely into the American idea of "manifest destiny," which inspired many Americans in the 19th century. It was the idea that the American people had a special mission, to remake the West in the form of agrarian America, and it was a destined duty for their people. Frederick

Star Trek, History and Us

Merk describes it as "a sense of mission to redeem the Old World by high example ... generated by the potentialities of a new earth for building a new heaven."[70] The history of the American frontier is described by Robert V. Hine & John Mack Faragher as "the story of the creation and defense of communities, the use of the land, the development of markets, and the formation of states. It is a tale of conquest, but also one of survival, persistence, and the merging of peoples and cultures that gave birth and continuing life to America."[71] Destiny and providence, combined with an almost religious sense of their mission, combined to instill America in the century before *Star Trek* with a belief that the frontier held a purpose for them, and this was carried through by Roddenberry in *The Original Series* and extended out to what he called the "final frontier," space as an extension of the American expansion westward from the 17th to the early 20th century.

Shatner literalizes this concept by calling his film *The Final Frontier*, in suggesting the end of that push into space culminates with finding God, even despite the scientific and secular goals of the Federation and Starfleet. It is quite at odds with *The Next Generation*, which launched in 1987 and which we will discuss in the next chapter, which saw Roddenberry re-install the 24th century as a utopian vision of a near-perfected humanity encountering gods as tricksters, such as the Q entity.[72] *The Final Frontier*, internalizing the search for God as a personal mission within the self, attempts to simultaneously hold to and undermine Roddenberry's vision of utopia. The Great Bird of the Galaxy himself disliked what Shatner was trying to say in the film, even while Shatner attempts to reflect the geopolitical realities of *detente* in Nimbus III, where diplomats from the *Star Trek* equivalents of America, Russia and China are all working to establish peace, even if that work is drowned in corruption and disenchantment.

Backed by another beautiful score from Jerry Goldsmith and a buoyant lack of self-awareness at how self-important the storytelling is, there remains something oddly charming about *The Final Frontier*. It would not have been the send-off Kirk, Spock and the original crew deserved at the end of the 1980s, as *Star Trek* was embracing a new era on television and considering options once again of prequels and taking the story back in time. However, Shatner's attempt to inject theme and substance into *Star Trek*'s narrative and create a film less about character and more about an idea feels like the inevitable, circular path back to the tone and style of *The Original Series* twenty years earlier, even if his efforts lack the subtlety, nuance or depth to explore these concepts without feeling trite or misjudged.

It was evidence that *Star Trek* was moving on, that by the end of the

2. The 1970s and 1980s

1980s the global and cultural paradigm was shifting, and Gene Roddenberry took the bold step in crafting an entirely new crew, ship and set of adventures for the franchise, with one eye on going where no one, as opposed to just no *man*, had gone before.

The Utopian Generation

In 1991, two years after he left office and not long before the death of Gene Roddenberry, former president of the United States Ronald Reagan visited the set of *Star Trek: The Next Generation*. While previous visitors, such as joint chiefs of staff, would ask Patrick Stewart, who of course played *Enterprise*-D Captain Jean-Luc Picard, if they could sit in the captain's chair, Reagan didn't ask. He just did it.

While Reagan may have graced the world of *Star Trek* with his presence after he was the leader of the free world, there is no doubt that the influence of Reaganism, and the American era he propagated across the 1980s, played a major part in where *The Next Generation* planted its flag politically and culturally.

The Next Generation launched in 1987, the first live-action *Star Trek* series in eighteen years and one weighted with a huge amount of skepticism and expectation. Roddenberry, his health in steady decline, never expected for Paramount to commission a new *Star Trek* series after years of false starts. Fans were dubious an entirely new cast, spearheaded by classically trained Shakespearian British actor Stewart, would be embraced in the manner *The Original Series* cast were. *The Next Generation* presented a new setting in the mid–24th century, a future *Enterprise*, and a resetting of the board for Roddenberry in how he wanted to present his vision of *Star Trek*.

Staff writer Hans Beimler, who wrote for the second season, was one of many staff members to take issue with Roddenberry's approach.

> On *Next Generation*, my argument with Gene Roddenberry was that he felt we were going to solve too many of our problems. Human characteristics like greed and that kind of thing were going to be gone. Captain Picard doesn't have any deep, dark secrets or fears. I always said to Gene Roddenberry that Shakespeare works three hundred years later because the things that motivated human beings then, still motivate us today. That's still going to be true in fifty, a hundred, or two hundred years.[73]

Much has been made of the phenomenon of the so-called "Roddenberry's Box," whereby Roddenberry approached the storytelling on *The*

Star Trek, History and Us

Next Generation with a strict, utopian edict he never as rigorously enforced on *The Original Series*. In the 24th century, humanity would have resolved all points of conflict. Picard and his crew would not bicker or fight with one another, nor would they experience grief or sadness or pain in the same way modern humans do. They would be examples of evolved humanity who had risen above such problems. This stemmed from Roddenberry's genuine belief that humanity would achieve a utopian state of being in the 24th century. It was his personal philosophy, and one which presented extreme difficulties for the writing staff in attempting to create drama around such limiting precepts.[74]

Everyone knows, roughly, the definition of a utopia. It is considered the ultimate goal of what humanity as a society can achieve, a world of peace and harmony in which every problem has been solved, every mountain overcome. It is a philosophical concept which goes all the way back to Plato's *The Republic* three centuries before the birth of Christ, even if the word itself wasn't coined until Sir Thomas More took it from the original Greek as the title of his 1516 book as the description of a fictional island in the Atlantic Ocean just off the coast of South America.[75]

In some sense, More's appropriation of the word can be considered the first recognizable use of Utopia to describe a fictional "world," though arguably the first historical version of this could be Panachea (or Panchaia) from Euhemerus' *Sacred History* around 300 BC, another island on which ethnic tribes in the Indian Ocean establish what is in essence a utopian, paradise society. The Greek original derivation of utopia actually means "no-place," or a non-existent society which was narrowed over time to describe a society *better* than our own—an ideal to strive for. It was in the 19th and 20th centuries that fictional works began to appear which correspond to the idea of utopian worlds.

One of the great formative writers of science-fiction in the late 19th and early 20th centuries, H.G. Wells, significantly explored the idea of utopian fiction in his work; *The Time Machine*, released in 1899, actively questions the idea of utopia given the Eloi in far distant 802,501 AD have become mindless, corrupted slaves to the subterranean, inhuman Morlocks after they rejected both technology and knowledge for a life of basic, simple pleasures. He would later in 1905 write *A Modern Utopia*, which subsequently combines those ideas of technology and social awareness into a consistently improving environment, but even Wells believed this could only be achieved in a progressively socialist, even perhaps Communist, "world state" in which resources and land were owned by the state and not the individual.

2. The 1970s and 1980s

Star Trek in the 1960s professed to portray a utopian future civilization of united humanity expanding America's "manifest destiny" outward from the West toward the stars, but *The Original Series*, grounded as it was during a tumultuous decade of social, political and cultural change, often struggled to truly reflect Roddenberry's vision of a so-called "masterpiece society."[76] Kirk's regular "gunboat diplomacy"[77] and flagrant refusal to hold to Starfleet's core stricture of the Prime Directive suggested the *Enterprise* and her crew held more to the cowboys of Roddenberry's original pitch of *Star Trek* as "Wagon Train to the Stars" than an enlightened assortment of "perfect" human beings. McCoy was a grumpy curmudgeon who later turned out to be a failed father.[78] Scotty is heavily implied, tapping into the clichés of Scottish life, to like his alcohol. We repeatedly see *Star Trek* challenge the idea it presents, as if in the 1960s it cannot quite square the circle of a humanity without imperfection with the aliens and moral, existential problems the *Enterprise* faces in space. As Kirk says in *The Final Frontier*, "I don't want my pain taken away! I need my pain!"[79] If Roddenberry's humanity of the future is accurate, Kirk would *feel* no pain to begin with.

This problem about conflicting the utopian values of *Star Trek*'s vision with the truth of character and drama is inherent in *The Next Generation*, which attempts to reset the core idea of the franchise in the 24th century and reclaim that utopian vision.

One of the key precepts of the *Star Trek* universe is that money no longer exists. Capitalism at some point between the 20th and 23rd centuries collapsed and was replaced by a secular system driven not by market forces but rather collective human endeavor. "The acquisition of wealth is no longer the driving force in our lives,"[80] Captain Jean-Luc Picard tells Lily Sloane in the second *Next Generation* movie, *Star Trek: First Contact*, when the *Enterprise* crew travels back to 2063 to prevent the Borg from changing Earth's history. Though intelligent and resourceful, Lily exists at a dark point in human history, after a Third World War in the mid–21st century which enabled the conditions from which the Federation ultimately sprung, as did the allied human race's ability to see beyond market wealth as a means of denoting success or security. By the 24th century, such a mindset is considered archaic.

Picard addresses this early in *The Next Generation*'s run, in the Season One finale "The Neutral Zone," written by Maurice Hurley, from a story by Deborah McIntyre & Mona Clee, where the *Enterprise*—in a similar vein to *The Original Series*' classic Season One episode "Space Seed"—discovers an ancient satellite containing 20th century humans who are cryogenically frozen. They are classic examples of the kind of regressive human beings the characters in *The Next Generation* have evolved beyond. "One had a heart problem, another had an advanced case of emphysema with extensive liver damage,"[81] Dr. Beverly Crusher reports of the deceased, frozen humans who through their capital bought their way into cryogenic freeze in the hopes of staving off death itself. They display health conditions it is intimated humans in the 24th century simply would not possess—liver damage being a clear sign of alcoholism, for instance. Their return to life in the utopian future is considered a mistake, one even Picard seems frustrated by. L. Q. "Sonny" Clemonds, the more boorish of the Americans thawed out, admits survival was a long shot, "but I figured what the hell, might as well give them the dough instead of leaving it to my ex-wives!"[82] again suggesting a privileged, entitled penchant for resolving human attachments through acquired wealth.

"The Neutral Zone" goes out of its way to make Sonny particularly vulgar in the context of the *Enterprise* crew members, as well as the money-obsessed Ralph Offenhouse, who has the temerity to use the ship's comm system to demand Picard see him, and is confused at why they are not readily used in such a way. "We are all capable of exercising self-discipline,"[83] Picard remarks in an almost patronizing fashion. The 20th century humans are portrayed as crude, gluttonous and obsessed with financial gain, Ralph in particular. He and Picard represent completely diametric points on the human scale. Picard tells him, "A lot has changed in the past three hundred years. People are no longer obsessed with the accumulation of things. We've eliminated hunger, want, the need for possessions. We have grown out of our infancy."[84] This entire episode underscores the mindset of *The Next Generation*, certainly at the beginning during the 1980s, and for much of the show's run. Picard and his crew are above the self-destructive, childish needs and desires, driven by capital, in what they consider to be "ancient" humanity. "The Neutral Zone" feels almost designed as an episode to hammer home the point, especially as Ralph attempts to equate the drive for capital gain as a means of controlling one's life and destiny through power. "That kind of control is an illusion,"[85] Picard counters, simply.

For these reasons, *The Next Generation* has been labeled Marxist by some scholars in the overtly "Communist" approach the series takes to the abolition of capitalism and the establishment of a utopian society based on equality and collectivist thinking. This is refuted by Alex Burston-Chorowicz as a fallacy:

2. *The 1970s and 1980s*

The destruction of capitalism through its own contradictions is nowhere to be seen in *Star Trek: The Next Generation*. There is no emphasis on class warfare or violent revolution. Picard and other Starfleet officers deplore the use of violence unless lives are directly threatened. Picard in particular always stresses diplomacy over a show of force. There is little reference to a collectivist ethos in the show apart from the Borg, whose collective consciousness crushes individuality and is an existential threat to the Federation. The entire point of eradicating market forces is justified as a means for individuals to reach their full potential without material incentive. The collective emancipation of the proletariat from the exploitations of capitalism gives way to a larger liberal sanctity of individualism.[86]

This is key to understanding *The Next Generation*'s values working as much as a rejection of Reaganite values, while embracing conservative aspects of social and foreign policy in the 1980s as *The Original Series* rejected the Johnson administration's hawkish stance in Vietnam while welcoming its encouragement of civil rights and acceptance of counter-cultural change.

The loss of individualism is a profound fear across much of *The Next Generation*. Ralph's determined stance, as a displaced 20th century capitalist, is one reflective of the modern American anxiety of state welfare and collective aspiration. However, Ralph's ability to spot an arrogant bluff comes in handy when Picard faces down a hawkish Romulan commander,[87] suggesting perhaps the 20th century mindset *does* have something still to offer the utopian future and we may not have reached that state of perfection without it. Yet Ralph has no idea how he will exist in a future without a sense of control over his own material wealth and gain, and asks what the challenge now is. "The challenge, Mister Offenhouse, is to improve yourself. To enrich yourself. Enjoy it,"[88] Picard tells him. The 24th century mindset of individualism is designed around personal, social and cultural achievements, a quasi-spiritual enrichment that serves the whole. As Picard tells Lily in *First Contact*, "We work to better ourselves ... and the rest of humanity."[89] Individual improvement serves the strident march of human and Federation prosperity across the final frontier. Burston-Chorowicz adds that this does seem in line with the idea of a utopian vision:

> If the *Star Trek* universe is a socialist utopia, it is more akin with technocratic Fabianism—the belief of gradual socialism without revolution—mixed with modern liberalism. Federationism is, at best, liberal or libertarian socialist in outlook. It is utopian, like Oscar Wilde's *Soul of Man* under Socialism, where Wilde contemplated a society based on equality that liberated people from menial work by advanced machines. This allowed for meaningful individualism to be realized.[90]

Star Trek, History and Us

The Next Generation's standpoint here at first feels at odds with Reaganite philosophy that had dominated the scope of the '80s, in the run-up to the imminent end of the Cold War, but is it, truly? Ronald Reagan sought to reverse the economic stagnation of the 1970s by returning America to the pre–World War II free enterprise, free market economy that existed before the Wall Street Crash and the Great Depression, and Franklin Delano Roosevelt's New Deal policies of welfare intervention. Both of these served as key triggers globally that helped furnish the rise of fascism, triggering World War II and the end of historic American isolationism. Reagan's slogan, "Let's Make America Great Again,"[91] sought a return to American economic *and* social values, a rebirth of the "nuclear family" and the strong moral ethics that had decayed in the years since counterculture. Across the '80s, his rejection of Keynesian economics and return to conservative values across culture, with significant crackdowns on vices such as drugs, combined America's financial prosperity with a widening equality gap and a focus on individualistic wealth and gain. He also firmly believed America's resurgent anti–Communist bent would see "the forward march of freedom and democracy will leave Marxism–Leninism on the ash heap of history."[92] Reagan believed predictions of the prosperity of the so-called "American Century" would bear fruit as the Soviet Union, in ideological opposition, began to decay.

Writing in *Life* magazine in 1941, publisher Henry Luce said of America:

> Throughout the 17th century and the 18th century and the 19th century, this continent teemed with manifold projects and magnificent purposes. Above them all and weaving them all together into the most exciting flag of all the world and of all history was the triumphal purpose of freedom. It is in this spirit that all of us are called, each to his own measure of capacity, and each in the widest horizon of his vision, to create the first great American Century.[93]

A phrase that subsequently entered the popular lexicon, the American Century is redolent of a belief in American global prosperity which without doubt influenced *Star Trek*, and certainly *The Next Generation*. As "neoliberalism"[94] transformed American life across the decade, and the country began bouncing back from the economic stagnation of the 1970s, *The Next Generation* represents an America convinced of its moral and economic superiority as the lone superpower, sensing the end of the Soviet Union. Reagan said in 1983, "Communism is another sad, bizarre chapter in human history whose last pages even now are being written."[95] Yet equally, Roddenberry's vision of utopian society champions a collective belief in individual betterment to achieve that

2. The 1970s and 1980s

superiority and hegemony. Swap out learning to play the flute for investing in a franchise of Quark's bar and the view could be distinctly Reaganite in nature!

The Next Generation therefore positions itself, at the tail end of the 1980s, in a far more rigid position of control and both individualistic, and collective, power. Kirk and his crew in the 23rd century really did feel like they were out on the frontier amid a largely unregulated and wild galaxy in which Starfleet, and the Federation, were but a small part. The 1960s reflected an era when America looked to the Moon and outer space as an uncharted aspect of their "manifest destiny." The universe of the 24th century as depicted in the 1980s feels less out of Captain Picard's control, and the frontier becomes increasingly across *The Next Generation*'s run into the 1990s a world in which Federation peacekeeping superiority and security are the by-word. Kirk was a cowboy; Picard is a diplomat. In the pilot episode of the series, "Encounter at Farpoint," he stands up to the omnipotent force of Q as the defense against his charge of humanity being a "grievously savage race" with no business exploring the galaxy with a robust counter. "We have a long mission ahead of us"[96] implies a level of dangerous exploration the show steadily begins to evade, particularly when Michael Piller takes over as showrunner and focuses the series more on morality plays, character deconstructions and tackling social and cultural issues in the manner *The Original Series* often did.

The early seasons of *The Next Generation* attempt to evoke *The Original Series* while consistently being hampered by the structural difficulties of the inherent lack of drama within its central premise. "The Naked Now" embarrassingly serves as a sequel to "The Naked Time," and uses alien influence to rob the staid crew of their inhibitions far too early to be effective, given we don't yet know them. "Where No One Has Gone Before" reboots early *Original Series* classic "Where No Man Has Gone Before" in order to explore Wesley Crusher's role as a savant and evoke the wonder and spectacle of the unknown *The Next Generation* initially wishes to probe. Q's return appearance establishes him in "Hide and Q" as a modern take on *The Original Series*' trickster god, and he would serve to menace the crew across all seven seasons,[97] appearing in deliberately eccentric stories such as "Deja Q" or "Q-Pid" which run against the safe, ordered grain of Picard's universe. Q, thanks largely to actor John de Lancie, always entertains when he easily could have irritated, but he deliberately appears chaotic, strange and out of place in a way he would never have been in *The Original Series*. These early seasons wrestle with how *Star Trek* should portray itself in the clearer, less unbalanced world of the '80s as opposed to the '60s.

Star Trek, History and Us

This uncertainty bleeds into the geopolitics established in *The Next Generation*'s prism too. The Klingons, thanks to the presence of Michael Dorn's Lieutenant Worf on the bridge of the *Enterprise*, are no longer the existential enemies they were in the 1960s, with relations having thawed with the Federation, as much as episodes such as "Heart of Glory" or "The Emissary" would initially toy with the difficulty of Worf's position as the only Klingon in Starfleet. This is a thread later seasons (and *Deep Space Nine*) would pick up on and make crucial to the broader politics of the 24th century universe. Instead, early on, the Romulans are re-established as ideological villains behind a Neutral Zone, emerging in "The Neutral Zone" from almost a century of isolation to investigate what would end up being foreshadowing for a deeper existential chaos introduced into the '80s *Star Trek* paradigm: the Borg. While the Iron Curtain with Russia was beginning to fall, China remained an unknown, moving toward a form of post–Maoist capitalist communism, and *The Next Generation* establishes a new cold front with a Romulan Empire intending to return to the galactic stage. If *The Next Generation* begins by suggesting there are no more enemies to fight beyond the bizarre (Q) or internally corrupt,[98] then the specter of Romulan ideological resurgence places the early years of *The Next Generation* within a Cold War paradigm. As Romulan Commander Tebok says in "The Neutral Zone," "Outposts destroyed, expansion of the Federation everywhere. Yes, we have indeed been negligent, Captain. But no more. We are back."[99]

This core sense of unshakeable individualism, set to a rigid Federation dominance within a more ordered utopian society, is thrown into chaos by the arrival of the Borg, who in "Q Who?," written by Maurice Hurley, are introduced when Q reappears, angry at Picard's hubris following his warning that humanity was not ready for what lay out there, and flings the *Enterprise* 70,000 light years[100] into a distant part of the galaxy and into the path of a monolithic Borg Cube. Picard even suggests that Q represents what the mission, as he previously described, is about, one that "Q Who?" begins even subconsciously to move away from. "You, by definition, are part of our charter. Our mission is to go forth to seek out new and different life forms, and you certainly qualify as one of the most unique I've ever encountered. To learn about you is, frankly, provocative. But you're next of kin to chaos."[101] That chaos is, undoubtedly, the Borg—a collective of parasitic mechanical droids made up of assimilated species as part of a hive mind, established through technology, and controlled by a Queen, as we eventually learn in *First Contact*, confirming them as a kind of technological apiary filled with consuming worker bees. Their Cubes

2. The 1970s and 1980s

are near indestructible black machines that travel the galaxy, assimilating species with their haunting, automated cry: "We are the Borg. Lower your shields and surrender your ships. We will add your biological and technological distinctiveness to our own. Your culture will adapt to service us. Resistance is futile."[102] They are the ultimate expression of anti–Federation values. They are designed to be in direct opposition of individualist freedom and personal expression. They assimilate, consume, adapt and move on, though the goal as the Queen later explains is disturbingly similar to the one Picard espouses for humanity: "We too are on a quest to better ourselves. Evolving toward a state of perfection."[103]

The utopian humanity of the 24th century seek perfection through collectivized individualist freedom working toward a future of tolerance, peace, understanding and knowledge of the universe. The Borg seek perfection through the unchecked absorption and consumption of that individualism, which makes them a twisted visage of a utopian society. The Queen believes "By assimilating other beings into our collective, we are bringing them closer to perfection."[104] We are therefore looking at two utopian ideals from opposing standpoints, and it makes the Borg the signature ideological enemy for the post–Cold War era in *The Next Generation*, and immediately renders the quasi-Soviet standpoint of the Romulans flexing their ideological might behind their invisible wall moot. The Borg hold no political standpoint. They cannot be reasoned or bartered with. You are either assimilated or they are destroyed, with no in-between, and in that sense, they constitute more of a virus than any kind of political or cultural alien threat. Anne Cranny Francis suggests, when Picard himself is assimilated by the Borg into "Locutus" in Season Three's cliffhanger "The Best of Both Worlds," those viral fears factored into how the Borg were presented at the end of the 1980s:

> This image carries a weight of cultural associations and meanings, including the dread of being fundamentally changed, indeed invaded, by technology. This was a particular concern in the late 1980s and early 1990s during the invasion of Western society by a series of viral vectors, biological and technological; including AIDS, (fears of) Ebola, flu viruses and digital viruses transmitted by email.[105]

While "Q Who?" introduces the Borg as an example of the chaotic danger within *The Next Generation*'s frontier, and heavily suggests they will one day return,[106] the Reagan era begins to pass. The Berlin Wall comes down in 1989, and the Russian promises by President Mikhail Gorbachev lean ever more closely toward *glasnost* and *perestroika* with the United States.[107] *The Next Generation* consequently starts to move away from Roddenberry's initial vision and, once Michael Piller establishes himself with a new writing staff and ethos for the series in 1989, begins to establish the controlled paradigm that would stay with the series throughout the early part of the 1990s.

The Romulans become less existential and more realistic as antagonists behind a crumbling Iron Curtain where the grass is not necessarily always greener. "The Defector" sees the *Enterprise* crew attempt to aid a Romulan officer exiled from his repressive regime, and this is after chief engineer Geordi La Forge in "The Enemy" works with a Romulan soldier on a world they have both crashed on in order to escape. Admiral Jarok's motivations in "The Defector" are born out of political realities he believes he can see and that his government refuses to: "There comes a time in a man's life that you cannot know. When he looks down at the first smile of his baby girl and realises he must change the world for her. For all children. It is for her that I am here. Not to destroy the Romulan Empire, but to save it."[108] Jarok believes war is to be avoided at all costs. Romulus may not be ready for *glasnost*, but men like Jarok are. Yet the Borg remain just around the corner, and when they finally do return, in what many believe to be the finest episodes of *The Next Generation* in "The Best of Both Worlds," right at the turn of the 1990s, they represent something deeper than simply an ugly utopian reflection. They are an inverse of the Federation's quietly colonial intentions as a different kind of hegemonic challenge to galactic individuality.

Lynette Russell & Nathan Wolski argue the point.

> Although the Federation is committed to a project we would describe as colonialist, a self-critique and reflection on this colonial mission develops through the seven seasons of STNG. In particular we see the Borg as a "post-colonial" mirror held up to reflect the nature of colonisation and assimilation. Episodes involving the Borg function as a post-colonial space within which the writers review the foundation narratives and the limits of their own perspectives. The colonising and assimilation functions of the Federation and the colonising and assimilating functions of the Borg are inverse reflections of one another. In reading the Borg in this way, we disagree with Weinstock's conclusion that "STNG's progressive thinking never reached the level of questioning its own authority." In fact, the Borg become the chief vehicle through which ideas of self and other, difference and sameness are explored and critiqued. The Borg function as the prism through which the colonial gaze of the Federation is reflected and intensified.[109]

Is the Federation inherently colonialist? There is strong evidence to suggest they assimilate cultures into their own collective much like the Borg, only with a mindset of sharing knowledge and jointly benefiting from collectivization, rather than robbing a culture of their individuality. Russell and Wolski build on this in their thesis, suggesting the Federation

2. The 1970s and 1980s

world view in the 24th century utopia, and of *Star Trek* at the end of the 1980s, is one defined by a one-world view—the Federation way or the highway, and the areas of the galaxy that do not fit into this paradigm are alien, lawless or to be avoided.

> Within *Star Trek*, recently encountered groups, perceived to be less advanced than the Federation, are frequently described in terms which suggest an expectation of unilineal evolution. The history of planets is often described in terms such as "stone age," or "bronze age" (as in the episode "Who Watches the Watchers"). It is as if the historical trajectory of these groups is expected to follow the path toward the advanced humans who represent the Federation.[110]

If Picard has been established as the *Star Trek* template for conservative individualism, for an era in which the Federation are controlling more of the frontier than they are now exploring it at the end of the American Century, then Picard's own colonization by the Borg is even more shocking, and it is why the events of "The Best of Both Worlds" subsequently carried through Picard's character and the legacy of *The Next Generation* right up to 2020s sequel series, *Star Trek: Picard*. In the way Spock's death in *The Wrath of Khan* thematically defines *The Original Series*, so does the Borg's corruption and assimilation define *The Next Generation* as a series that balances a utopian vision in the one hand and a powerful sense of individualist, American and Reaganite determinism on the other. At the time, Michael Piller had no idea how they would get Picard back to who he was after being assimilated. There were question marks as to whether Patrick Stewart would remain in the series from Season Four onwards, with Jonathan Frakes' Commander Riker being promoted to leading man. And for an entire summer, audiences were left wondering if Picard's assimilation into Locutus would be permanent, and if the Borg had done more than simply colonize and destroy the Federation. They had personalized this dual conflict between the two visions of utopia and assimilated our diplomatic, assured hero.

Without realizing it, *The Next Generation*, with this uncertainty and the existential trauma of what the Borg represent, helped usher in a decade in the 1990s in which all of the political and cultural certainties that defined *Star Trek* would be washed away, and the franchise would push and challenge what it believed possible, while reflecting on its own past, like never before. It would be, for a time, the end of its own history.

3

The 1990s

Though *Star Trek* was an enlightened, progressive projection of humanity born in the ashes of war, it would live long and prosper during an age of geopolitical stability balanced tentatively alongside dynamic social change.

By the 1990s, at the second apex of *Star Trek* amid a rapidly changing televisual landscape, the anxiety of nuclear Armageddon had been replaced by a post–Cold War guilt about World War II and its global consequences.

Many nonetheless consider the 1990s as the "Golden Age" of the *Star Trek* franchise.[1] No other decade saw as much *Star Trek* produced and as many series under the same umbrella on air at once. In 1996, *The Next Generation* had graduated into the cinematic realm, *Deep Space Nine* was reaching its apex four seasons in, and *Voyager* was by now well-established. It would take almost twenty-five years before audiences were again exposed to as much *Star Trek* on television, and the next significant era has yet to fully be contextually appreciated as a concrete entity. The 1990s is as iconic a decade for a generation of *Star Trek* fans as the 1960s was to the generation before them, despite existing within and reflecting two distinctly different eras of American and global geopolitical history.

The Cold War ended in 1991, bringing down the (iron) curtain on almost half a century of tensions that defined the post-war generation within which the democracy that permitted the existence of *Star Trek*, and the television world constructed around it, existed. With it, appropriately timed, came the final collective voyage of *The Original Series* crew in *The Undiscovered Country*, within a narrative where Kirk, Spock et al. on the eve of retirement work to bring down the *Star Trek* universe's own divide between East and West. With *The Next Generation* continuing the ongoing mission of less exploring strange new worlds and more appropriately securing the now unipolar quasi-American, Federation landscape, the *Star Trek* universe would initially be concerned with establishing a homogenous status quo that was rejected by certain scholars in the wake

3. The 1990s

of Francis Fukuyama's assertion that the West had reached "the end of history."

Fukuyama's argument, which we will explore in more depth during this chapter, was questioned at the time by fellow scholar Samuel Huntington, who believed religion and culture would form a stronger influence on Western society than Fukuyama's belief that liberal democracy had finally, definitively, won out. Robert W. Merry codifies this argument, as Aaron Haviland discusses:

> Merry places the discussion in the greater context of a debate between the "Idea of Progress" and "Cycles of History." The Idea of Progress, which aligns with Fukuyama's thesis and of which Merry is critical, posits that humanity as a whole is moving toward a unified civilization of universal principles. Cycles of History, on the other hand, was an idea developed by the German historian Oswald Spengler. Spengler put forward that history can only be divided into separate civilizations, such as Western, Orthodox, and Sinic, that rise and fall in cyclical patterns. It is impossible to conceive of a universal human civilization, as the cultural underpinnings that define each civilization are simply too different.[2]

Star Trek, without a doubt, falls on the side of Fukuyama. What is the Federation but not a civilization of "universal principles"? The 1960s struggled to fully articulate a consistent, solidified base for the Federation as an entity, while the 1980s gestates it in utero with wizened, old Federation presidents, one of whom, in *The Undiscovered Country*, directly counteracts the assertion of Richard Nixon during the Watergate scandal by declaring, "This President is not above the law."[3] He is encouraged by less principled agents of other alien empires to prey on the vulnerability of the ailing Klingons, but he refuses. As Reagan and Gorbachev seek alliance while the Soviet Union crumbles under decades of economic stagnation, so the Federation aids the Klingons when they need it most, breeding the conditions that *The Next Generation* would sail under: a geopolitically stable future, troubled only by existential "viruses" such as the Borg, or malevolent tricksters à la Q.

What happens subsequently, as the initial hope of the early 1990s starts giving way to the suspicion that perhaps neoliberal prosperity has birthed an all-consuming American "Empire" who have made it their mission to not seek out new civilizations but rather police those they know about, is that *Star Trek* begins to question *The Next Generation*'s familial unipolarity. It becomes increasingly troubled with the looming specter of Western history, and how despite the collapse of the 20th century's defining existential conflict, the causes and legacies of the tumultuous first half of the century have not been dealt with by society.

Star Trek, History and Us

Following Roddenberry's death, the second *Star Trek* spin-off series, *Deep Space Nine*, would focus specifically on the Holocaust in a seven-season long narrative with the Bajorans as a Jewish analog, recovering from years of planetary occupation by the fascistic Cardassians, with the Federation as an American or UN proxy providing aid and recovery. While Roddenberry explored conceptual fears and aspects of war in a futuristic paradigm across *The Original Series*, *Deep Space Nine* devoted entire storylines, main character arcs and years of nuanced development into the psychological, physical and political trauma of genocide and conflict, before taking the brave, almost anti–Roddenberry step of plunging the Federation and its idealism into a devastating, destructive and costly galactic war.

Star Trek had the luxury during the '90s of being able to look back and examine the cost of war by re-telling the story through its own narrative. The Dominion, a powerful alien union led by a xenophobic race of shapeshifters who believed in racial purity, assembled an allegorical group of Axis powers (including the Cardassians) to conquer the "Allies," with the Federation now working with former enemies the Klingons and Romulans to push back against the invaders. *Deep Space Nine*'s war added a solemn, yet hopeful footnote to the *Next Generation–era*, which began amid Reaganite neoliberalism at the end of the Cold War, and ended with the dawn of the Bush Administration as prequel series *Enterprise* becomes embroiled in the consequences of the post–9/11 "War on Terror." While throwing the ordered, *Next Generation–era* into chaos, it nonetheless believes that an allied struggle against perpetual war can, like in 1945, prove triumphant.

Beneath these examinations, however, there lies a growing distrust and uncertainty about the morality and veracity of the post–Cold War franchise, typified in how *Star Trek* begins to engage quite readily with conspiracy culture.

As '90s pop culture glanced back to the '60s counter-cultural color, updating science-fiction concepts and B-movie aesthetics with a postmodern sheen—be it the alien invasion blockbuster cheese of *Independence Day* or remakes of enjoyably kitsch '60s concepts such as *The Saint* or *Lost in Space*—the decade also found space to indulge in a growing sense of post–Watergate paranoia as American geopolitical domination truly turned into an empire, and a deeper engagement with the '70s. *The X-Files* served as the chief proponent of the West growing weary of its own, supposedly virtuous leaders, weaving a grand mythological tale which chimes readily with *Deep Space Nine*'s exploration of post-war guilt and manifest legacy, in contrast to destiny. Indeed, it is telling that *Deep Space Nine* is the

3. The 1990s

series to truly introduce these anxieties into *Star Trek* in the Season Six episode "Inquisition," which reveals the existence of Section-31, a secret Federation black ops agency buried inside its original charter which does not, officially, exist.

This contrasts with what Ross Douthat calls the middlebrow conservatism of '80s culture in America, one the '90s sought to invert with cautious trepidation:

> During the '90s, the expansion of cable TV and independent filmmaking began to change this middlebrow-or-bust equation: HBO's *Oz*, the brutal prison drama that paved the way for *The Sopranos* and *The Wire*, debuted in 1997; the "indie" craze kicked off by Steven Soderbergh's *Sex, Lies, and Videotape* (1989) built steadily to 1996, the Year of the Indie, when four of the five Best Picture nominees were produced outside the major studios. But the thing that actors and directors seemed to miss the most about the 1970s—the mood of the decade, the mix of paranoia and pessimism and ambivalence about America itself—made for a poor fit with the optimism of the Clinton boom. What nihilism there was came across as winking rather than bone-deep—Tarantino, not Polanski—and even the strongest forays into subversion and social criticism, such as David Fincher's *Fight Club* (1999) and David O. Russell's Gulf War tragicomedy *Three Kings* (1999), felt somewhat weightless.[4]

Before this re-engagement with mistrust and paranoia which touched *Star Trek*, the Federation's purpose was deemed inviolate in Roddenberry's supposed utopia. Analogues of the Soviet KGB could be found in the Cardassian Obsidian Order or the Romulan Tal'Shiar, who would often plot machinations designed to disturb the stable geopolitical order of the Alpha Quadrant, but the Federation had no apparent equivalent. Starfleet kept the peace, explored, made first contact, and continued the Federation's "soft" colonization of space beyond their territory, but they never deigned to dirty their hands in covert operations, assassinations, and worse. The '90s changed all of that, delivering characters such as Luther Sloan into the *Star Trek* universe, who describes to Julian Bashir the philosophy behind their role as keepers of the Federation's virtue, albeit secretly: "The Federation needs men like you, doctor. Men of conscience. Men of principle. Men who can sleep at night…. You're also the reason Section 31 exists—someone has to protect men like you from a universe that doesn't share your sense of right and wrong."[5]

If the '90s era of *Star Trek* begins with the Federation as righteous custodians of a utopian future whereby all of the major conflicts have receded into history, the decade ends with the same organization turned inside out through unexpected and brutal conflict, one which strongly echoes the anxiety that history repeats, that trauma operates in cycles.

Deep Space Nine's bittersweet conclusion fears that the end of history is less than definitive, even if *Voyager*—the only *Star Trek* series to carry through from the '90s into the 21st century on television—attempts to pretend America's unipolar destiny remains inviolate.

To understand where the decade ends, we must first understand *Star Trek*'s place within its beginning, and how it celebrates the conclusion of one journey while glancing toward the start of another.

The End of History

At the end of *Star Trek VI: The Undiscovered Country*, after the joint crews of the USS *Enterprise* and USS *Excelsior* have foiled the conspiratorial machinations of Klingon General Chang to assassinate the Federation president on the eve of a historic peace summit between the two long-feuding states, Captain James T. Kirk delivers a powerful speech to the stunned chamber and new Klingon Chancellor Azetbur about the near miss on her Federation compatriot's life. "It's about the future, Madame Chancellor. Some people think the future means the end of history. Well … we haven't run out of history quite yet."[6]

These are quite profound words from the soon to retire, legendary Starfleet Captain of *Star Trek*'s most iconic ship and crew, but they borrow from and echo the words of political historian Francis Fukuyama. His 1989 essay "The End of History?" would later be expanded into a political science book, *The End of History and the Last Man*, which serves as a defining text on the socio-political climate at the end of the conflict which defined the second half of the 20th century: the "Cold War," fought ostensibly between the two ideological superpowers of that century—the United States of America and the Soviet Union.

Fukuyama asserted that humanity, as the Berlin Wall fell and the Soviet Union collapsed, was experiencing

> not just … the passing of a particular period of post-war history, but the end of history as such: that is, the end point of mankind's ideological evolution and the universalization of Western liberal democracy as the final form of human government.[7]

There is little doubt that across the span of *Star Trek*, as produced between 1966 and 1991, the Cold War was represented by the political sphere inside and out of the United Federation of Planets. If Gene Roddenberry's initial conception of Starfleet was a future entity of NASA-style explorers, by 1991 under the command of Rick Berman's Paramount division in *The Next Generation* era, the Federation and Starfleet very much

3. The 1990s

emerged as an idealized 23rd and 24th century version of a liberal, tolerant and forward-looking United States of America; indeed *The Undiscovered Country*'s writer-director Nicholas Meyer initialized this transition in his aforementioned adjustment of Starfleet into a naval enterprise.

With the hindsight of decades, we readily describe the *Star Trek* universe in the context of the United Federation of Planets, the governing construct of future Earth under which Starfleet sits as the military umbrella, but it was only from Season Two onwards that *The Original Series* introduced this key aspect to the *Star Trek* fabric as a way of contextualizing its exploration of the future through the lens of the Cold War.

The final two seasons of that show establish three key allegories: Starfleet and the Federation as the United States; the Klingon Empire as the Soviet Union; and the Romulan Star Empire as Communist China. Rick Worland suggests these broader geopolitical developments in *Star Trek* change the series.

> The appearance of the Klingons causes the final frontier to shrink dramatically. Once the Federation mission became basic to the series, many stories began to revolve around the ideological competition between the two superpowers, taking place not on barren rocks in the far corners of the galaxy, but on and around populated planets of varying industrial development where the Federation had important economic, political or military stakes. The Federation was not, therefore, an outer space United Nations—after all the Soviet Union, Libya, Cuba and other American adversaries are UN members—but was more akin to the Cold War conception of the 'Free World,' with Starfleet as its NATO.[8]

While the Federation existed as a quasi-America, forwarding their economic and territorial objectives across the galactic map under an umbrella of peaceful exploration and indeed expansionism, then Roddenberry created distinct oppositional forces to represent the Soviet opposite in the minds of 60s Americana. If the enigmatic and nebulous Romulan Empire represented a shadowy, emergent China—at this point approaching the Great Leap Forward and the iron Communist grip of the infamous Chairman Mao—then the Soviet bear was analogized in the Klingon Empire.

Their development across the first half-century of *Star Trek* very much worked in step with how the Soviet Union's relationship with American society undulated. First introduced in *The Original Series* episode "Errand of Mercy," the Klingons are free of the ridged foreheads that in part would cement them as an iconic science-fiction species in 20th century popular culture, and as exemplified by the fearsome Commander Kor, they are an expansionist warrior species whose values appear directly at odds with that of Starfleet's mission of peaceful exploration.

Star Trek, History and Us

They are precisely what American society would have considered the Russian threat to be in 1967—pervasive, bellicose and a direct ideological challenge to their own post-war sense of determinism.

"We are similar as a species. Here we are on a planet of sheep, two tigers, predators, hunters ... killers. And it is precisely that which makes us great. And there is a universe to be taken," Kor claims to Kirk, attempting to mediate the fate of a defenseless planet with the shadow of a Klingon war looming. "It's a very large universe, Commander, full of people who don't like the Klingons." Kor retorts, "Then it shall be a matter of testing each other's wills, and power. Survival must be earned, Captain."[9]

That "very large universe" Kirk mentions here could just as easily be modern America in relation to a Soviet state they found it impossible to trust and, just a few years after the Cuban Missile Crisis of 1962 inflamed tensions between the superpowers to a level unbearably close to triggering thermo-nuclear conflict, were no closer to accepting in terms of what would later be known as *detente*.

Attitudes were, however, changing among Americans. In the end, Kirk and Kor reached a common accord which avoided war, thanks admittedly to the help of an ancient, enlightened, non-corporeal alien species known as the Organians. Tensions defused. *Star Trek* never depicted a period during the 1960s of the Federation and the Klingons in open conflict. They had been at war—a war we most recently saw in the first season of prequel series *Discovery*—but they were both resolved to not take their respective powers down that destructive route again.

> The long rule of Leonid Brezhnev (1964–1982) is now referred to in Russia as the "period of stagnation." But the Soviet stance toward the United States became less overtly hostile in the early 1970s. Negotiations between the United States and the Soviet Union resulted in summit meetings and the signing of strategic arms limitation agreements. Brezhnev proclaimed in 1973 that peaceful coexistence was the normal, permanent, and irreversible state of relations between imperialist and Communist countries, although he warned that conflict might continue in the Third World.[10]

Star Trek was cancelled in 1969, on the eve of the Apollo 11 Moon landings, perhaps the single most iconic scientific achievement in the 20th century for mankind. The "space race" fought between America and the Soviets was won by the former, yet this renewed interest in the galactic frontier did not save *Star Trek*, nor did it allow for attempted live-action revivals across the decade as the show's posthumous reputation gained popularity among a burgeoning fandom community, as we have earlier discussed. We did not see a Klingon again until briefly at the beginning of

3. The 1990s

The Motion Picture. By then, their ridges were in evidence and their guttural, cod-Germanic language was under burgeoning development, but culturally they remained a distant antagonist, if one less inclined to strike fear into the audience.

Oddly enough, while the Klingons loom larger in *The Original Series* as nefarious antagonists, we meet the Romulans first, halfway through Season One in "Balance of Terror," which ranks among the most iconic episodes of *Star Trek* from the 1960s for a number of different reasons.

"Balance of Terror," written by Paul Schneider, sees the *Enterprise* investigate the loss of contact with Earth outposts along the Neutral Zone, here established as *Star Trek*'s analogy for the so-called "Iron Curtain,"[11] which formed under the peace treaty established after the "Earth-Romulan War" of a century earlier. Kirk is plunged into a battle of wills as a result on the border with an unnamed Romulan commander,[12] leading to a deadly game of cat and mouse between the *Enterprise* and the cloaked Romulan bird-of-prey, one in which—unusually for *Star Trek*—we see the Romulan commander characterized in scenes devoid of the *Enterprise* crew, as he counter-strategizes against Kirk, Spock and company. Ultimately, he would rather destroy his ship than be captured by Starfleet when he loses the battle.

While the Klingons end up characterized with names, it is telling that the Romulans are intentionally devised as a mysterious race. We never learn the name of the commander, unlike we do Kor or Kang or Koloth. If as a species they are analogous to communist China, they also have as much in common with the regal imperialism of the Roman Empire, from which Schrader borrowed their mythology. The commander's second is named, intriguingly, with the distinctively Roman name of Decius. They serve a "praetor" as opposed to a "president" or even "chancellor." No human, incidentally, has ever seen a Romulan visually to this point, after the treaty was signed over sub-space audio communication and the war was fought with atomic weapons. "Earth believes the Romulans to be warlike, cruel, treacherous, and only the Romulans know what they think of Earth,"[13] claims Spock, who given his Vulcan ancestry likely has greater knowledge of the Romulan Empire than he chooses to share with Starfleet.

The difference with the Romulans is that they approach by stealth. The Klingons eventually utilize cloaking technology, but subterfuge is bred into Romulan psychology, particularly when they are reimagined in *The Next Generation* era. Though there has been a war between the Federation and the Klingons, there exists no all-encompassing hard border as there does with the isolationist Romulans. Yet there exists a fear on the side of the Federation at their power. The Romulan commander attempts to deploy a nuclear device to destroy *Enterprise*. The aforementioned war was fought with weapons of mass destruction that, at the height of the Cold War when this episode aired, were a key anxiety within the mind of the American public. It is traditionally saved "only for self-destruction"[14] as Decius claims, but the commander actively deploys it here, in a move that does ironically lead to his own doom.

In that sense, "Balance of Terror" plays into certain deeper theories about how *Star Trek* holds a distinctly liberal, anti-communist view of the Cold War in the 1960s, as espoused by Mike O'Connor when discussing "Errand of Mercy."

> What originally appears as the Organians' unwillingness to recognize the significance of the Klingon threat, and their lack of appreciation for Kirk's noble sacrifice, shifts to a perception of Kirk himself (and, presumably, the Federation he represents) as being far too quick to pull the trigger. The Organians reveal Kirk, who claimed that it was only the militaristic impulses of the Klingons that force him to advocate violence, to be as primed for war as his enemies. Later on, the captain tells Spock that he is "embarrassed. I was furious with the Organians for stopping a war I did not want." In this episode, it is Ayelborne, not Kirk, whose values are most worthy of the viewers' respect. Kirk is positioned as the hero not because he is willing to fight for Federation values, but because he grows beyond that position, which is to say, beyond Cold War liberalism.[15]

As we saw in an earlier chapter, when discussing *Star Trek*'s treatment of Vietnam, itself a proxy war of the broader Cold War conflict, the push-pull between conservatism, liberalism and indeed countercultural pacifism was clear, and the same is true of episodes which provide a direct allegory for the ideological conflict raging at this point. *Star Trek* presents races such as the Romulans and the Klingons but often struggles with the question of where the Federation, or perhaps where Kirk and the *Enterprise*—at times, given his willful ignorance of the "Prime Directive"[16] of his needs, being two different things—stand in relation to their enemies. Does the 23rd century represent a place of peaceful coexistence? Or does the utopian "end of history" suggest the Federation must win the war, as the United States wish to do in the '60s? In that sense, Roddenberry's vision of an idealized future in the '60s is a falsehood. Their Cold War exists just as profoundly as ours did at the time, even if Earth is a supposed paradise.

The Klingons truly re-entered the *Star Trek* universe fully in the third movie sequel, *The Search for Spock*, in 1984—two years after the death of Brezhnev, and at the point the Soviet Union was on the cusp of significant change. *Detente* having been firmly established in the 1970s, with the Russians keen to depict themselves in a less fearfully Stalinist light and an

3. The 1990s

American population reeling from the calamity of the Vietnam War and the impeachment and subsequent resignation of President Richard Nixon after the Watergate scandal, *glasnost* was about to become the new normal between these two historical enemies.

The Search for Spock's ultimate villain is Kruge, a vicious Klingon commander of a lethal Bird of Prey who keeps a slavering pet "targ" and is wont to execute his own crewmen the moment they fail in their tasks or disobey his orders. Worse still, after capturing Kirk's estranged scientist son on the formative planet Genesis, Kruge presides over the young man's quite vicious and sudden execution—arguably one of the darkest and emotionally devastating moments in *Star Trek* history, and particularly for Kirk's character. Kruge, however, is a lone wolf; there is never any sense that he truly represents the Klingon Empire's direct orders and simply wants to attain the secrets of the Genesis Project for his own personal gain.

The Voyage Home (1986) feels the more appropriate depiction of the allegorical tensions between the Federation and the Klingon Empire. While Kirk's theft of Kruge's Bird of Prey in the previous film and the Klingons' assumption that Kirk murdered the entirety of his crew lead to a fiery denouncement of *detente* from a blustering Klingon Ambassador: "There shall be no peace … as long as Kirk lives!."[17] *The Voyage Home* never truly carries through its underlying threat that Kirk's actions to save Spock's life could tip the galaxy into an interstellar war. By 1986, Mikhail Gorbachev was in power in Russia. He and U.S. President Ronald Reagan would begin a fruitful relationship with the singular goal of reducing nuclear armaments to the point the Cold War would no longer be necessary. The beginning of the end for the Soviet Union was unknowingly in evidence.

Star Trek reflected the growing American acceptance that perhaps the day would come when the Communists would not be considered the greatest threat to their civilization and could even integrate into Western society—at least on Federation terms. Nowhere is this more apparent in Roddenberry's vision of the future than in the creation in 1987 for sequel series *The Next Generation* of Worf, Starfleet's first Klingon-born officer, as Peter B. Orlik discusses:

> "One of *Star Trek*'s constant messages is that strangers, even enemies, can become friends. Less obviously, the message is about cultural imperialism, the assumed irresistibility of American culture and institutions. Even communist nationals (Chekov) can be seduced and captured by an expansive American culture. Spock, although from Vulcan, is half-human, with human qualities. We learn, therefore,

that our assimilationist values will eventually rule not just all Earth but extend to other planets as well. With *The Next Generation*, Klingon culture, yet more alien than Vulcan and personified by Bridge Officer Worf, has joined the melting pot.... Inevitably, American culture will triumph over all others—by convincing and assimilating, rather than conquering."[18]

Worf's character existed in a future some seventy years after the end of *The Original Series* era which concludes with *The Undiscovered Country*, and this meant for *The Next Generation*'s first four seasons its portrayal of the mid–24th century would overlap with the end of the 23rd century. Worf's inclusion in Starfleet, despite being frequently pointed out as an aberration which resulted in him being shunned by traditionalist Klingon culture, nonetheless directly corresponds to a universe where the old tensions between the Federation and the Klingons have cooled to the lightest of simmers. If Pavel Chekov in the 1960s on the bridge of the original *Enterprise* was progressive wish fulfillment by Roddenberry, Worf's inclusion as part of the status quo is an even deeper recognition that the old world has fallen apart.

The Federation, the Americans, won.

How did *Star Trek* get there? This is a question posed by *The Next Generation* through the inclusion of Worf in its first few seasons, if not directly. By the end of its first season in 1988, the fifth motion picture *The Final Frontier* depicted the Klingons as antagonists with almost a knowing wink to an audience aware the paradigm had changed. Captain Klaa is a softer version of the Kruge character in *The Search for Spock*—a young warrior seeking to prove himself in battle by besting the legend of Captain Kirk but, ultimately, he works with the Starfleet crew to save Kirk's life from a power-hungry alien being. Even the Klingon Ambassador in that movie is a tired, often drunk old man. *Star Trek* now considers the Klingons on a par with how the James Bond franchise in the 1980s would frequently have Russian intelligence tsar General Gogol sipping tea with his British opposite in Whitehall. The Klingons and the Russians were no longer to be feared.

The Undiscovered Country was not only the final film to feature *The Original Series* crew of the *Enterprise* together, it also answered the question of the Klingon homogenization within the Federation universe and was released in the very year everything changed: 1991. The year the Cold War finally ended as the Soviet Union, following a failed coup against Gorbachev's regime, collapsed. Fukuyama's "end of history" began with two key events that shook the very pillars of Soviet hegemony. One was the collapse of the Berlin Wall in 1989, in which Germans in both West and East Berlin tore down the very core of Churchill's Iron Curtain which had existed since the defeat of Nazism and the end of World War II in 1945, paving the way for a reunified Germany.

The other happened three years earlier in 1986, in a place called Chernobyl, and it was the event which most acutely proves to be the end of over two decades of *Star Trek* history, and the beginning of the next.

An accident at the Chernobyl reactor in the Ukrainian town of Pripyat, since abandoned, led to the release of tons of radioactive material into the atmosphere, which had a direct effect across Western Europe and principally the Soviet Union, with significant political consequences for the Kremlin. *The Undiscovered Country* chooses to portray Chernobyl within the *Star Trek* universe with an explosion on the Klingon moon of Praxis, one of the key energy production facilities for the Klingon Empire, following a similar devastating accident. As a consequence, the Federation concludes that without their direct support, and a cessation of the decades of "cold" hostilities between their two societies, the Klingons may be wiped out within the next half century. As Spock states: "We believe it was the result of over-mining and insufficient safety precautions. The moon's decimation means a deadly contamination of their ozone layer. They will have depleted their supply of oxygen in approximately fifty Earth years. Due to their enormous military budget the Klingons do not have the resources to combat this catastrophe."[19]

The conscious parallels to the Soviet Union and Chernobyl are striking in Spock's address to the Federation Council once the realities of Praxis become clear. KGB documents subsequently declassified by the Ukraine after the dissolution of the Soviet Union between 1971 and 1988 point directly to initial construction negligence or structural problems, many of which were catalogued, few of which were acted on in order to make Chernobyl more secure. The "deadly contamination of their ozone" parallels the fission material released into the Russian atmosphere and the fallout which has estimated to have affected millions of people across Eastern and parts of Western Europe. On Praxis the consequences of such an environmental disaster are even more severe—complete extinction of their society, of the Klingon way of life.

The Undiscovered Country therefore directly parallels the imminent collapse of the Soviet Union with the fall of the Klingon Empire. As a huge military power, they have for decades maintained a significant presence on the border of the Federation Neutral Zone and consequently do not have the financial recourse to prevent their own societal collapse. Much like how the Soviet Union concentrated significant military prowess in

Eastern Europe, attempting to shore up states under the Soviet yoke—many increasingly keen on democracy—the Klingons' defensive mobilization to guard against Federation attack leaves them vulnerable to internal problems. With the Soviets it was political unrest, yet with the Klingons it serves as their own ecological and environmental downfall.

The ultimate signing of the Khitomer Accords at the end of *The Undiscovered Country* marks as seismic a socio-political shift in the *Star Trek* universe as the collapse of the Berlin Wall in post-war Germany, or the eventual collapse of the Soviet Union itself. The Klingons are forced, intractably, into peace accords which allow Federation support, internal reconstruction, and the end of the Neutral Zone. Their chancellor, Gorkon, who inspires this historic moment between these two powers in concert with Starfleet's legendary Captain Spock, may not be removed in a coup following the historic nuclear disarmament treaty Gorbachev signed with the United States, but in a plot with more than a few shades of John F. Kennedy about it, he is assassinated by a conspiracy made up both of Starfleet intelligence officers and Klingon Generals—neither of whom want "peace in our time."

Gorkon, indeed, is considered comparable to the British Prime Minister Neville Chamberlain, who famously waved a white flag of appeasement to Adolf Hitler ahead of World War II; he is viewed by the hawkish General Chang as weak, a figure who would hand over the Klingon Empire to the hegemonic Federation. Kirk, displaying worrying white supremacist tones in his racist consideration of the Klingons throughout the movie, makes the callous response to Chang's suggestion they need the "breathing room" of "Earth. Hitler. 1938."[20] Kirk's racial antipathy, heavily influenced by the murder of his son, mirrors the continued distrust inherent among American society for their Soviet opposites, even in an era of *glasnost* and *perestroika*. The old paranoia remains. "If there is to be a brave new world, our generation will have the hardest time living in it,"[21] Gorkon wisely opines before his assassination.

The "brave new world" would come to pass both for American society and indeed the Federation, at least for a time. Following the collapse of the Soviet Union, former Russian states would begin to flex their democratic muscles, while the 1990s exists as one of the more ideologically peaceful eras in modern global geopolitics, with the super power states working toward shared nuclear disarmament and forward thinking, progressive policies in which the *Next Generation–era* had the space to breathe.

The Next Generation, arriving just before and during the end of Cold War, believed in the conflict as an ideological battle that could be

3. The 1990s

understood and solved. In the late 1980s it presented the Romulans as a worrying unknown factor, but swiftly resolved, in episodes such as "The Enemy" or "The Defector," to unpick their monolithic culture and suggest co-operation between their two world views could be possible. *The Undiscovered Country* arrives in the same year that *The Next Generation* introduces the Cardassians, another race whom the Federation had once waged war with in the intervening years between *The Original Series* and *The Next Generation* that we didn't witness as audiences. While they are presented initially as warlike and aggressive, *Deep Space Nine* subsequently transforms them into fascists who lost their own World War II and pay the ultimate price for their xenophobia and hubris.

The final *The Original Series* film, equally, overlaps with the Season Four into Season Five two-part episode "Redemption," in which Captain Picard becomes "arbiter of succession" for the Klingon Empire as the Romulans, covertly, attempt to influence the accession of a new leader of the empire. It is a tale which cements Picard's role as a diplomat, unlike Kirk's position as more of a political loose cannon amid a rougher Cold War paradigm. He works to influence Klingon politics in a positive manner and establish the Federation as an arbiter of fairness and righteousness, working to prevent the manipulation of a free and fair electoral process. In this sense, as Alex Burston-Chorowicz argues, *The Next Generation*'s approach to Cold War politics was harder to define and often filled with deeper shades of grey:

> *Star Trek* offered its audiences a glimpse into a future where a utopia took shape, loosely infused with values that were now held up as humanity's ideological pinnacle. Nonetheless, prickly issues of power politics, nationalism, dictatorship, and exploitation remained. *The Next Generation* attempted to deal with these issues with Captain Picard serving as the Federation's voice to explore America's new place in the world, just as he explored the galaxy. The dilemmas Picard faced throughout the show mirrored developments in the post–Cold War period. *Star Trek*, once again, was used as a vehicle for social and political commentary.[22]

While there would be a brush fire war briefly during the *Deep Space Nine* era and plenty of internal political issues of succession and rule during *The Next Generation*, the Klingon Empire—having been ecologically supported by the Federation—became more often wary allies than fierce enemies, aiding Starfleet in their near-catastrophic war with the Dominion toward the end of the 24th century. It was only following the existential trauma of 9/11 that the brave new world come to an end, reflected in both the real and fictional universes.

As 9/11 saw the specter of a new enemy rise in Afghanistan and the

Middle East (or rather an emerging threat waiting for decades to fully assert itself), prequel series *Enterprise* in 2001 onwards looked back to the 22nd century and recast the Klingons as a powerful warrior race not to be trifled with. Later, most recently in *Discovery*, the Klingons are represented in the form of a religious sect of extremists who, in the name of a martyred religious figure, begin a war with the Federation in the mid–23rd century—the war, indeed, first referenced in "Errand of Mercy"—designed to destroy their enemy. They see the Federation the way that Al-Qaida and Isil see the West and America—a "Great Satan" with imperialist ideals looking to eradicate their culture and religion.

Star Trek may have believed in 1991 that we were approaching the end of history but, in truth, history was just getting started, and the franchise looked to the past, the legacy of 20th century human history, as a way of figuring out the way to our bold new future.

Darkness and Light

If *Star Trek* was influenced heavily by wartime experiences across the 1960s as the series emerged from the shadow of post-war depression, by the franchise's second era experience had turned to melancholic reflection about not just what caused the conflict but what it took to resist the forces of darkness that drove it.

The 1990s sees *Star Trek* move away from simply depicting Nazism in a literal form such as in "Patterns of Force" and developing entire fictional races and internal histories devoted to exploring fascism, genocide and the aftermath of how these political shocks rippled through societies. Nowhere is this more keenly observed than on *Deep Space Nine*, the second spin-off series set in the *Next Generation* era which debuted in 1992, a year after Gene Roddenberry passed away. These aspects are baked into the show's DNA, a hard-wired part of the unique corner of the *Star Trek* universe that *Deep Space Nine* would mine.

It established a direct parallel between the Jewish experience and the Bajoran people, a deeply religious, largely agrarian species who had just emerged from a half-century long occupation by the Cardassians, a proud, reptilian-looking race of entitled conquerors who would spend decades squeezing vital resources from Bajor and surrounding territories. They enslaved many Bajorans in labor camps and space stations—including *DS9*, so renamed from its Cardassian designation "Terok Nor" after, following the Cardassian withdrawal, the Bajorans requested

3. The 1990s

Federation assistance in stabilizing their territory and assisting them in establishing a provisional government as they begin reconstructing their broken society.

Producer Ronald D. Moore has stated that Bajor is not meant to exist directly as a Jewish analog.

> Depending on the episode, you could also call Bajor Israel, or Iran, or even America and the Cardassians could be Germans, or Russians or several other examples. While these parallels do enter our discussions and sometimes are more overt than others, we don't really try to make Bajor a direct analogy to any specific contemporary country or people. Blending the experiences of many Earth peoples and races into our storytelling allows us to comment on these subjects without advocating a particular political point of view, while at the same time allowing us to view the topics in a different light without the baggage of contemporary politics.[23]

Despite this, the plight of the Bajoran people most directly parallels the treatment of Jews in World War II,[24] while Bajor itself aligns with France during the war, a territory invaded, conquered and subjugated within which a clear and concise program of resistance builds in the Bajoran people.

Resistance becomes the byword for many of these stories within *Deep Space Nine* and later certain episodes from subsequent spin-off series *Voyager* and *Enterprise*. *Deep Space Nine* introduces a main character in Major Kira Nerys, an officer in the Bajoran Militia working as a liaison between the Provisional Government and Starfleet in the role of station Commander Benjamin Sisko's first officer, who was previously a significant player in the Bajoran Resistance movement against the Cardassians in the final days of what is colloquially known by Bajorans simply as "The Occupation." *Deep Space Nine* plays with the question, particularly in Season Five's "The Darkness and the Light," of whether Kira should be treated as a war hero or a terrorist, given how she was part of a cell who took lives as part of the greater good.

Moore again adds that this was a complex and nuanced question:

> Typically, when you get into a scene like this in television or even film, your heroine is confronted by the man from her past who's been wronged by her in some way, and usually she'll say, "You know what? I feel bad, too. You're right. I wish I didn't have to do those things that I did. Can't we all just get along?" But that would have been so phony, especially in this situation. So, I respect the fact that Kira looked at Prin and said "Screw you! You expect me to feel sorry for you? Fifteen million Bajorans died in the Occupation. You people were on our land, you didn't belong there, and you were all guilty!" I mean that's pretty bold. You can't say whether it's right or wrong—it's the stance of a terrorist. But it's what I felt Kira absolutely believed at the core of her being.[25]

Star Trek, History and Us

Deep Space Nine for the most part comes down on the side of Kira being a freedom fighter attempting to free her people from the yoke of fascism, yet the very fact the series makes this argument, that it even suggests that Kira—a character who five seasons in has mellowed into a devoted feminist heroine and team player—could have committed crimes that in any other scenario we might consider her analogous to fundamentalism or extremism, is telling in how the series exists in a paradigm where it is prepared to throw a spotlight on the victors of history. Do we, as Western audiences, consider freedom fighters in the same way as other cultures? Is our concept of "resistance" less nuanced that we have considered? *Deep Space Nine* suggests there may be shades of grey within our traditional post-war definitions of good and evil, righteousness and intolerance.

The first season of the show is heavily concerned with the fallout on the Bajoran people following the Cardassian withdrawal, and how their people attempt to recover and regain their own sense of identity. Their political system may represent Vichy France, but Bajor itself could be a ravaged Poland, littered with scores of concentration camps and haunted survivors. Their subjugated religion based around a litany of incorporeal alien beings known as the "Prophets" becomes a focal point for their cultural restoration, as does the rescue of Li Nalas, an iconic figure in the Bajoran Resistance languishing in a Cardassian prisoner of war camp. He is considered a symbol not just of resistance but heroism, and his recovery chiefly by Kira is seen as a major psychological boost to Bajoran society. In the end, however, Li finds it impossible to live up to the legend surrounding him, giving his life to prevent a government coup in "The Siege" by anti-alien extremists.

Deep Space Nine is even this early on a series which understands that legends, for good or ill, do not automatically line up with accepted reality. Americans, in the wake of World War II, mythologized many of the heroes and crusades against the Axis war machine as indicative of a true-blue battle against the darkness, yet the show questions the veracity of these beliefs. Heroes are not always what they seem. Kira might have killed Cardassians who simply followed orders and didn't give them, while Li Nalas' acts of bravery were outweighed by the need for a symbol of survival. Equally, the cruel enemies perpetrating these crimes exist in more complex circumstances; in the episode "Duet," supposed Cardassian war criminal Gul Darhe'el, aka "The Butcher of Gallitep," expresses deep remorse and regret for his genocidal actions, despite the episode establishing him as a cross between Hannibal Lecter and Dr. Josef Mengele. In truth, the

3. The 1990s

man questioned on *DS9* is Aamin Marritza, a lowly filing clerk who has convinced himself he *is* Darhe'el as punishment for his own inactivity. "I covered my ears every night, but… I couldn't bear to hear those horrible screams. You have no idea what it's like to be a coward. To see these horrors and do nothing."[26]

Aside from the Bajoran Resistance and the reality of Cardassians who may have struggled under the weight of their own fascist regime, *Deep Space Nine* also works hard to establish the Maquis as a significant example of morally conflicted resistance in *Star Trek*'s idealized future.

Introduced in "Pre-emptive Strike," one of the final episodes in the seventh and last season of *The Next Generation*, the Maquis are an organized group of freedom fighters behind the so-called Demilitarized Zone, an area of space filled with unclaimed colonial worlds in the wake of a border war between the Federation and Cardassia (some ten years or so before the beginning of *Deep Space Nine*). Captain Jean-Luc Picard is particularly rankled by his protégé, Bajoran security officer Ro Laren, when "Pre-emptive Strike" reveals her as having Maquis sympathies, and she ultimately leaves her role in Starfleet to join their cause.

She becomes a bellwether of future Maquis storylines in which the organization is considered more of a dangerous irritation to Federation values than the allegorical French Resistance they are named for, who banded together in occupied Vichy government northern France in order to take on the Nazi machine. We never see Ro Laren again, mainly due to production realities of the actress being unavailable to reprise the role, but she is parlayed into various Maquis characters across *Deep Space Nine* and into *Voyager*, where they serve as part of the core series concept of a Starfleet and Maquis crew, lost in a distant part of the galaxy, having to integrate with one another and co-exist.

Their first true introduction comes in the Season Two episode of *Deep Space Nine* called "The Maquis," a two-part story in which Sisko works with his "cold" enemy, the former *DS9* (or *Terok Nor*) Cardassian station commander Gul Dukat, investigating Maquis attacks on Cardassian ships in the Demilitarized Zone. The key twist in the tale is how Sisko's old friend, Starfleet Captain Cal Hudson, turns out to have turned to the Maquis cause, positioning him in conflict with Federation peace-keeping values. Sisko is strong in his condemnation of the Maquis, at least initially. "There is a treaty currently in place between Cardassia and the Federation. If you make yourself an enemy of Cardassia, you make yourself an enemy of the Federation."[27] But equally, thanks to how the Maquis are personalized to him through his relationship with Hudson as opposed to an ideological challenge to Federation peace-keeping efforts, Sisko comes to understand the situation is complicated: "On Earth, there is no poverty, no crime, no war. You look out the window of Starfleet Headquarters and you see paradise. Well, it's easy to be a saint in paradise, but the Maquis do not live in paradise. Out there in the Demilitarized Zone, all the problems haven't been solved yet. Out there, there are no saints—just people. Angry, scared, determined people who are going to do whatever it takes to survive, whether it meets with Federation approval or not!"[28]

You can clearly understand how this could apply to the historical Maquis in the French resistance and how the Allies, attempting their own clandestine operations from London and Washington in the years before the D-day invasion of France, could have grown frustrated at their efforts, as well they did. Charles de Gaulle, later a major post-war French political figure and president, became particularly disenchanted with the Maquis' headstrong determination to combat the Vichy collaborators and their Nazi rulers. This is certainly how Admiral Nechayev, representing Starfleet Command, feels about the Maquis efforts to compromise the unsteady peace between the Federation and Cardassia, who as we have already established given their historical relationship with Bajor, are the allegorical face of Nazi fascism in *Star Trek*. To a pragmatist like Nechayev, the Maquis are a fly in the ointment who threaten a bigger picture, and the stability of the broader quadrant. To a realist like Sisko, at first at least, they are flesh and blood Federation citizens fighting for their freedom in a difficult world.

The entire episode was built on the foundation of Sisko's comment about being a "saint in paradise," with showrunner Ira Steven Behr keen to explore the fantasies of Federation life against the realities of distant colonial existence. "I'd been waiting to say that line in *Star Trek* for a long time. We need to dig deeper and find out what, indeed, life is like in the twenty-fourth century. Is it this paradise, or are there, as Harold Pinter said, 'Weasels under the coffee table'?"[29] Subsequent *Star Trek* series, up to and including the most recent as of this writing, *Star Trek: Picard*, have challenged Gene Roddenberry's concept of a utopian future. Earth may well be free of internecine conflict, tribal nationalist war and fighting for key resources, but over time the idea that such Federation peace has spread like a flower bud across the known galaxy has grown increasingly akin to a fantastic piece of anti-realism. *Deep Space Nine* led the way in suggesting the *Star Trek* universe remained one of wars, powder-keg treaties, conflicted and complicated systems of government, and a galactic landscape of fragile peace that could be shattered by external forces. Behr had this come to pass with the eventual Dominion War.

The Maquis, however, remain a symbol of human resistance in a progressively alien *Star Trek* universe, yet they become increasingly more unsympathetic as the franchise continues. Sisko ends up locked into a psychological battle with the man who essentially replaces Hudson following his death in "The Maquis"—Michael Eddington. Introduced as a headstrong Starfleet security officer at the tail end of Season Three, he nevertheless commands the respect of Sisko before revealing his true Maquis affiliations in Season Four's "For the Cause," abandoning his Starfleet career and his role on *DS9*. If Sisko felt a fondness for Hudson and his predicament based on their friendship, Eddington's perceived betrayal challenges Sisko's own sympathy toward the Maquis at large, especially when his girlfriend, Kasidy Yates, is also implicated in smuggling for the Maquis, and he has to send her to prison. "You know what, Mr. Eddington? I don't give a damn what you think about the Federation, the Maquis, or anything else. All I know is that you betrayed your oath, your duty, and me. And if it takes me the rest of my life, I will see you standing before a court-martial that'll break you and send you to a penal colony, where you will spend the rest of your days growing old and wondering whether a ship full of replicators was really worth it."[30]

This declaration comes after an impassioned statement from Eddington on how he considers the Federation from the viewpoint of the Maquis.

> Why is the Federation so obsessed with the Maquis? We've never harmed you. And yet we're constantly arrested and charged with terrorism. Starships chase us through the Badlands and our supporters are harassed and ridiculed. Why? Because we've left the Federation, and that's the one thing you can't accept. Nobody leaves paradise. Everyone should want to be in the Federation. Hell, you even want the Cardassians to join. You're only sending them replicators because one day they can take their "rightful place" on the Federation Council. You know, in some ways you're even worse than the Borg. At least they tell you about their plans for assimilation. You're more insidious. You assimilate people and they don't even know it.[31]

Can you imagine that speech ever being given in *The Next Generation*? Picard was affronted enough at Ro Laren's abandonment, but Sisko is deeply wounded by Eddington's betrayal of himself and of the Starfleet values he lives by.

Eddington is roughly analogous to the Maquis figure of Jean Renoir, a key figure in the resistance movement who bound numerous cells across France together in a coordinated effort to fight the Nazis within their occupied borders, much to the chagrin of Allied forces and commanders such as Churchill and de Gaulle. In *Star Trek*, the face of the Maquis in many ways *becomes* Eddington, and the writers have been clear in how they were inspired by Victor Hugo's classic piece of revolutionary fiction *Les Misérables* in the relationship between Eddington and Sisko, as Jean Valjean and Javert respectively, to the point Eddington even suggests this in Season Five's "For the Uniform." He understands that Sisko has personalized a conflict that should be broader and ideological, angry and affronted that Eddington abandoned Starfleet principles to lead a group considered, by Federation standards, as terrorists. Would we have considered the French Maquis along similar lines had the Allies made an alliance with the Nazis to jointly rule occupied France as opposed to returning the country to democratic rule? At what point do resistance fighters become terrorists in the eyes of the military and peacekeepers? These are challenging ideas that *Deep Space Nine* puts on the table in a manner that almost makes the utopian concept of *Star Trek* uncomfortable. Sisko's uncertainty about how he truly feels regarding Eddington, and the hardline Federation edict of refusing to help the human colonists in the Demilitarized Zone, reflects how the writers didn't really know which side to fall on either. It takes the Dominion alliance with Cardassia to provide a safe and easy set of villains to destroy the Maquis as a resolution to a difficult ideological problem.

Eddington *does* have a point in how the Federation operates in a post-war paradigm. Numerous writers and theorists have suggested the Federation colonized worlds by stealth, through peaceful efforts and missions of exploration, but in just as insidious a manner as aggressive alien species or egocentric fascists such as the Cardassians. The third *Next Generation* movie, *Insurrection*, builds an entire narrative around Picard standing up to a secret Federation plan with an aggressive race to force the relocation of natives on a planet rich in resources. *Star Trek: Picard* has the *Enterprise* captain—or by then, admiral—resign his commission in protest when Starfleet, following a devastating terrorist attack on Mars, refuse to provide aid and resources to the Romulan people in advance of their sun going supernova. Starfleet and the Federation may have created a utopia on Earth and extol lofty peacekeeping goals of unity backed by exploration and scientific discovery, but when challenged by external forces or a lack of resources, they act much like historical Earth states. They defensively refuse to help the Maquis. A conspiracy within Starfleet top brass attempts to sabotage efforts to help the Klingons following the explosion of their moon Praxis in *The Undiscovered Country*. Sisko even

3. The 1990s

later in *Deep Space Nine*, against his better judgment and manipulated by Cardassian spy Garak, in "In the Pale Moonlight" in Season Six, actively fakes evidence and is complicit in the murder of a Romulan official to bring the Romulans into the Dominion War when projections suggest the Federation will lose. Eddington was many things, and crossed boundaries, but there was a moral objectivity about his cause that the Federation simply didn't like. As he put it, "Nobody leaves paradise."[32] The Maquis resistance was considered as much a resistance to Federation authority as Cardassian rule.

That same institutionalized, privileged Federation hegemony bleeds into *Voyager* too, a show which from the very beginning refuses to truly engage with the Maquis as an entity. The concept forces an entire group of Maquis, led by the noble but driven Native American-born colonist Chakotay, to work alongside Captain Kathryn Janeway's Starfleet crew as they travel the 75,000 light years back to Earth, on a journey they all know could take the rest of their natural lives. At no point, however, does *Voyager* capitalize on the natural enmity between these two ideological stances. *Voyager* had, after all, been sent into the Badlands—the stormy area of plasma and asteroids in the Demilitarized Zone where the Maquis hide, akin to how French Maquis soldiers would hide in forests and hill valleys between attacks—to find and capture Chakotay's cell with the help of undercover Starfleet security agent Tuvok and the newly released ex-Maquis prisoner Tom Paris.

Yet by the end of the pilot episode "Caretaker," Chakotay has neatly slotted into the role of Janeway's "Number One," the Riker to her Picard, and the difficulties of integration rarely raise their head bar the odd grumbling moan from characters such as chief engineer B'Elanna Torres, as *Voyager* instead embraces the science-fiction *Star Trek* formula of exploration and discovery. It was a mistake co-creator Ronald D. Moore found difficult to take and led him to quit the writing staff:

> I don't know what the difference is between *Voyager* and the *Defiant* or the *Saratoga* or the *Enterprise* or any other ship sitting around the Alpha Quadrant doing its Starfleet gig. That to me is appalling, because if anything, *Voyager*—coming home, over this journey, with that crew—by the time they got back to Earth, they should be their own subculture. They should be so different from the people who left, that Starfleet won't even recognize them anymore. What are the things that would truly come up on a ship lost like that? Wouldn't they have to start not only bending Starfleet protocols, but throwing some of them right out the window?[33]

Ultimately, should the Maquis cell forced by Janeway's choice at the end of "Caretaker" to help the Ocampa aliens that strands them in the

Star Trek, History and Us

Delta Quadrant have resisted Starfleet control and homogenization? This is the crux of what Moore was frustrated the show didn't challenge, even while having all of the necessary elements in place. Ultimately on some level, you sense he revived *Battlestar Galactica* successfully a few years later as a response to *Voyager*'s refusal, nay fear, of challenging the core conceits of what made a human, Starfleet crew exploring the galaxy. It found the Maquis' resistant impulse, their challenging of Federation rules and passionate defense of the worlds they did not want to see under a Cardassian yoke, to be an impertinence the show very quickly seeks to burn out of the main Maquis characters on the show. Chakotay becomes Janeway's trusted friend and adviser. B'Elanna falls in love with swaggering flyboy Tom Paris. Tuvok was always a Starfleet spy working against the Maquis. One of their cell even turns out to be, in Lon Suder, a telepathic Betazoid serial killer, albeit one who finds some level of redemption. *Voyager* rejects, fundamentally, the Maquis world-view, paying lip service only to it in gimmick "what if?" episodes such as Season Three's "Worst Case Scenario." When, on receiving messages from the Alpha Quadrant from Season Five onwards, the Maquis crew members learn about the Dominion destruction of the entire organization, they mourn and question whether or not they should even retain any sense of their Maquis identity ... which is rich, given the show has largely ignored these aspects of their characters for five years!

These choices make it all the stranger that *Star Trek* remains fascinated by resistance, and particularly Nazi resistance, even when it seems unable to countenance any form of challenge to Federation—read Western—cultural norms and values. *Voyager* literalizes Nazi resistance in Season Four's "The Killing Game," a two-part episode which traps the crew inside a holodeck simulation of Vichy-occupied France, stalked by aliens called the Hirogen who have seized control of the ship and are using the program to play out their nomadic cultural reality of hunting "prey." It is, in a sense, a 1990s evolution of "Patterns of Force," except without having to awkwardly supplant Nazi Germany on an alien planet in step with an alien race which nevertheless looks human. *Voyager* was obsessed with the holodeck and utilizing familiar human characters and constructs to tell science-fiction stories, and "The Killing Game" is perhaps the most pointed reaction to the ideas of war and resistance conveyed on any of the series. *Deep Space Nine* bathed in allegory. *Voyager* actually dresses up the *Predator*-esque Hirogen in Nazi uniforms in a holographic re-creation of 1940s France.

Crucially, the writers invent for "The Killing Game" a piece of holodeck

3. The 1990s

magic technology called a "neural interface" which allows the Hirogen to convince the captured Starfleet crew they are the characters within the simulation. Hence Janeway truly believes she is Katrine, the headstrong Resistance agent and owner of a cafe in the small Vichy town of Sainte-Claire, and Seven of Nine—*Voyager*'s aloof yet physically beautiful de-assimilated Borg drone—believes she is a sultry, Nazi-coveted lounge singer. This is partly a narrative technique to extend the concept but it also, strangely, works to replicate the personalities of the crew inside these fictional archetypes resisting Nazi rule. Tuvok therefore is Katrine's loyal bartender, B'Elanna the feisty Resistance agent, Neelix the friendly courier between Nazis and the French and so on. *Voyager* doesn't seem to embrace allegory in the same context when it comes to sympathetic resistance. Half of the crew, being Maquis, have an built-in intolerance of oppression and fascism that inspired them to become militant freedom fighters, yet *Voyager* works to reduce these impulses. *Deep Space Nine* dared to suggest the Federation might be as complicit in crushing resistance to their hegemony as the Nazis or Cardassians attempted to be, if in a democratic manner. *Voyager* reduces these ideas to playful archetype and literalizes the Nazi as part of an alien sport. Joe Menosky's rationale behind the story betrays the simplicity. "When I got back from Europe, I wanted to do a World War II show [...] I thought it would be real cool to do a World War II episode with our characters, and have a little French town and tanks and our people in GI uniforms."[34] We're a long way from saints in paradise, here.

This is not to say "The Killing Game" is a bad episode of *Star Trek*. Quite the contrary in fact, and it forms part of *Voyager*'s strongest season; however, it exemplifies how differently *Voyager* and indeed *Enterprise*, at the end of the '90s and early into the '00s, approach war and resistance compared to *Deep Space Nine*. *Enterprise* essentially repurposes aspects of "The Killing Game" in Season Four opener "Storm Front," in which a sinister alien race called the Na'khul manipulate Earth's history to seize control of the Nazi war machine during World War II, forcing Captain Archer and his crew back in time to save them and repair damage to the timeline. It ends up a story much more about the complex Temporal Cold War narrative of that series than making any particular commentary on fascism. *Deep Space Nine*, conversely, toward the end of its seven-season run, cyclically angled back toward the initial ideas of resistance, war guilt, and economic and social recovery from the trauma of holocaust and fascist rule, by invoking a cruel irony. Cardassia, the perpetrators of the decades-long war crimes on the Bajoran people, suffer a similar—if less protracted—occupation and systematic elimination by the Changelings of the Dominion and their Jem'Hadar shock troops in the final days of the conflict, as the Federation-Klingon-Romulan alliance close in, having turned the tide and with plans—à la the Allies reaching Berlin—to liberate Cardassia and end the war.

"Citizens of Cardassia, this latest wave of vandalism directed against your Dominion allies must stop. We know that these disgraceful acts of sabotage were carried out by a mere handful of extremists. But these radicals must come to realize that their disobedience will not be tolerated. That you, the Cardassian people, will suffer the consequences of their cowardly actions. Which is why I must inform you, just a few moments ago, Dominion troops reduced Lakarian City to ashes. There were no survivors. Two million men, women and children … gone in a matter of moments."[35] So broadcasts Changeling stooge Weyoun during series finale "What You Leave Behind" as a justification for an immediate, horrific war crime perpetrated by a cornered foe aware of their own impending defeat, and in response to the efforts of *DS9*'s first officer Kira Nerys, now working—in the bitterest of ironies—with the secret Cardassian resistance movement on Cardassia Prime to try to sabotage the Dominion from the inside.

It is, quite simply, a brilliant narrative choice, to put Cardassia through the same sins they previously perpetrated, and it suggests a true recognition of the legacy of war. The Cardassians are explored in depth as a culture in *Deep Space Nine*, after their introduction as relatively one-dimensional intergalactic fascists in *The Next Generation*, and are counterpointed with the Bajorans—a peaceful, spiritual culture ground into the dirt through occupation and slavery—as a militant, unimaginative and egotistical race convinced of their own superiority and exceptionalism. By the end of "What You Leave Behind," if the Bajorans have learned with the help of the Federation to find some peace with their own trauma, the Cardassians are humbled by their own hubris in the shadow of the bitter, dominant Dominion, and are offered their own path to redemption after suffering some of the horror they previously inflicted upon others. Neither race nor culture are the same by the end of *Deep Space Nine* as when it began.

Come the 1990s, *Star Trek* therefore is capable of engaging more readily with the continuous trauma of fascism, resistance and war, but it still struggles with accepting—constructed by the descendants of the victors—the West's own role in the legacy prescribed by the 20th century's most defining period of history. It will explore and struggle with accepting the cultural trauma of World War II across the 1960s and into the 1990s,

3. The 1990s

and grapple with whether we are ready, as a society, to truly accept the difficult answers and unpalatable truths at the heart of it.

Little Green Men

In July of 1947, an extra-terrestrial spacecraft slammed into the desert near the town of Roswell in New Mexico, or so goes one of the more well-known American legends of the 20th century. The United States Army claimed, and still maintains more than seventy years later, that the "Roswell incident" was a crashed weather balloon, but millions for decades believed, and continue to believe, otherwise.[36]

The universe of *Star Trek* certainly holds true to the myth that aliens *did* in fact crash at Roswell, and the U.S. Army covered up the evidence in perpetuity. *Deep Space Nine*'s Season Four episode "Little Green Men" posits that the Roswell aliens were in fact *DS9*'s Ferengi bartender Quark, his brother Rom, and his nephew Nog, who landed thanks to a time-travel accident and subsequently attempt to manipulate the Army into purchasing futuristic weapons of mass destruction, before shape-shifting *DS9* head of security Odo—aboard ship secretly, having suspected Quark of smuggling—aids U.S. Army sympathizers in helping the Ferengi family escape before the Army can begin insidious experiments on them.

This is one of numerous examples of *Star Trek* buying into the modern religion of "UFOlogy" which took root among particularly the American psyche in the wake of World War II and spread across European democracies in various ways. The concept of the "unidentified flying object" did not exist in the same manner before World War II, with examples of the same mysterious phenomena either going unreported or having even more overtly mystical or religious connotations. In the era of science, tragically brought to bear by the creation of the atomic bomb, the survivors of World War II looked to the heavens—to alien life—for their enemies, their explanations, and even their gods. Roswell happened just two years after Hiroshima, after all.

Star Trek, long before "Little Green Men" aired in 1996, explored the growing interest and fascination in UFOlogy and the so-called "Foo Fighter," the name coined by pilots during World War II to describe encounters in the air with phenomena they could not explain, often attributed to the moniker of the UFO.

"Tomorrow Is Yesterday," which aired in the first season of *The Original Series* in 1967, written by D.C. Fontana, sees the *Enterprise* fall through a black hole into a time vortex which throws them out into the skies of the United States, circa 1967, where they are classified as a UFO by the United States Air Force and pilot Captain John Christopher is sent to intercept. The disoriented *Enterprise* uses a tractor beam on his jet to prevent him from launching potentially nuclear warheads at the ship, but it explodes, forcing them to beam Christopher aboard. Kirk is at first curious and cavalier about their suspicious but amazed visitor, until Spock reminds him that the knowledge Christopher possesses, if returned, could be exploited and threaten to change the future. Kirk and the crew have to protect the secret of their existence from the U.S. Air Force whilst figuring out a way to slingshot around the sun and go back, as it were, to the future.

Fontana's episode is one acutely aware of UFO culture which, by the time *Star Trek* was created, had become embedded in American folklore. The case in 1961 of Betty and Barney Hill, a New Hampshire couple who claimed to have been abducted while driving and experimented upon by extra-terrestrials, recalled via hypnosis, had made them UFO celebrities.[37] More UFO sightings in Exeter, New Hampshire,[38] the Lonnie Zamora sighting in New Mexico,[39] and the folklore surrounding the legend of the "Mothman"[40] all brewed together with Roswell and multiple accounts of lights in the sky and UFO encounters (which had significantly increased in reportage and popularity since World War II), made "Tomorrow Is Yesterday" quite contemporary, even if Fontana approaches the subject, as does "Little Green Men" some three decades later, with a clear Vulcan-esque quirk of the eyebrow. Though the stakes, akin to the fate of Edith Keeler later in the season in "City on the Edge of Forever," are significant in terms of changing the entire future of humanity, the episode approaches the concept more with a light-hearted curiosity than the kind of serious, frightening, other-worldly threat we would see in later television series and movies, particularly in the 1990s.

Though never one to hold fast to the principles of the Prime Directive and Starfleet's non-interference policy, Kirk is remarkably blasé about Christopher seeing the technology of the future—even giving him a Starfleet uniform to wear! On one level, it is a nice reflection of how Starfleet might consider any military or naval officer from Earth's relatively recent history as worthy of serving on a Starfleet crew, but on another it is surprisingly tone-deaf to the concerns Spock quite rightly points out: "I do not specifically refer to Captain Christopher, but suppose an unscrupulous man were to gain certain knowledge of man's future? Such a man could manipulate key industries, stocks, and even nations, and in so doing, change what must be."[41] This does hold true to *Star Trek*'s

3. The 1990s

determinism that the utopian Federation future we know from the series must be protected at all costs, as we later see in Harlan Ellison's more serious time-travel conundrum, and also questions the moral turpitude of 1960s man as something less than inviolate. Christopher proves himself to be relatively noble, grateful and respectful to Kirk and crew, if by the end he is returned to the original timeline and he remembers nothing of the experience, but his Air Force colleagues are much less enlightened and far more suspicious. When Kirk himself is captured by the Air Force, he plays with them with a level of simplistic innocence and willful ignorance, refusing to be drawn into their questions. "The truth is, I'm a little green man from Alpha Centauri. A beautiful place. You ought to see it."[42]

The fun of Fontana's story, of course, is in how it inverts the legend already established in UFO culture. It makes the *Enterprise* and her crew the extra-terrestrials. We, the audience, are John Christopher in this scenario, initially unable to fathom the situation he is in, having been taken aboard an "alien" ship. Director Michael O'Herlihy intentionally stages moments in which Spock's "alienness" is made apparent to the 20th century humans, again mainly for comic effect, but equally with the occasional trace of menace, such as when Spock, Kirk and Christopher are discussing the problem of returning the latter to Earth. "I have run a computer check on all historical tapes. They show no record of any relevant contribution by John Christopher."[43] The inference, that the future would not miss Christopher if he disappeared at the hand of the mysterious UFO, is downright sinister. Kirk at first is prepared to never return him, even though Christopher is a husband with two children. He is a virtuous example of the human, certainly American, ideal in the 1960s. You could almost see the genetic string of a Jonathan Archer leading from him. Yet he is disposable to protect the "alien" secrets of the *Enterprise* and the Federation. It's fortunate they happen upon a science-fiction time gambit to return Christopher and reset the timeline, even if in reality it has more in common with magic than any real science, even for *Star Trek*.

Lawrence M. Krauss suggests that the frivolity with which Kirk and his crew deal with their sojourn into the past reflects their own lack of understanding when it comes to the consequences of time-travel:

> Perhaps the most fascinating aspect of time travel as far as *Star Trek* is concerned is that there is no stronger potential for violation of the Prime Directive. The crews of Starfleet are admonished not to interfere with the present normal historical development of any alien society they visit. Yet by travelling back in time it is possible to remove the present altogether. Indeed, it is possible to remove history altogether![44]

Star Trek, History and Us

The enjoyable central image of the *Enterprise* sailing over the skies of North America and being spotted on radar is even repurposed in the 1990s with *Voyager*'s third season two-part story "Future's End," where the ship and crew are transported back to Earth 1996 by a 29th century time ship. Part one ends with a shot of *Voyager* flying low over the skies of Los Angeles in 1996, having been captured not by radar in this case but rather by home video camcorder. The image plays off the growing number of UFO sightings filmed by the public, from surprised civilians to dedicated sky-watchers, that would appear on a litany of TV series across the '90s from *Unsolved Mysteries* through to *Sightings*. *Voyager* is just as "alien" here as the *Enterprise* was, and Captain Janeway and her crew have to work very hard to stop the devious influence on history by tech billionaire Henry Starling without compromising the timeline. While Janeway is far more concerned with preserving history than Kirk ever was, you can understand why by the 24th century, as we discovered in *Deep Space Nine*'s "Trials and Tribble-ations," Starfleet has a Department of Temporal Investigations who do not think highly of James T. Kirk!

"Tomorrow is Yesterday" speaks to how *Star Trek* engages with the counter-cultural phenomenon of UFOlogy. It approaches it as myth to be debunked. It exposes our own beliefs in the possibility of alien life as primitive and, frequently, completely out of touch with reality.

"Little Green Men," written by Ira Steven Behr and Robert Hewitt Wolfe, takes a strong cue from the aforementioned *The Original Series* episode in tone and style, approaching the Roswell incident from a deliberately comedic perspective, arriving in the wake of documentaries on the subject during the '90s, a 1994 dramatic retelling of the story starring Kyle MacLachan and Martin Sheen—not to mention *Roswell High*, an angsty teen drama revolving around aliens in the town.[45] There was also the popularization of underground, supposedly real alien autopsy videos, and of course the pop culture '90s phenomenon that was *The X-Files*, a series which dominated early-internet, message board and fan discourse with its labyrinthian mythology and deep suspicion of government, state and the suggestion the American public were being conspired against by their own leaders. *The X-Files* varies on whether Roswell was a hoax or a key part of its own mythology,[46] but it always considers the incident as a serious moment in American cultural history, whereas *Star Trek* considers the event a joke. "Little Green Men" plays up to the historical ideas of strange alien beings landing on Earth in the wake of World War II and the Army's baffled, primitive attempts to understand them.

3. The 1990s

Even the title of that episode is a reference to the legion of reports from Americans who claim to have experienced alien activity, who described "little green men," often with bulbous eyes and heads, as indicative of whatever race these extra-terrestrials hailed from. This term, and the image of the so-called "Grey," swiftly became synonymous with UFOlogy and had a significant impact on the '90s boon of TV shows and movies that explored alien invasion, alien abduction and alien conspiracy, led in popularity by *The X-Files*. The year of 1996 saw *Independence Day*, with similar-looking entities invading the planet in gigantic saucer-shaped discs with explosive abandon, recalling science-fiction B-pictures such as *It Came from Outer Space* on a mega budget with an emphasis on action set pieces, though it too exploits the Roswellian mythology in American folklore and the idea of Area 51.[47] Then 1997 gave us a deliberately comedic take on similar ground, combined with H.G. Wells' *War of the Worlds* in Tim Burton's *Mars Attacks!* That film plays the aliens for bulbous headed comedic purposes, but they are no less sadistic and brutal—one sequence sees them detach the head of Sarah Jessica Parker and attach it, living, to the body of a small puppy![48] Later that year, *Men in Black* entirely reinvented another key aspect of conspiracy and UFO folklore in the sinister government agent who would call upon witnesses to so-called alien activity and threaten them into silence. Will Smith and Tommy Lee Jones re-cast them as defenders of the galaxy, protecting Earth from all manner of alien scourges, replete always with a one liner and a tongue firmly in cheek. Even *The X-Files* itself would go to the movies in 1998 with big screen version *Fight the Future*.[49]

The craze for alien conspiracy culture was reaching its apogee by 1996, when *Deep Space Nine* had the confidence in its flexible storytelling to turn the Roswell legend into a "Ferengi comedy,"[50] and hence "Little Green Men" very deliberately plays into its audience's knowledge and understanding of the Roswell lore, squeezing it to fit the "future history" narrative of the *Star Trek* universe. By making the Ferengi characters the more enlightened creatures in parallel to the ignorant, hawkish U.S. military of the mid–20th century, *Deep Space Nine* here inverts *Star Trek*'s own sense of allegory, in that *Deep Space Nine* positions the Ferengi as analogous to 20th century capitalists, interested only in profit, lacking gender equality, considering women to be sexual objects and placing the self before all else. The Ferengi were tailored, in *Deep Space Nine*, to reflect our own avarice and self-obsession, but the central joke of "Little Green Men" is that we're even worse than they are! As R.J. Lambourne, M.J. Shallis and M. Shortland state:

A film like *Them!* might suggest that such problems had been resolved in favour of the military authorities; according to Twentieth Century, its theme was unequivocally to "Place trust in the FBI." Science fiction incorporated with great ease much of the retinue of war films, and a lot of the visual apparatus from such films passed unnoticed, if substantially transformed, into science fiction. Dog fights, air travel, weapons, mass destruction and aerial bombardment were sure audience pleasers. The same was true for crisp, clean military personnel. In many films, overall command comes from the barrel of a gun. The army calls the shots and fires them too.[51]

One of the more controversial choices made in the later seasons of *Deep Space Nine* is one that further calls into question the enlightened and utopian veracity of 24th century humanity. Perhaps inspired by a resurgent interest in the cultural and folkloric landscape in UFO and conspiracy culture, it appeared in the Season Six episode "Inquisition," written by David Weddle & Bradley Thompson: the creation of Section-31.

Amid the all-encompassing Dominion War, one we learn in the subsequent episode "In the Pale Moonlight" that the Federation is effectively losing, a mysterious Starfleet officer from the Department of Internal Affairs called Luther Sloan arrives on *DS9* claiming that they believe the Dominion have a spy on the station. Sloan subsequently begins a ruthless interrogation of Julian Bashir, under heavy suspicion given numerous points across the series' own internal history[52] when he was potentially compromised, only for Sloan to later reveal himself as part of a covert organization called "Section-31," that existed at the beginning of the Federation's charter and now answers to no one. It was all an attempt to recruit Bashir into the organization and Sisko, concerned Starfleet haven't confirmed nor denied their existence, asks him to eventually accept the offer when they come calling again.

Section-31 is, in no uncertain terms, a Starfleet version of the covert intelligence agencies *Star Trek* in the 1990s felt comfortable introducing initially for the allegorical alien versions of the American "Other." The Romulan Tal'Shiar or the Cardassian Obsidian Order—both of whom play key roles in the political machinations behind many *Deep Space Nine* stories, particularly the latter—are established as analogous to the Soviet Union's KGB, the East German Stasi during the Cold War, Israel's Mossad or even the Chinese Ministry of State Security. From a Western, particularly American, point of view, they are not to be trusted and sow galactic discord through their plotting. The half human/half Romulan agent Sela in *The Next Generation*'s "Redemption" attempts to rig the election of the Klingon Chancellor, and later in "Unification" works to undermine Ambassador Spock's attempts to foment a reunification movement between

3. The 1990s

Romulus and Vulcan. On *DS9* the Obsidian Order regularly attempt to undermine station operations from behind the scenes—in "Second Skin" they surgically transform Kira and attempt to make her believe she is the daughter of a Cardassian military leader they distrust. Later in "The Die Is Cast," they and the Tal'Shiar team up for an unsuccessful, covert strike on the homeward of the Founders, the Changeling rulers of the Dominion. The Obsidian Order also regularly try and undermine or combat the Maquis, and it's from the "It's easy to be a saint in paradise" line from "The Maquis Part 2" that Ira Steven Behr first envisaged what would become Section-31. "Why is Earth a paradise in the twenty-fourth century? Well, maybe it's because there's someone watching over it and doing the nasty stuff that no one wants to think about. Of course, it's a very complicated issue. Extremely complicated. And those kinds of covert operations usually are wrong!"[53]

The very concept of Section-31 directly works in opposition to Gene Roddenberry's established precept of humanity having evolved beyond conflict, and Earth operating as a paradise. Season Four's two-parter "Homefront" and the aptly named "Paradise Lost" join as the first shot across the bow from Behr as to the invalidity of Roddenberry's vision, as a group of Starfleet officers work to stage a military coup on the Federation by creating a fake Changeling on Earth threat. It's a conspiracy directly designed, from the angle of the conspirators led by Admiral Leyton, to protect the Federation: "There will be some dissenters at first, but they'll fall in line once they realise that strengthening Earth is the first step toward strengthening the Federation."[54] Sloan has precisely the same mindset when it comes to Section-31, and their validity operating as, effectively, a black-ops CIA organization deep within Starfleet, so secret most people no longer even know they exist. "We deal with threats to the Federation that jeopardise its very survival. If you knew how many lives we've saved, I think you'd agree that the ends do justify the means."[55]

Roddenberry would have argued, of course, that the ends would *never* have justified the means, and the Federation would never have dreamt, at its foundation, of allowing an organization named after a specific clause in its charter to ever exist. As Weddle admits, many of the fans concurred:

> There were many that were screaming for our heads over that show, (saying) that it betrayed everything that *Star Trek* stands for and the value system that Gene Roddenberry promoted. Others said that of course, the Federation would have to have an organization like this. Fans would get into these long ethical and political arguments, really struggling with issues like that, which was great to see.[56]

Star Trek, History and Us

In Roddenberry's utopia, there would be no need for Section-31. The Earth was a place of peace and the galaxy, the frontier, was out there to be explored, not to be feared. By the end of the 1990s, and the decades of political and social upheaval since *Star Trek* began, those beliefs were harder to maintain.

The X-Files not only helped revive interest in UFO and conspiracy culture in popular entertainment, but also invoked the specter of conspiracy thrillers from the 1970s, as inspired by the American trauma of Watergate and the resignation of President Richard Nixon as the films of Alan J. Pakula[57] and such were. Oliver Stone's *Nixon*, a searing biopic of the man, was released in 1995, while television and cinema were flooded with a new market of stories in which the United States government and its institutions particularly were not to be trusted. It didn't help that during Bill Clinton's tenure as president while *Deep Space Nine* was on the air, he not only was forced to apologize for secret radiation tests conducted on the American people decades previously,[58] but he was only the third president in history to himself be impeached, in his case for sexual impropriety with his aide Monica Lewinsky, though he was later acquitted. Though the Clinton era was, in hindsight, a time of relative peace and domestic prosperity for America and the West between the end of the Cold War and the shock of 9/11, Americans were finding reasons to distrust constructs of power once again. Oliver Stone in 1991 also brought us his towering dramatic investigation of the Kennedy assassination in *JFK*, which alongside *Twin Peaks* partly inspired *The X-Files'* paranoid cultural approach, and laid the foundation for conspiracy theories to resound: JFK and the Lone Gunmen, CIA covert operations, MK-Ultra mind-control experiments, the death of Marilyn Monroe, aliens in Area 51. These were believed by many to be secrets being kept by government forces from the American people at the highest levels of power. Section-31 ends up becoming a natural extension of that uncertainty and paranoia at the tail end of the 1990s.

Aside from Section-31 on television, cinematic *Star Trek* also leaned into the concern of Starfleet becoming embroiled in conspiracy which betrayed their core values. *Insurrection*, written by Michael Piller, saw the crew of the *Enterprise*, seemingly at the tail end of the Dominion War we never saw them embroiled in, investigate when Data goes rogue and exposes a secret Starfleet project on a world inhabited by the Bak'u, a peaceful people of small number whose planet's rings exhibit a rare kind of metaphasic radiation that heals and regenerates human tissue. Picard, upon learning Starfleet—represented by Anthony Zerbe's

3. The 1990s

grouchy Admiral Dougherty—are conspiring to secretly relocate the Bak'u to another world with the Son'a, a neighboring alien race looking to benefit from the radiation, leads his crew in the titular insurrection against the Son'a to protect the Bak'u and their rights.

Though not one of the finest *Star Trek* movies, it is fundamentally the kind of moral hill Picard would die on, and he is outraged at the very idea the Federation would betray their principles and act in such a covert and devious fashion, in order to gain an advantage. "Some of the darkest chapters in the history of my world involve the forced relocation of a small group of people to satisfy the demands of a large one. I'd hoped we had learned from our mistakes, but it seems that some of us haven't,"[59] Picard tells a Bak'u woman, Anij, part of a group of particularly human-looking aliens who represent more of the Roddenberry utopian ideal at this stage than Starfleet does.

Picard can see his own resolute principles siding with the Bak'u rather than Starfleet, which makes *Insurrection* quite a key touchstone in the steadily eroding faith in *Star Trek*'s utopian future, but is in retrospect crucial to Picard's eventual loss of faith in the Federation years later, which we see in *Star Trek: Picard*. Dougherty, exasperated, tells the principled captain that they're only moving six hundred people. "How many people does it take, admiral, before it becomes wrong?" is Picard's simple question. Dougherty has no answer. "It was for the Federation," he says ultimately. "It was all for the Federation…."[60]

Star Trek had even, historically, suggested that the '90s themselves would have been a decade of political turmoil in "Space Seed," where the legendary Khan Noonien Singh is revealed to have played a part in the "Eugenics Wars." "Your Earth was on the verge of a dark ages. Whole populations were being bombed out of existence,"[61] Spock claims, suggesting a 1990s of a very different kind than actually came to pass in Earth's history, but a future *Star Trek* was initially anxious about given strides in eugenics and technology since World War II. Though *Enterprise* develops the first story since *The Wrath of Khan* to pick up on the Eugenics Wars and their legacy in the Arik Soong arc starting with "Borderland," *Deep Space Nine* certainly investigates the anxiety and paranoia over genetic experimentation in revealing Bashir was "enhanced" as a child, breaking laws in the Federation that expressly ban any form of eugenics. Starfleet Rear-Admiral Bennett lays it out in the episode "Dr. Bashir, I Presume": "Two hundred years ago we tried to improve the species through DNA resequencing, and what did we get for our trouble? The Eugenics Wars. For every Julian Bashir that can be created, there's a Khan Singh waiting in the wings. A superhuman whose ambition and thirst for power have been enhanced along with his intellect. The law against genetic engineering provides a firewall against such men."[62] These are the kind of not just alien, but superhuman, threats that "Inquisition" argues 24th century humanity still needs to be concerned about, with Section-31 existing as a bulwark against such aberrations, doing the "dirty work" behind the scenes so Starfleet never has to. Odo admits he's surprised, once they learn about Section-31, that the Federation *wouldn't* have their version of the Tal-Shiar or the Obsidian Order. Bashir is the one who pulls things back to the perhaps flawed *Star Trek* ideal: "But what does that say about us? When push comes to shove, are we willing to sacrifice our principles in order to survive?"[63]

In some ways, "In the Pale Moonlight" proves the point by forever compromising Benjamin Sisko himself. Written by Michael Taylor, from a story by Peter Allan Fields, it serves as a confession of sorts by Sisko into camera, recounting the story of how he is corrupted into working with Garak on a plan to fake evidence the Dominion are planning to attack the Romulan Empire in order to bring them into a war the Federation are losing. Garak manipulates Sisko and is successful, but it leads to the covert murder of a Romulan senator which Sisko never intended. While the Romulans enter the war on the side of the Federation, Sisko erases his confession, covering up his own conspiracy. It is, essentially, Sisko's Watergate.

Celebrated as one of the most powerful and thought-provoking episodes *Deep Space Nine* ever did, "In the Pale Moonlight" is also the final nail in the coffin in terms of the inviolate nature of Starfleet and their officers. The thought of Picard or Janeway, or even Kirk, doing what Sisko does here is almost unthinkable. Sisko acts in pure desperation in the face of a devastating war, seeing his values and belief systems corrupted as part of pursuing the kind of ends justifying means Section-31 undertake on a daily basis. If Kirk can be seen as a Ronald Reagan cowboy leader, with Picard as a veritable Woodrow Wilson for the late 20th century,[64] and even Janeway as a nascent Hillary Clinton (though this is much more debatable), then Sisko is confirmed in this episode as the Richard Nixon of the *Star Trek* universe. If not corrupt in the same way, his actions motivated in an attempt to serve the greater good, Sisko nonetheless ends up tainted by his own actions as a leader and serves as the ultimate example of a future bastion of utopian humanity who has been utterly compromised. "If your conscience is bothering you, you should soothe it with the knowledge that you may have just saved the entire Alpha Quadrant, and all it cost was the life of one Romulan senator, one criminal … and the self-respect of one Starfleet officer. I don't know about you, but I'd call that a bargain,"[65] Garak tells him, justifying their actions. Sisko ends his log trying to convince himself he can live with what he has done. The sense you get is … only just.

These are the kind of areas you can only imagine *Star Trek* exploring at the end of the '90s, at the conclusion of a decade which promised the "end of history." The wall came down as the Soviet monolith crumbled, but the decade struggled to pay off the brave new world Americans, and the West, believed might come to pass. The new Russian Republic was swiftly corrupted by oil baron gangsters and the underworld mafia. Brush fire wars in Iraq or Kosovo, including the kind of ethnic cleansing not seen since World War II, continued to sprout up, with rising turmoil in the Middle East. Domestic terror attacks on U.S. soil by right wing militia actively turned against a supposedly corrupt federal government, with scions such as Timothy McVeigh or David Koresh rising on a troubling right who waited in the wings. The '90s may have been economically fertile, with growing civil and minority rights and protections and the West governed by largely progressive democracies working, theoretically, toward the Federation's bright future. However, a dark underbelly lurked beneath, one that perhaps the rise in conspiracy culture and folklore about alien forces and secret shadow governments in fiction suggested was closer than we might have imagined. Even *Star Trek* was losing faith in Roddenberry's utopian vision for humanity.

Francis Fukuyama, in his aforementioned seminal essay about the turning point the '90s represented, was more prescient in his thinking than he realized at the time about what lay around the corner at the turn of the 21st century:

> The end of history will be a very sad time. The struggle for recognition, the willingness to risk one's life for a purely abstract goal, the worldwide ideological struggle that called forth daring, courage, imagination, and idealism, will be replaced by economic calculation, the endless solving of technical problems, environmental concerns, and the satisfaction of sophisticated consumer demands. I can feel in myself, and see in others around me, a powerful nostalgia for the time when history existed. Such nostalgia, in fact, will continue to fuel competition and conflict even in the post-historical world for some time to come. Perhaps this very prospect of centuries of boredom at the end of history will serve to get history started once again.[66]

Star Trek, **History and Us**

Little did Fukuyama realize history would get started again after the end of the 20th century, sooner rather than later. The dawn of the new millennium brought with it the greatest existential shock to Western civilization since World War II, and a brand new global paradigm *Star Trek* would have to navigate, as the promise of the final frontier ebbed steadily further and further away from reality.

4

The 21st Century (So Far)

If you had been considering the *Star Trek* franchise on "Millennium Eve" in 1999, you could be forgiven for believing the future of Gene Roddenberry's universe was bright going into the 21st century.

The Next Generation was now well-established in cinematic terms, even if 1998's *Insurrection* had achieved less critical acclaim and a lower box office than 1996's *First Contact*. *Deep Space Nine* concluded in the summer of 1999 with a dramatic flourish, beloved by a devoted core of fans, even if it failed to break out into the mainstream to quite the degree of *The Next Generation* or *The Original Series*. *Voyager*, now entering its sixth season, was flying the flag for the franchise on screen, and rumblings were already underway about the next spin-off series, a prequel to the entire franchise that would become, in 2001, *Enterprise*. Audiences might have expected a decade as rich and full of *Star Trek* content as the 1990s, a decade in which the franchise had been on air, and in cinemas, constantly.

Voyager, after all, continued the trends established in the *Next Generation* era by existing, essentially, as a by-product of that same show, extrapolating the sense of Federation order and control over the distant Delta Quadrant, despite the obvious contradictions within the series' premise. Darren Mooney, who has written extensively about *Voyager* as a whole, believes the show was expressly capturing the ideological American moment at the end of the 1990s:

> There was a sense that Starfleet and the Federation would always be around, expanding their role as galactic peacekeepers to protect the time itself. There was no sense that anything would ever challenge the status quo. Not only did *Voyager* extrapolate the American Century into the twenty-fourth century, but also suggested that the ensuing political stability would extend well beyond that. This was a reflection of the prevailing mood in the nineties. The liberal democratic ideals championed by the United States and the Federation had won and would never be challenged. It is interesting to contrast this with the War on Terror anxieties that permeate *Enterprise*.[1]

Star Trek, History and Us

Voyager would come to an end in the summer of 2001, a matter of months before the existential trauma of the Twin Towers attack on September 11, the ripple effects of which are still being felt in society and culture across the West two decades on. Indeed, they may come to define much of the 21st century as the assassination of Archduke Ferdinand in Sarajevo in 1914[2] defined the previous century's devastating course. It is hard to imagine how *Voyager*, with its view of American exceptionalism perhaps even more obsessed with the traumatic legacy of war and memory than *Deep Space Nine*, could have existed in the form it did in the post–9/11 paradigm. Captain Janeway and her crew sailing home, bringing civilized moral values and principles to a routinely chaotic and savage part of space, would no doubt have seemed trite. It could have resorted to doing the "Year of Hell" season, after all.[3] These issues no doubt contributed to the troubled start faced by *Enterprise*, a series both designed to bring a freshness to *Star Trek* while, on the other hand, in misjudged fashion attempting to simply continue the tone and style of the franchise of the 1990s. Mooney has also written extensively about *Enterprise*, and expands on this further:

> When *Enterprise* first debuted, it was a stunningly conservative show, from both a narrative and political standpoint. Television was undergoing a massive evolutionary leap at the turn of the millennium, shifting away from a rigid episodic format and towards more ambitious storytelling approaches. Serialisation had already worked very well on cable networks like HBO, but it was creeping into the mainstream. *Enterprise* premiered in the same season as *24*. However, the first two seasons of *Enterprise* were distinctly uninterested in embracing serialised storytelling. Instead, they hewed rather close to the rigid "done-in-one" episodic format that had defined so much of *Voyager*.[4]

Initially, *Enterprise*—which in an attempt to stand alone, ditched the *Star Trek* moniker for the first two seasons—was designed to ground *Star Trek* in an earlier age closer to the modern day. Captain Archer and his crew would dress more like astronauts, watch movies, and generally talk and act more like modern day, 21st century humans. In principle, this earthiness in the storytelling and characterization bore fruit but, in practice, *Enterprise* failed to bring anything new to the universe, and given it premiered weeks after 9/11, at the same time the aforementioned *24* was pushing stylistic boundaries and expressly dealing with American shock and awed fury at the attack on New York, *Enterprise* for the first two years simply tried to pretend the year was still 1997.

That all changed with, in response to falling ratings, the Season Two finale, "The Expanse," which kickstarted a third season built not only

4. The 21st Century (So Far)

around a serialized narrative that fulfilled *Star Trek*'s promise of exploring new worlds, but directly—even if the writers deny it—saw Archer and his crew respond to the War on Terror by attempting to stop the launch of a super-weapon after a devastating terror attack on Earth. By default, *Enterprise* darkened. Characters made moral compromises. They dealt with addiction and grief. Many of these themes were played out on *Deep Space Nine*, but the context on *Enterprise* was different. These people were designed to be more like us, and so began *Star Trek*'s reluctant attempt to engage with the pulse of an age no longer defined by steady geopolitical conflict or unipolar superiority, but rather our own wounded reaction to the trauma of ideological terrorism and, by default, rising nationalism.

It was too late to save *Enterprise*, ultimately, which suffered a similar fate to *The Original Series*, becoming only the second *Star Trek* series to be cancelled. However, it opened the franchise up, fully, to the possibility of not simply existing beholden to a utopian future worldview by Roddenberry which, with each passing year, was looking more distant and less relatable to Western audiences.

Star Trek, on some level, reacted to this trauma by indulging nostalgia. The effect began with *Enterprise*'s final season, which eschewed a war against terror for serialized cluster arcs that tapped into the internal mythology of the franchise, particularly *The Original Series*. Episodes such as the Augments arc explained why Klingons had ridged foreheads by the time of *The Next Generation* when this was not the case in *The Original Series*.[5] We met the man who created the transporter device, which has helped writers cut corners and save time for half a century. These storylines were designed to appeal to *Star Trek* fans who had long explored these ideas in fan fiction, filling holes in continuity in a manner the 1990s era often ignored in charting new territory.

Before the same trend continued in 2017's TV revival *Discovery*, after over a decade in which *Star Trek* disappeared from television screens entirely, Hollywood came to the rescue with an alternate kind of nostalgia: the reboot.

J.J. Abrams' 2009 film, simply called *Star Trek*, found a clever narrative device to recast *The Original Series* crew and the iconic duo of Kirk and Spock without sacrificing forty plus years of continuity. However, the entertaining, big-budget gloss of Abrams' action-adventure take on Kirk and Spock's origin story was designed less as a way to advance *Star Trek* as a franchise, and more to appeal to the box office vicissitudes of a public who, in the wake not just of 9/11 but wars in Iraq, economic crises and a growing fear of random acts of terrorism, sought a safer past for comfort,

Star Trek, History and Us

filled with situations and characters they understood and could relate to. David Sims describes Abrams' intentions in comparison to the franchise he would later revive, *Star Wars*:

> When he set out to make a new *Star Trek* and drag that moribund cinematic franchise back into blockbuster territory, he cheerfully swapped in some very familiar visual language to help it over the hill. Early on in the film, James Kirk (Chris Pine), nursing a desire to transcend his farmboy life, rides a motorcycle to see the USS *Enterprise* being built at a shipyard, and gazes up at it longingly. *Star Wars* fans would connect the scene to one at the beginning of the first 1977 film, when Luke Skywalker wistfully watches the dual suns of his home planet set; *Star Trek*'s producers even called the scene "our Tatooine moment."[6]

The gambit worked. *Star Trek* 2009 made over five times what 2002's limp *Nemesis*, the final *Next Generation* big-screen adventure, did at the box office,[7] and set in motion sequels that equally made money, if not to the degree Paramount would have wished, which has resulted in the cinematic arm of the *Star Trek* universe existing in limbo since 2016's *Beyond*. The so-called "Kelvinverse" films, nonetheless, rebooted *Star Trek* in the popular consciousness by returning to what fans understood, on a teleological basis, from the 1960s. It had come full circle, with a contemporary twist, as the second film, *Into Darkness*, certainly worked to react to a growing conservative "hawkishness" in American foreign policy following the war in Iraq. These films may have been produced in the Obama era, yet they retain the echo of responding to terror by seeking to reassure audiences that familiar worlds and characters exist. The same would be true of *Star Wars* in *The Force Awakens* onwards.

Star Trek finally returned to television following the powder keg of Donald Trump's 2016 election and struggled to entirely convince audiences that nostalgia was enough. *Discovery* delved into the sinister, fascistic Mirror Universe, ruled by dictators who seemed comical in the '60s and '90s but who feel worryingly possible in the early 21st century. *Picard*, a series built entirely on a nostalgia for the early 1990s sense of control and order, places Patrick Stewart's iconic *Enterprise* captain in a chaotic, post-terror, post-climate change late 24th century where utopia, at least outside of the boundaries of an insular Federation, seems to have completely dissolved. The late 2010s spawned what could be another "Golden Age" for *Star Trek* on television, another decade where the series was rarely off air,[8] but there are questions about what kind of universe it will be.

In a fractured climate, fuelled by conservative trench digging on one hand and liberal, ideological protest on the other, all exacerbated by online discourse, is *Star Trek* still on course for Roddenberry's utopia? The first

4. The 21st Century (So Far)

two decades of the 21st century have told a story of decline, both within the franchise and without, yet as the year 2000 began, the future looked bright. Everything was about to change.

Remember the Journey

Before we place the *Star Trek* franchise in the prism of the world after September 11, 2001, it is worth reflecting on the space it inhabited at the turn of the year 2000, the new millennium.

Unless *Star Trek* and television truly live beyond the final frontier, it is entirely possible the year 2000 will be the only millennial epoch the franchise sees, and as the 1990s receded into memory, the franchise stood at a crossroads. *Deep Space Nine* ended in 1999 to critical acclaim, drawing to a conclusion a reflective examination of the circularity of conflict and personal destiny, while projecting anxieties about the future to come. It was a series that, deep down, did not truly believe in Gene Roddenberry's utopian vision for humanity and the extended galaxy, or believed at least we would need to fight to retain it.

Voyager, entering its sixth year of a seven-season run, was devised by creators Rick Berman, Michael Piller and Jeri Taylor with an entirely different approach, as Berman explains:

> "*Star Trek* by definition, the original series and *The Next Generation* as well, are series dealing with people who are traveling or going off on adventures, as opposed to people who are trying to come back from adventures. That's a spirit that we realized had been somewhat lacking in the show, because there had been so much focus and concentration on getting home. What we wanted to do was shift the focus of the characters in the sense that they had confidence that they would be finding a way home, whether it's going to be in four months or four years, we didn't know. But there was going to be less brooding and a sense of the excitement of exploration, which is the reason they all joined Starfleet in the first place."[9]

The Original Series had focused on exploring the final frontier. *The Next Generation* established the final frontier as, largely, a utopian landscape on which to reflect the human experience. *Deep Space Nine* was about surviving a final frontier that was far less agreeable to Roddenberry's vision. *Voyager*, according to Berman's thesis, was about *enjoying* the final frontier; about recapturing a sense of adventure and excitement for the unknown that *Star Trek*, suffused by Borg invasions and interplanetary wars,[10] had begun to lose. The irony lies in how *Voyager*, more perhaps than any *Star Trek* series before or since (including *Enterprise*), felt the safest of all journeys that took place in the wider universe. It assumes cultural dominance and superiority over the final frontier, confident enough as it is to explore uncharted regions of the galaxy while determined to run back to the very place the crew originated: Earth.

It could be argued that *Star Trek*, at this point, was retreating from the broader mission statement that *Deep Space Nine* pushed further than any series to date. *Enterprise* followed *Voyager*, a series which didn't simply return the franchise to Earth but took the series back further than it had ever gone to explore the origins of Starfleet, the Federation, and the legend that was the *Enterprise* as a vessel. Until *Picard* returned viewers to the end of the 24th century, *Voyager* was the furthest into the future, as a main series setting, *Star Trek* had ever ventured.[11] It travelled farthest from where *Star Trek* began, geographically, while moving deeper into the *Next Generation*–era utopian future, but when it came to style, tone and texture, *Voyager* ended up the most homogenized and generic series the franchise ever delivered. It was a patchwork of the first two *Star Trek* series combined and remained committed to rarely ever pushing out of that sandbox and challenging what *Star Trek* could be, or could mean, as we approached a new century.

Darren Mooney argues thus about the cultural context of *Voyager* in the late 1990s:

> *Voyager* was tasked with defining *Star Trek* for the Clinton era. The economy was strong. Crime was in decline. Although the United States would involve itself in conflicts in places like Haiti and Bosnia, the global climate was largely stable. The United States had won the Cold War. For the first time since the start of the Second World War, it could unequivocally be argued that the United States was at peace. Liberal democracy had triumphed. Although the show's relative stability made little sense in the context of the high-concept premise of a bunch of explorers trapped alone on the far side of the galaxy, it reflected the general mood of America in the nineties. More than any other *Star Trek* series, *Voyager* invested in the idea of the status quo. Nothing ever changed.[12]

Voyager premiered in 1995, toward the end of Bill Clinton's first term in office. The franchise existed at the height of its power and popularity, with *Deep Space Nine* beginning a third series in which the show began to layer in the narrative and character aspects that built a complex tapestry over the next four seasons, and *The Next Generation* crew had kickstarted a successful movie franchise. Paramount wanted *Voyager* to be the flagship for the United Paramount Network,[13] an entirely new channel the show could help give birth to, and one they wanted to develop against the better judgment of Berman and Piller initially.[14] *Voyager* was to represent the apex of what *Star Trek* meant, how *The Next Generation* particularly had defined television science-fiction across the last decade and returned *Star*

4. The 21st Century (So Far)

Trek to the public consciousness. It would work to encapsulate that same spirit of progressive exceptionalism *The Original Series* inspired—Asian, Latino, even Native American main crew members, and for the first time a female captain in command of the ship.[15] There was a confidence about *Voyager*'s position, upon its launch, which reflected American existential brio during the middle of that decade.

Douglas Coupland speaks wistfully of it as "the good decade":

> At the very least, in North America and Europe, the 1990s possessed a sense of happiness that seems long vanished. Money still generated money. Computers were becoming fast, easy and cheap, and with them came a sense of equality for everyone. Things were palpably getting better everywhere. History was over and it felt great. I also remember working at *Wired* magazine, though, in 1993, and having a discussion about the internet with one of the editors, Kevin Kelly. The thrust was that there was an internet, sure, but there was nowhere to go.[16]

Yet just one year after the USS *Voyager* set sail for the "Badlands" under Captain Kathryn Janeway to hunt down a group of Maquis rebels, only to become stranded thanks to an alien being 70,000 light years (aka around 75 actual years of travel) away in the distant Delta Quadrant, author Chuck Palahniuk published *Fight Club*. This seminal novel, later made in 1999 into a celebrated film from director David Fincher, cut deep into a sense of post–Cold War, nihilistic cynicism about American culture and the future at the end of history. He wrote: "We're the middle children of history, man. No purpose or place. We have no Great War. No Great Depression. Our Great War's a spiritual war ... our Great Depression is our lives. We've all been raised on television to believe that one day we'd all be millionaires, and movie gods, and rock stars. But we won't. And we're slowly learning that fact. And we're very, very pissed off."[17] Though captured well by Fincher's film, the book itself, decades on, is a gut-punching indictment on the underbelly of white male rage still troubling America today and serves as a remarkable counterpoint to *Voyager*'s confidence in *Star Trek*'s mission. It may be stranded, but it refuses to believe it is heading in the wrong direction.

Though the show is enjoying some level of critical re-appreciation during its 25th anniversary celebrations,[18] *Voyager* nonetheless remains far less venerated than *Deep Space Nine*, itself having recently celebrated a quarter-centenary with a significant reminder thanks to documentaries and convention events, of how well that series had held up in the context of changing television styles and attitudes. One of the primary criticisms of *Voyager* from the very beginning was in how, from pilot episode "Caretaker" onwards, the series welched on the conflict hard-wired into the central premise. Not only was *Voyager* thrown the furthest from home of any Starfleet crew, they were flung *with* the Maquis rebels they were sent to arrest, and Janeway—having lost Starfleet crew members in the long distance travel—is forced to integrate the rebels into her crew, making their leader Chakotay her first officer. Internal character conflict that appears baked into the DNA of the series is, however, very quickly cast aside by Berman, Piller, Taylor and their writers.

Brief series writer and producer Ronald D. Moore expands on this:

> When the Maquis put on those Starfleet uniforms at the end of the pilot, the show was dead. That was the biggest mistake, because they went through this whole thing to bring on their enemies. We made up the Maquis on *DS9* just so that they could appear on *Voyager*. Here are Starfleet officers who had become terrorist resistance fighters, guerrilla warriors. The Federation has got them on the run and both of these groups are thrown in a ship on another side of the galaxy and forced to live together. You'd think that's the setup for a major show about conflict, but at the end of the pilot they all put on the Starfleet uniforms and that's it. It was a huge mistake. It should have been these two sides that were forced to work together that still don't like each other and still are gunning for each other, wondering who's going to come out on top. Who's going to betray who? It should have been gold, but they got scared.[19]

That fear of *Voyager*'s premise, with more distant eyes, seems bizarre to behold. Moore parlayed a great many of the ideas he brought into *Voyager* when he briefly joined Brannon Braga's staff during the sixth season, which premiered late in 1999, into his reimagining of *Battlestar Galactica* during the next decade. Yet the calls for deeper conflict and added serialization in *Voyager*'s narrative are now deep-baked into modern *Star Trek* series such as *Discovery* and *Picard*, which feature mutineers, failed officers, mercenaries and murderers among their crew complements. *Voyager*, however, existed in the dying age of syndicated network dominance, whereby it was required to achieve a round one-hundred-episode number filled with episodes that could be sold to local networks and aired out of sequence. It overlapped the arrival of *The Sopranos*, and the birth of the cable era spearheaded by HBO, which itself helped engineer the streaming era of the late 2010s into the 2020s, which has entirely revolutionized television. The entire medium has fluctuated wildly over the last two decades, in tandem with the upending of the geopolitical and cultural sphere in the Western world by economic shock, terrorism and the embrace of social media, but *Voyager* existed in a space defined by one word: stability.

Berman, as the steward of the *Star Trek* universe following Roddenberry's death, saw his duty to hold to the precepts of *Star Trek* in how stories within the universe were told. *Voyager*, therefore, could never diverge too steeply from the template laid down by *The Next Generation*, unlike how *Deep Space Nine* had forged its own direction in defiance of those edicts.[20] It was designed to capture the premise of *Star Trek* audiences understood: a ship, a crew, space exploration and adventure. While *The Next Generation* explored a range of deep, fascinating philosophical and scientific concepts, it was a series defined by a lack of inter-personal conflict or development. After *Deep Space Nine*'s deliberate inversion of those precepts, building an inter-connected mythological world of consequences, *Voyager*'s determination to follow *The Next Generation*'s footsteps, especially given the conceptual ideological conflict between the two crews thrown into the Delta Quadrant, reflects the position of the show within a pre-millennial decade itself defined by stability. Nothing changed, existentially, between 1991 and 2001. *Voyager* exists at the end of the beginning of history.

Mooney considers this key to how *Voyager* questioned the nature of its own existence and reality in much of its storytelling.

> All of this captures an anxiety that permeated late nineties culture, finding expression in a variety of pop culture from *The Matrix* to *Dark City* to *The Thirteenth Floor* to *Harsh Realm* to *eXistenz* to *The Truman Show*. There was a palpable anxiety at the end of the nineties that the world wasn't actually real, and that nothing actually existed. It was perhaps a response to the collapse of the rigid ideological framework of the Cold War, the collapse of that ordering principle opening the popular consciousness to more abstract existential queries.[21]

Order was something that existed during the era of *The Next Generation* and for the adventures of Captain Picard and his crew. The universe the *Enterprise* explored, which later became defined as the Alpha and Beta Quadrants, was largely colonized and understood by the Federation and a range of familiar galactic powers who dominated the landscape—Klingons, Vulcans, Romulans, Andorians, later Cardassians and so on. *The Next Generation* explored, and it encountered new lifeforms, but the *Enterprise* never truly felt alone, never took too many risks in exploring the final frontier. There was always a starbase to contact. There was always another Starfleet ship in the near distance. *The Next Generation*'s world was a contained, ordered sense of exploration and adventure, a world of understood futuristic stability. *Voyager*, by virtue of its very premise, never took the opportunity to explore the chaos of uncharted space, despite the fact the Delta Quadrant is unquestionably different from the world of the Federation and their allies or "cold" enemies.

Mooney considers the Delta Quadrant to be an area of the galaxy haunted by species living in the ruins of greater, long departed civilizations:

> There is a sense that the Delta Quadrant was populated by species living amid the ruins. Before it was destroyed in "Hunters," the Hirogen laid claim an impressive communications network designed by a long-lost civilisation. The Trabe had collapsed decades before the start of the series, leaving the Kazon to fight over what remained in stolen ships. The Talaxians had been humbled and conquered by the Haakonian Order. The Vidiians had been a bastion of artists and creatives, before a highly contagious disease turned them into scavengers and predators. As such, the Delta Quadrant represents what George H.W. Bush described as the "new world order" of the era following the Cold War. The Soviet Union had collapsed, leaving a number of smaller states scrambling to hold themselves together. The United States was the world's only superpower. Some even began to use the word "hyper-power" to properly quantify the amount of influence that the United States held. *Voyager* reflected this sense of shifting global perspective.[22]

The argument constructed in Mooney's work is that *Voyager* represents, within the Delta Quadrant, a pure example of America's status as a sole hyper-power at the end of the 20th century, having "defeated" Communism, having reached a point of corporate and economic stability and liquidity, while culturally leading the way in entertainment to a degree never before experienced. *Voyager* is never humbled by the Delta Quadrant. There are rarely episodes in which Janeway and her crew are confronted by the dark majesty of the universe or a Lovecraftian sense of cosmic power.[23] The Hirogen, a powerful group of seemingly amoral hunters are provided with advanced Federation technology which quells their quadrant-wide search for prey. The Vidiians began as equally amoral scavengers, compromised by the desire to cure their horrendous "phage" by pillaging the organs of healthy species, but *Voyager*'s heroic Emergency Medical Hologram gives them the tools to find a cure. The crew are able to uphold the principles of Starfleet and the aims of the Federation amid a lawless area of space with no sense of cohesive, collective history, and filled with dangerous tribes and scavengers.

One of the most telling examples of how *Voyager* refuses to divert from the sense of its own superiority lies in the two-part episode "Year of Hell." A powerful, action-based story, it takes place across the span of a year in which *Voyager* is repeatedly beaten and brought to near destruction by Annorax, a commander in the Kremin Imperium, a powerful Delta Quadrant race who has a ship capable of repeatedly changing the fabric of time. Brannon Braga, newly destined to inherit the role of showrunner from the retiring Taylor, envisaged the story as a season-long narrative, presaging the rise of serialized television that *Enterprise* would

4. The 21st Century (So Far)

later reluctantly embrace in its third season. However, as Bryan Fuller explains, the idea was reduced to one of numerous two-part episodes which Braga encouraged as a means to make *Voyager*'s adventures on a more epic scale:

> In season four, the entire season was going to be *Voyager* getting its ass kicked and the show was really going to go to a gritty and rich place of "We are out of our element and we are in danger and all we have is ourselves," Janeway being this situational, ethical leader who was willing to do whatever it took for her people to survive in these circumstances. And it was so much bolder than what you saw. That's not to say that there weren't some great episodes in that season. You had the "Year of Hell," but Brannon had so many bold visions that were brushed aside by Rick just not seeing it and not wanting *Voyager* to be as gritty and bold as *DS9*.[24]

These "bold visions," as suggested by Fuller, suggest *Voyager* was a series stymied by the need to retain the sense of order *The Next Generation* had imposed on the broader universe of *Star Trek*, and a narrative formula that the writing staff were frequently keen to break away from. The result, despite Season Four arguably being *Voyager*'s strongest season, filled with well-constructed singular and two-part stories, was a reinforcement of *Voyager*'s place as an inviolate starship that just happened to be travelling in uncharted space. Initial villains, the Kazon, originally designed as a youthful, tribal culture, descended into a hybrid of Native American–style nomads who fought back against monoculturalism and the recognizable antagonism of the Klingons, and they were quickly dropped by the third season. *Voyager* would consistently attempt to tell stories that tethered the show to the Alpha Quadrant and Earth—"Message in a Bottle" or "Future's End"[25]—and as the series progressed, and the closer they came to home, the more *Voyager* became determined to replicate the style, and even borrow from the world, of *The Next Generation*.

The omnipotent Q, such a staple of *The Next Generation* who only appeared on *Deep Space Nine* once and very quickly felt aberrant to the world of the space station, appeared repeatedly on *Voyager* and fit like a glove. He swapped his barbed irritation with Picard for sleazy flirtation with Janeway as the series attempted to unpick, and even humanize, the Q Continuum in stories such as "Death Wish,"[26] while "The Q and the Grey," "False Profits" directly tethered to *The Next Generation*'s "The Price" and brought in the Ferengi. "In the Flesh" was set in an alien recreation of Starfleet Academy. The Borg, and *First Contact*'s Borg Queen, were introduced as regular antagonists, and their impact was consistently lessened thanks to overuse, in no small part due to the creation of *Voyager*'s breakout character Seven of Nine.[27] The series increasingly relies on "the holodeck episode," a staple of *The Next Generation* as previously discussed, to tell stories. *Next Generation* characters such as Geordi La Forge, Deanna Troi and Reg Barclay appeared, the latter pair becoming recurring characters in later seasons. *Voyager*, at every turn, worked to re-orient and point the series back in the direction of the Alpha Quadrant and the comfortable, ordered universe of *The Next Generation* rather than present the Delta Quadrant as a dangerous, difficult region of space where they would have to fight to stay alive.

This, again, speaks to *Voyager*'s confidence as representative of America's dominance. If the United States by the late 90s was a "hyper power," then *Voyager* was a "hyper powered" starship. Rather than be forced to adapt and change and develop and grow as a vessel marked by an alien, unknown region of the galaxy, *Voyager* remains precisely the same across seven seasons. It somehow manages to create sleek new shuttles like the Delta Flyer. It gains "ablative armour" from Borg technology to strengthen it. It often meets alien beings who help propel the ship further back in the direction they came rather than keep them alienated, remote and humbled. When *Voyager* even encounters a second starship in "Equinox" that was thrown into the Delta Quadrant at the same time, it serves as simply a dark, morally compromised reflection of Janeway and her crew, as opposed to a complicated group of officers who were forced to make troubling choices to survive. The show consistently reinforces *Voyager* as steadfast, morally secure and filled with a conviction in its manifest destiny to find a way home. The outcome given in series finale "Endgame" is never in doubt. "If" within a couple of seasons becomes "when," and the when was always going to line up with the traditional seven-season run for *The Next Generation* era that allows for syndication.

The man who coined the term "hyper power" to describe the United States in the late '90s was French foreign minister Hubert Vedrine, who when asked how the "steamrolling" nature of American dominance could be curtailed or reckoned with, said: "Through steady and persevering work in favor of real multilateralism against unilateralism, for balanced multipolarism against unipolarism, for cultural diversity against uniformity. None of that will happen automatically and our influence in the world isn't going to grow all by itself. A strategy, a tactic, a method, are necessary. It's possible."[28] The future of *Voyager*, however, assumes the unilateral confidence of American cultural, political and economic dominance by projecting the Federation forward as a consistent state of galactic being.

Deep Space Nine questioned whether the Federation could survive

4. The 21st Century (So Far)

the cyclical nature of history and the perpetual state of war. The Dominion, a society built on xenophobia and fear based on their own persecution by "solids" aka humanoids, sought control and order through means of dominance, and forced the Federation into a war they never imagined they would need to fight in their sense of utopian, 24th century world-building. Starfleet had brushfire wars over the decades since *The Undiscovered Country*, since the construction of peace with the Klingons, but the Cardassians or the Breen or the Tzenkethi were never species who presented a threat to the Federation's way of life. The Romulans, while always problematic, stayed behind their own iron curtain until *The Next Generation*'s "The Neutral Zone," only pulled out of their isolationism by the encroachment of the Borg. Yet even they, for all their collectivized terror and rampant hive power, were a menace to be beaten back by the Federation. At great cost, as "The Best of Both Worlds" suggests, yes, but the Borg would come and go akin to a plague, an ideological pandemic to be controlled until the next flare up. Only *Deep Space Nine* brought the Federation to the brink of genuine destruction. The Dominion and their allies actually attacked Earth in "The Changing Face of Evil," in an act that would have been the equivalent of the Nazi machine launching an attack on Washington, D.C., during World War II.[29]

Voyager, lost in the Delta Quadrant, entirely skips this conflict. It starts after they have vanished and is over by the time they return, but the Maquis are wiped out by the Dominion and, thanks to communications from the Alpha Quadrant (another example of how the show tethers to home), characters such as Chakotay and B'Elanna Torres are marked by losing their fellow rebels in a conflict they have completely lost touch with. "Those were our friends, good people willing to put their lives on the line for something they believed in and now you're telling me that they are gone, that they are slaughtered,"[30] Torres says, and later swears vengeance. In "Extreme Risk" she creates a holo-program where she intentionally injures herself to try and feel emotion for the death of her friends. These are rare moments where *Voyager* acknowledges the Maquis loyalties in a crew just as homogenized by Starfleet and the Federation ideal as the many races they create. As such, *Voyager* is unaffected by the Dominion War to a similar degree as *The Next Generation*, who merely pay lip service to it during their big-screen adventures.

Yet the 1990s ended with *Star Trek*, through *Deep Space Nine*, faced with the biggest existential threat to the sanctity of the Federation for perhaps centuries. Worlds are invaded and destroyed. Millions are killed. Cardassia suffers a literal Holocaust. *Voyager* returns to a world, in 2001, in "Endgame," that is completely changed, even if the series never recognizes it and, in fact, suggests the Federation will eternally endure. "Future's End" introduces the idea that in the 29th century, the Federation utilize "timeships" to explore history as well as space, and "Relativity" later follows up on this as *Voyager* introduces one such timeship, showing how the Federation half a millennia later have mastered time as well as space, able to exert some level of order and control over both. It is a marked contrast to *Deep Space Nine* which, predicting the tides of history in the century to come, believes the Federation and its utopia is far from eternally secure. *Voyager*, and later *Enterprise* with the Temporal Cold War narrative, establish the Federation as surviving for at least 700 years since its inception, and only *Discovery*'s upcoming (as of writing) third season set in the 32nd century seems to suggest the Federation has been reduced to near dissolution, if not outright destruction. *Voyager* undoubtedly would not have characterized that century the same way. Their Federation would have remained stable and exceptional.

Voyager's obsession with projecting forward to an unshakable, uniform future, even in the face of new worlds and threats and unknown regions of space, almost appears to contradict the very idea that the show was a return to Roddenberry's original idea of *The Original Series* as "*Wagon Train to the Stars.*" The galaxy of *The Original Series* was filled with lawless worlds ruled by machines or gods or dictators, without any sense of the Federation structure *The Next Generation* gave the 24th century. However, *Voyager* is presented with the chance to replicate that disorder and chooses to run back, conservatively, toward the stability it understands and believes will be represented everywhere for years to come. Michael Piller discusses the thought processes behind the show's conception in this regard:

> When we hooked on this idea, we realized in a sense that we were talking about a journey that is very much like the journey that all of us in this country are on. It seems clear that the kind of problems that this country is facing are not problems that are going to be easily solved in our lifetime. We have to begin working on solutions that may take more than one generation to see the final result of. In fact, our children might be the ones who get to see the results of our hard work if we start now. In a sense, the ship franchise of *Voyager* is that kind of journey, because we are on a ship of men and women who are beginning a journey that conceivably we may not see the end of—and we are working in the best interests of everybody on board to try to solve our problem and to make the best life we can for ourselves on this ship, to find the way back home.[31]

The irony of this statement is that *Voyager* does the opposite. It never assumes the Delta Quadrant is home. It never assumes the journey

4. The 21st Century (So Far)

will take the rest of their lives, and the crew never plan accordingly. It assumes the next Caretaker or wormhole or advanced technology is around the corner. It assumes that home is a world that will always exist as it was, as the world they knew and were ripped away from, and while the writing staff may have encouraged the characters to enjoy the sense of adventure in their experience, Janeway and her crew are never truly explorers. They are trapped by their own sense of history, and indeed *Voyager* is as obsessed with history as *Deep Space Nine*, only in a different context.[32] *Voyager* cannot let go of the past as part of its drive to return to a world it understands and is terrified of looking ahead at the future. Perhaps America was at this point too. Perhaps the millennium, after a century of war and cultural, technological, societal change unlike anything in human history, was too great an epochal moment for the franchise to deal with.

Interestingly, *Voyager* is the only *Star Trek* series to expressly touch on the transition from 1999 to 2000 (or more accurately 2000–2001) in the Season Five episode "11:59," and it deals with the fragmented nature of the history of that transition. In it, Janeway learns that her ancestor Shannon O'Donnell, whom she believed to be a female pioneer on a mission to Mars, was in fact a down on her luck engineer who married a kindly bookstore owner in a small Indiana town who fought to stymie the creation of the Millennium Gate, a structural icon representing the dawn of the new millennium. Janeway always believed she represented part of humanity's stride into the future when in reality, she prioritized home and family, security and stability, and a false legend about her journey persevered over the centuries through oral history.

This feels a fitting metaphor for *Voyager* as a series. It is a show that approaches the end of the 20th century pulling away from the final frontier as opposed to pushing forward, obsessed with the preservation of memory and the continuation of a conservative, ordered set of principles to the *Star Trek* universe at the supposed "end of history." America, and *Voyager*, and the Federation, were a fixed point in space, and indeed time.

Voyager ended in the summer of 2001 as the crew finally, as they always deep down expected, made their way home. We never saw what happened next. We never saw their interactions with an Alpha Quadrant scarred by the Dominion War. *Star Trek*'s journey was further into the past, taking its obsession with history to a new level as the franchise began exploring its own internal past, its own mythical story, never expecting that the world around it was about to change for good, as the 21st century truly began.

Star Trek, History and Us

Shock, Awe and Terra

In the year 1947, almost two decades before *Star Trek* began, the United States changed the world through the use of atomic weapons on the Japanese cities of Hiroshima and Nagasaki to bring about the end of conflict with Japan in the wake of World War II.

Robert Oppenheimer had, just two short years earlier, developed the atomic bomb in Los Alamos, New Mexico, leading a team of theoretical physicists in creating the most powerful weapon ever devised by human hands. "I am become death, destroyer of worlds," he famously said, watching the test detonation of the H-bomb, quoting from the Bhagavad-Gita[33] as he recognized that he had opened a metaphorical Pandora's Box. Just two years later, President Harry S. Truman sanctioned the only use of such a weapon in the theater of combat since its creation, an apocalyptic event which wiped two cities instantly off the map and killed hundreds of thousands of civilians. In the many dark days in the American history, Hiroshima and Nagasaki remain among the bleakest.

America has never experienced the kind of trauma they visited upon the Japanese that day, which quickly led the nation to surrender in the eastern theater of war that raged after the official end of World War II in 1945 following the collapse of the Nazi regime. No nuclear weapon has ever been detonated on American soil. Yet in September of 2001, the United States faced, in microcosm comparably, their own Hiroshima or Nagasaki, when the World Trade Center at the heart of New York City was destroyed as part of a coordinated terrorist attack by fundamentalist Muslim organization al-Qaeda. The "twin towers" fell as hijacked planes crashed into the buildings, and elsewhere the Pentagon, home of the U.S. military and intelligence forces, was also hit and a fourth plane crashed in rural Pennsylvania while the world watched in real-time thanks to cable news. Thousands died. Millions more wept.

The world changed that day, particularly for *Star Trek* as a franchise, even if it took Rick Berman, Brannon Braga and the writers around them time to reconcile it in the only remaining series now on air: *Enterprise*. Braga explains the initial concept:

> We wanted to show what happened in the period in *Star Trek* history between *First Contact* and Kirk. How did we end up building the first warp ship? What was it like to meet a Klingon for the first time? People had ball caps and walked dogs and wore tennis shoes and are more identifiable as people than, say, a Captain Picard, who is more of an idyllic man of the future that you probably wouldn't recognize as a person that you could ever meet today.[34]

130

4. The 21st Century (So Far)

Enterprise began life as a radically different concept than the show that ended up on screen. We did see Scott Bakula's Captain Jonathan Archer in a baseball cap and sneakers on a ship which had more a submarine than starship esthetic; even the title ditched the *Star Trek* prefix at first,[35] and they chose to place a soft-rock song over the credit sequence rather than the traditional orchestral beat.[36] Very quickly network directives and the conservatism of Berman began, however, to fashion the series in the same mold that *Star Trek* had successfully maintained since 1987. Stories were self-contained, eschewing serialization, which was already beginning to strike a chord with audiences after HBO series such as *The Sopranos* displayed what was possible, as Fox's action series *24*—perhaps the most deliberately serialized television drama outside of a soap opera ever—became an overnight sensation the same year *Enterprise* launched. Many of the plots recycled ideas that had been used over the 600+ *Star Trek* episodes to date. The show felt dated even before the end of its first season.

Crucially, the series debuted just two weeks after the shock of what became known colloquially and in media circles and nascent social media on the internet as "9/11," and it was attempting to project, as *Star Trek* always does, toward a bright, optimistic future in the shadow of a time filled with, particularly for Americans, fear, anger and skepticism about the century to come. It had almost sanctified TV series such as *The X-Files* or *Millennium*,[37] which displayed all kinds of pre-millennial anxiety, or the turn of the millennium doomsayers who believed the 21st century would be an unknown, frightening era for mankind as they stepped from the 20th. Barnaby J. Feder wrote about these fears in the *New York Times* in 1999, particularly concerning the "Y2K" bug:

> The early fears about the Year 2000 computer problem featured all sorts of machines driven haywire by their inability to read dates in the new year: computer networks that control power, water and phone systems freeze; railroads, airlines and trucks are idled as dispatch and traffic safety systems crash, and the financial universe, from stock markets to payroll systems to automated teller machines, goes on the blink. That was before tens of billions of dollars were spent on computer repairs and upgrades. Now, a chorus of regulators, Year 2000 project managers and other authorities warn that Americans fearing the worst may end up inflicting more serious damage on themselves, their neighbors and the economy than anything the computers do. Planning experts say those scenarios could include bank runs, hoarding of food and gasoline, fires caused by misuse of newly acquired wood stoves and generators, and a rise in gun violence stemming from the surge in firearm sales to those fearing civil unrest.[38]

In such a climate, *Enterprise* immediately appeared old fashioned in attempting to stylistically depict the *Star Trek* universe, over its first two seasons, in the same manner. Archer and his crew were designed to relate more to 21st century humanity, with largely a human crew much like *The Original Series* of mixed ethnicity taking cautious baby steps into uncharted space, against the protestations of their conservative, irascible guides the Vulcans. However, the series soon descended into telling stories that merely felt tweaked from *The Next Generation* or *Voyager*, tales that Picard or Janeway's crews could have experienced two centuries hence. *Enterprise* did include an ongoing, overarching narrative concerning the Temporal Cold War being fought between a 31st century Federation and 22nd century aliens the Suliban, and this did deliver episodes such as "Shockwave," which depicted a particularly post-apocalyptic Earth of the future, but beyond that 9/11 and its existential trauma were avoided. While *24*'s Jack Bauer was serving as a proxy for conservative Americana and battling fundamentalist Muslim terrorists on U.S. soil, *Enterprise* was producing episodes such as "Precious Cargo," in which Trip Tucker is kidnapped and escapes with a spoiled alien princess.

However, everything changed in the summer of 2003, in the wake of George W. Bush's promise of "shock and awe" as the U.S. military invasion of Iraq—a direct response to 9/11 in the eyes of many[39]—began in March of that year, with the second season finale "The Expanse."

The second season ends with the Earth being attacked by an alien probe which cuts a swath across Florida, killing millions of innocent civilians, including Trip's sister. Archer learns the probe was sent by the Xindi, a race who live inside a dangerous, unpredictable region of space called the Delphic Expanse, who have been manipulated by a 26th century race in the Temporal Cold War called the Sphere Builders into believing Earth is going to destroy their civilization. They are building a super-weapon to attack and destroy Earth in advance, thereby preventing the founding of the Federation and the Sphere Builders' eventual defeat in a 26th century war with the Federation. The season ends with a re-tooled *Enterprise*, transformed from nascent ship of exploration into defensive battlecruiser, entering the Expanse on a desperate mission to find the Xindi and destroy the weapon. So begins the first seasonal arc in *Star Trek* history, as *Enterprise*'s third year was designed from the ground up over twenty-four episodes to revolve around the Xindi, the Expanse and their weapon.

Bizarrely, both Berman and Braga have denied that 9/11 was an influence on "The Expanse" as a story, despite the fact the "War on Terror" had now begun to rage as American forces stormed Afghanistan in search of al-Qaeda and the Taliban, and concocted a pretext to invade Iraq over their fear of weapons of mass destruction. Both *Enterprise* creators attest

4. The 21st Century (So Far)

that the Xindi arc was a response to a network edict to liven up the series, which like *Voyager* and *Deep Space Nine* before it was suffering from falling ratings, and as Berman describes based on looking at previous, successful *Star Trek* narratives:

> I think one of the things that motivated us is in analysing the 10 existing *Star Trek* movies, we were looking for something that would help torque up our series and add a little dimension to get a little added excitement towards the end of the season. We did a little analysis of our own, and we saw that two of the most popular movies ... were *Star Trek IV* [*The Voyage Home*], which was the one about whales, and *Star Trek VIII*, which was *First Contact*. These were both films that had to do with the future of Earth being at stake. And we decided that that would be a great place to start. ... It wasn't literally for a long time that we suddenly realized [the parallel]. But the idea of aliens coming to destroy Earth has been around a lot longer than 9/11.[40]

The key difference with the other examples Berman cites here is that the attack on the Earth was not in the wake of global events in which there had been a fundamental, earth-shattering vulnerability exposed in the national security of the West, one which across the next decade fundamentalist terrorists of varying nations would see as open season on the established systems of American civilians and institutions. *The Voyage Home* presented the Earth under threat from the consequences of reckless environmental ignorance in the 20th century (a lesson we still have not learned). Before it, *The Motion Picture* saw Earth threatened by an intelligence on a religious odyssey, unaware of the human cost, while *First Contact*'s return of the Borg, a hive mind comparable to a disease that simply requires containment, had been pre-figured in *The Next Generation* seven years earlier in "The Best of Both Worlds" (and oddly, after the fact, Season Two of *Enterprise*) and was simply based on attempts to scale up the threat level for Picard's crew to face. "The Expanse" is different. It presents an attack by an unpredictable force, out of the blue, on a believed inviolate part of Earth, which massacres innocent people. It is impossible to consider, written almost two years after 9/11, that it was not in some way a reaction.

The Xindi arc was *Star Trek*'s first, fundamental challenge to Gene Roddenberry's utopia since the Dominion War in *Deep Space Nine*. In that show, the Dominion allies, the Breen, manage to attack San Francisco, but their target is Starfleet Headquarters, and it is part of a declared, ongoing state of war. It is more Pearl Harbor than 9/11. The Florida attack is brutal, unexpected and sees *Star Trek*, for the first time, have civilians pay the price. *Enterprise*, tethered a little more to our modern reality than its predecessors, is a logical place to display such horror, especially given Roddenberry's future has not quite been reached at this point. The "post-atomic horror" of World War Three (which we will discuss later) has come and gone, Earth has made contact with alien lifeforms and developed warp drive, and Starfleet has now been formed. However, we remain some years away from the foundation of the Federation, and there remain serious social issues on Earth among its citizenry as the fourth season depicts in "Demons" and "Terra Prime," suggesting that xenophobia has not quite yet been eradicated on Earth by the mid–22nd century.

For the first time, *Enterprise* sees *Star Trek* adapting to realities around them in the same manner *Deep Space Nine* factored in pre-millennial anxieties about the century to come. That show even prefigured the corrupted sanctity of Earth's utopia as early as its fourth season in "Homefront" and "Paradise Lost," in which fearful Starfleet conspirators whip up mass hysteria about Changeling invasion and Earth-based terrorism, declaring martial law to give Starfleet more hawkish, aggressive militaristic powers as a means of "protecting" Earth. They are ultimately exposed by Captain Sisko as, much like the conspirators in *The Undiscovered Country*, misguided and not in line with Starfleet's ethos, but there is a sense *Enterprise* would have been more forgiving in the wake of 9/11. If in the mid–90s, a decade fuelled by anti-government conspiracy theory as the zeitgeist questioned American history, *Deep Space Nine* took a dim view of conservative protectionism, then *Enterprise* exists in a decade where Americans were, largely, behind government strides to secure and protect the home front against the threat of terrorism.[41] *The X-Files* ended, its brand of government suspicion giving way to *24*'s ultra-conservatism of the one-man army Jack Bauer protecting American cities from both internal and external extremists who would threaten America's largely centrist way of life.

The Xindi arc represented the *Enterprise* as a ship entering the Expanse as comparable to American forces in Afghanistan, "going it alone"[42] in the face of international and domestic criticism on their hawkish foreign policy, which many considered to be driven by some level of vengeance against the attack on New York. Trip in *Enterprise* is certainly driven by a need for revenge for the death of his sister. Archer becomes increasingly hardened across the third season, at one point in "Anomaly" torturing an Oosarian pirate for information, which triggers the specter of Abu Ghrayib or Guantanamo Bay in the wake of 9/11 and the rendition of suspected terrorists who would be exposed to disturbing treatment by American forces which, seemingly, goes against the fundamental ideals of Starfleet and the nascent Federation. Yet, much as the American people

4. The 21st Century (So Far)

remained behind Bush's invasion of Iraq initially in the wake of UN condemnation, Starfleet and their allies remain behind Archer's mission. One suspects Earth's citizens at that point, if canvassed, would have considered the ends justifying the means in more of the extreme lengths Archer and his crew must go to in order to stop the second Xindi attack.

Earlier in this chapter, we discussed Robert Oppenheimer and his weapon of mass destruction, and while *Enterprise*'s chief allegory across the third season is a response to the War on Terror, it also reflexively plays out an Oppenheimer parable in the character of Degra, the Xindi-Primate scientist who develops the super-weapon, as Darren Mooney suggests:

> The show rather explicitly parallels Degra to Robert Oppenheimer rather than Osama Bin Laden or Saddam Hussein, a very clear indication that the character is not so different and reinforcing the idea that the Xindi are not a metaphor for a nebulous terrorist "Other." Instead, the Xindi are a mirror to the Federation and to the audience. The Federation has always been presented as an idealised version of the United States, while the Xindi present a more fractured and unstable iteration of the same idea; perhaps reflecting anxiety in the face of a changing world.[43]

Voyager, in Season One's "Jetrel," had presented the Oppenheimer-figure of a scientist who constructed a weapon that led to the genocidal destruction of another culture, but it presented the character of Jetrel in a historical context. It worked in the same manner as *Deep Space Nine*, exploring the Holocaust and Nazi war crimes through the prism of Bajoran Occupation, as an event which occurred in the recent history of a species. On *Enterprise*, the threat is real and imminent. If the Xindi are analogous to the militant fundamentalist arm of the Taliban, with the Federation their "Great Satan," then Degra does not serve the same function as Osama bin Laden, the figurehead of extremist terrorism. Degra is a man with a wife and children building a weapon, under pressure from militant forces within his society, that he knows can do terrible harm: "I was ordered to begin designing the weapon. I devoted years to it. I made so many sacrifices. So did my wife."[44]

Degra is presented as a complicated, sympathetic figure caught up in the hawkish response from his own society as a means, in part, for a particular caste of his people to seize internal power. *Enterprise* attempts to suggest that the Xindi are not unlike us, that their experiences in relation to Starfleet and Earth are simply through an altogether different prism. Unlike in *24*, where the villains largely remained fairly one-dimensional archetypes for Jack Bauer to destroy in the pro–American crusade against the "Other," *Enterprise* reaffirms the very *Star Trek* ideal, even in the face of rampant conservatism and American hurt and anger which subsequently devastates the Middle East and plunges their armed forces into a modern-day Vietnam, that we can reconcile our differences. Archer, in "The Council," *does* manage to make many of the Xindi understand his point of view. It ends up being a Xindi extremist who forces the *Enterprise* into a last-ditch battle to prevent the use of the super-weapon. *Enterprise*, a show not destined for a long life or the critical acclaim of its forebears, approaches the "War on Terror," even subconsciously, with the hope we can resolve our ideological differences and forge a path to peace.

As *Star Trek* passes through what could be considered its "Second Dark Age," a period between 2005 and 2008 where no *Star Trek* film or TV series was on air or being produced for the first time since 1979, there is a sense that the franchise's transformation toward the modern era of *Star Trek* loses, on some level, that sense of optimism.

Enterprise was cancelled after the end of its fourth season in 2005, following poor ratings and despite a critical upsurge during a final season which truly lived up to the original intended mission statement of depicting the continuity of *Star Trek* before *The Original Series*. With it the Rick Berman era came to an end. *Star Trek* was fairly swiftly revived by J.J. Abrams' Bad Robot production stable and returned as a blockbuster, high budget Hollywood film with an all new cast portraying the now iconic *The Original Series* characters Kirk, Spock, McCoy and so on. The film managed not to invalidate the original 1960s series or subsequent franchise entries by utilizing Leonard Nimoy, returning to play Spock for the first time since 1992's *The Next Generation* episode "Unification," in a story which via the magic of time-travel allowed writers Roberto Orci & Alex Kurtzman to create a new timeline separate from any existing continuity to tackle the origin stories of the first *Enterprise* cast and crew.

Though at times they feel more in line with *Star Wars*' fantasy than *Star Trek*'s measured sense of philosophical adventure, the 2009 *Star Trek* film and subsequent two sequels to date, *Star Trek Into Darkness* in 2013 and *Star Trek Beyond* in 2016, all follow in the *Enterprise* slipstream of placing the franchise in a post–9/11 context. Abrams (and *Beyond*'s director Justin Lin) works to rediscover a nostalgic sense of 1960s derring-do, propelled with narratives that keep the action moving, but each story sees the *Enterprise* and its crew face an existential threat to not just the Federation but the human race. *Star Trek* 2009 has Nero, a revenge fuelled Romulan extremist from the late 24th century who is thrown back in time and destroys Vulcan, and later tries to destroy Earth, with a weapon of mass destruction that sucks a planet into an antimatter vacuum. *Star Trek*

4. The 21st Century (So Far)

Into Darkness reimagines the character of Khan Noonien Singh[45] less as an exiled, mad prince but a fanatical eugenicist turned Section-31 weapon who transforms into a terrorist extremist and strikes at the very heart of Starfleet, plunging a starship into the San Francisco skyline in a climax designed to deliberately evoke 9/11. And even *Star Trek Beyond*, which takes the *Enterprise* further into deep space for a planetary adventure, *The Original Series*–style,[46] features a seemingly alien villain in Krall—the monstrous, corrupted visage of a Starfleet captain lost since the *Enterprise*-era (even referenced as fighting in "the Xindi wars"), who intends to release a devastating biological weapon on Earth.

Each of these villains are driven by anti–Federation vengeance, as indeed was the antagonist in the final *Next Generation* film from 2002, *Nemesis*, in Shinzon, the new Romulan Praetor who seized control in a coup and who turns out to be the revenge-seeking clone of Captain Picard, a dying man who wants to attack Earth. After 2001, in cinematic terms as well as in *Enterprise*, the direct threat to Earth becomes a staple of *Star Trek* storytelling as the stakes become higher and more directly focused on challenging the utopian security of humanity's cradle. *Nemesis*, a film which failed at the box office much like *Enterprise* failed on television, sought to replicate the unique alchemy of *The Wrath of Khan*, and in that sense, it relates particularly to *Into Darkness*, which actively replicates and reimagines certain moments and scenes from Nicholas Meyer's 1982 film. They are both driven by characters who, from their extreme points of view and created by warped human (or in Shinzon's case, Romulan) science, are aberrant psychopaths who operate in direct opposition to the heroes facing them, be it Picard or Chris Pine's Kirk. *The Wrath of Khan*'s villain is, of course, a Khan driven by vengeance, but his is personal and relates directly to Admiral Kirk. Meyer never voices Khan's desire to use the Genesis Device on Earth, even if that was his ultimate intent.

It was only after the shock and trauma of 9/11 that *Star Trek* becomes *about* the antagonists actively seeking to destroy "paradise," and constantly until the arrival of *Star Trek: Discovery* in 2017 plays out the same underlying fear. Utopia can now be compromised, and it was certainly a notion on the minds of Abrams and his writers in crafting *Into Darkness*, as Orci states:

> We wanted to explore the notion of the utopia of the Federation. A utopia is supposed to be a society without conflict, but how do you aspire to a utopia while also acknowledging the barriers to utopia? No matter how advanced the Federation is and no matter how advanced the twenty-third century is, there are still going to be things that intrude, that make it difficult. We're the most advanced nation, we are

prosperous, and we are powerful and plentiful, and yet there's a lot of darkness and a lot of things we have to overcome. Although our ideals are right and although our lip service to what we want is worthy, there are real barriers, both from within and externally.[47]

Into Darkness reacts to this threat in the most overtly hawkish, pro–American, conservative standpoint of any *Star Trek* product since 2001, particularly in the character of Admiral Marcus, played with razor-like grit by Peter Weller. When the threat of Khan, under the alias John Harrison, stages a terror attack on Starfleet and kills Kirk's mentor Admiral Christopher Pike, Marcus goes further in his rhetoric than even the most staunch Starfleet Admirals the franchise had presented to that point: "For unknown reasons, John Harrison has just declared a one man war against Starfleet. And in the name of those we lost, you will run this bastard down. This man has shown willingness to kill innocent people, so the rules of engagement are simple. If you come across this man and fear for your life or the lives of those nearby, you are authorised to use deadly force on sight."[48]

This is a Starfleet Admiral actively advocating for Starfleet captains to "shoot to kill" a terrorist without any trial or due process, talking to them as a military commander might on a wartime footing. Marcus is the next stage on, over a decade later, from *Insurrection*'s Admiral Dougherty. He compromised his ethics and morals to help give the Federation a medical boon that would have prolonged or saved lives. Marcus has no morals or ethics and is willing to commit cold blooded murder to protect the vision he has for Starfleet and the Federation, one driven by perpetual conflict in the wake of terror. He considers war with the Klingons "an inevitability." He enlists Khan, after being the one to discover the S.S. *Botany Bay* in deep space as opposed to the *Enterprise* in "Space Seed," to help him engineer weapons to defeat the Klingons, to defeat "an uncivilized threat in an uncivilized time."[49] As if to underscore the fairly on-the-nose point, Marcus' huge, powerful, black-skinned starship is named the USS *Vengeance*.

Into Darkness very much presents Marcus as an extremist in the same vein as Khan, an officer willing to destroy the *Enterprise* and murder the entire crew to protect the secret of his machinations, but he represents the apex of the compromised Starfleet officer we have seen the franchise portray for decades. Whether it was Ron Tracey in "The Omega Glory" going native, Benjamin Maxwell in *The Next Generation*'s "The Drumhead" killing innocents in Cardassian space, Captain Ransom in *Voyager*'s "Equinox" killing alien creatures to preserve his crew, or even Benjamin Sisko being manipulated into complicity to murder (see chapter 4), *Star Trek* has always played with the idea of the ethically challenged Starfleet

4. The 21st Century (So Far)

officer. However, Marcus' manipulative, calculated operation is in direct response to the post–9/11 world *Star Trek* now inhabits: a world of growing geopolitical tensions between America and Russia (and China), an imploding Middle East, particularly in Syria, with the backdrop of rising totalitarianism and populism that would emerge fully formed in 2016 with the election of Donald Trump as president of the United States. "War is coming! And who is going to lead us? You? If I'm not in charge, our entire way of life is decimated!"[50] Marcus barks at Kirk, entirely convinced his amoral ends justify the means.

Interestingly, in retrospect, Marcus is faced down not by a steadfast Picard, a righteous Sisko, or even a stalwart, morally upstanding Archer, but rather a youthful Kirk so unsure of his place in the world, *Into Darkness*' entire arc has him question whether he should even command the *Enterprise*. In the world of rising political and societal tensions, our only hope is the cowboy captain who still has a lot to learn, and a long way to go.

It turned out that Marcus was right, in one sense. War with the Klingons was indeed coming, to *Star Trek* anyway, as the franchise's long-awaited return to television in 2017 with *Discovery* began with the Federation in the 23rd century, a decade before *The Original Series* in the series' original timeline, at war with a freshly unified Klingon Empire.

Discovery, despite the show's title, begins in a similar manner to previous series pilots before entirely deconstructing the very premise of a *Star Trek* series. From *The Next Generation* through to *Enterprise*, every pilot episode established the concept of the show, the ship or space station setting, and ended with our crew established and ready for character development and whatever parables they would face out in the final frontier. *Discovery* does the opposite: it begins with those in place, with Commander Michael Burnham on the USS *Shenzhou* under experienced, Picard-esque Captain Phillipa Georgiou, rounded off by their anxious alien science officer Saru, and the second episode concludes with Georgiou killed in action, the *Shenzhou* dead in space, and Burnham sentenced to life in prison after an attempted mutiny. These events inadvertently trigger conflict with the Klingons after Burnham kills T'Kuvma, a religious fundamentalist who believed in Klingon purity and isolationism, and was ready to destroy the Federation to prevent the homogeneity of his culture. We don't even see the eponymous USS *Discovery* until the third episode.

The entire "modern era" of *Star Trek*[51] has worked to decrypt how *Star Trek* can remain relevant at a time where, globally, society is faced with an escalating series of political, environmental and cultural problems

139

that seem increasingly insurmountable. Burnham has to fight in order to regain some semblance of respect and rank from the crew who consider her a mutinous pariah, making her far from the respected, often inviolate protagonists of series past.

T'Kuvma is a clear representation of regressive, fanatical politics at work in the *Star Trek* universe. We had never seen a Klingon quite like him until *Discovery*. In *The Original Series*, the Klingons presented themselves as hawkish Soviet allegories who countered Starfleet's American idealism with territorial bullishness, before evolving during *The Next Generation* era into a proud, noble, if still unpredictable and stubborn warrior race who, from a societal perspective, clashed with the Federation's inclusive utopian sensibilities but on a political level, in terms of galactic stability, aligned through a sense of mutual respect, especially during the reign of Chancellor Martok toward the end of *Deep Space Nine*. Humans and Klingons might never entirely understand one another, but by the end of the 24th century, enough bridges had been constructed to ensure they could live peacefully alongside each other. *Discovery*, despite being set over a century earlier, intentionally disrupts this paradigm and casts the Klingons as unpredictable adversaries once more.

The religious cult constructed around T'Kuvma, who worships the teachings of the legendary Klingon warrior Kahless, is formed around the same kind of fear that drives fanatics in organizations such as al-Qaida or Isil: fear of cultural dominance and appropriation by a liberal, expanding entity. If Admiral Marcus feared alien expansion and control in *Into Darkness*, T'Kuvma represents the opposite: Federation homogeneity. "Atom by atom, they will coil around us and take all that we are. There is one way to confront this threat. By reuniting the twenty-four warring houses of our own empire. We have forgotten the Unforgettable, the last to unify our tribes: Kahless. Together, under one creed, remain Klingon! That is why we light our beacon this day. To assemble our people. To lock arms against those whose fatal greeting is … we come in peace."[52]

These are the opening lines in the entire *Discovery* series, and they serve almost as an ideological flag being planted in the ground in 2017, a year after the election of Trump and the growing election victories of anti-migrant demagogues around the world, from the UK to Brazil to Hungary (not forgetting Russia), began to calcify amid democracies over the next few years. T'Kuvma is willing to radicalize the entire Klingon race, divided by internal, tribal politics, in order to wage a war to secure an isolationist worldview. This seems counter-intuitive, but it speaks to the same rejection of Federation expansionist, idealist policies as we saw

4. The 21st Century (So Far)

in 2016's *Star Trek Beyond*, where alien (or rather biologically human) villain Krall declares, having attacked and destroyed the *Enterprise*: "This is where the frontier pushes back!"[53] Krall, T'Kuvma, Khan—they are all antagonists who could just as easily represent the post–9/11 terrorist in the American worldview, but they equally serve as anti-colonialists, fanatics who refuse to accept the Federation—read: American—way of life, and will go to extreme, genocidal methods to destroy it.

This rising trend of nationalism is perhaps best personified in *Discovery* by how the series chooses to set part of its first season not just around war with an ideologically fearful Klingon Empire, but inside the so-called "Mirror Universe" which since the 1960s has represented the dark inversion of our age.

An almost comic-book notion presented in the 1960s, "Mirror Mirror" played with the dark side of our nature, plunging Captain Kirk into an alternate universe where the Federation was, in fact, the Terran Empire, and humanity had not reached out into the stars as a progressive, humanistic race of explorers and scientists, but rather a repressive, genocidal, hateful species more analogous to a thousand year Reich. Nobody much considered in the 1960s that such a world could probably exist, and it was a device primarily designed to allow the main cast to enjoy portraying "evil" alternate versions of themselves.[54] That trend continued in the 1990s when *Deep Space Nine* revived the idea for a number of episodes across four seasons which, by the 24th century, recast Terrans as a baleful resistance movement, with their empire having been crushed by an equally malevolent "Alliance" of alien races they formerly had subjugated as slaves—Bajorans, Cardassians, Klingons etc…. *Deep Space Nine* suggests the Terrans might yet see the error of their ways and one day create a Federation much like our own.

Come the era of *Discovery*, that faith in the Terrans has collapsed. The Mirror Universe is once again bleak, dark and murderous, built on a hierarchical command structure in which officers kill to reach the top, and ruled by the iron fist of a merciless Emperor, who in this instance turns out to be the mirror image of our universe's compassionate, late Phillipa Georgiou. *Discovery* actively seems to question the validity that "our" universe, in fact, was ever the Federation future. Airing in late 2017, with rising violence, inequality and challenges to democratic ideals, *Discovery* wonders if our future might not more accurately represent the Mirror Universe. Here, Starfleet's finest fail to realize that the Discovery's own captain, Gabriel Lorca, is a replacement from the Mirror Universe until it is almost too late, despite the fact that across Season One we see the

141

character exploit innocent lifeforms and push harder against the Klingons during the war than any other captain we had previously seen: "When I took command of this vessel, you were a crew of polite scientists. Now, I look at you. You are fierce warriors all."[55] Lorca is proof we have blinkers on. The extremists are now among us every day, and if we exist in a "new normal," it is one in which what would have been considered regressive, dangerous thinking has now reached a global, mainstream platform.

Discovery, by the end of Season One, projects toward that hopeful future people watch *Star Trek* to see. War with the Klingons ends, Lorca is exposed, and the Mirror Universe is left to the future we had previously seen take place, but *Star Trek* has forever been changed by the post-trauma of 9/11 and the challenges of the 21st century. We continue to see that reflected in the movies and television shows that balance portraying an idealistic human utopia with a realistic, character-driven near-future filled with almost insurmountable strife.

This is perhaps why, alongside reacting to 9/11, *Star Trek* has also worked hard to look back wherever possible and indulge in comforting nostalgia, as we edge further into the 21st century, perhaps as a shield to the challenges of our world today.

Re-Discovering Nostalgia

In 2016, *Star Trek* celebrated a vaunted anniversary.

It had been fifty years since the debut of "The Man Trap," which launched Season One of *The Original Series*, and propelled Kirk, Spock, Bones and the crew of the *Enterprise* into the mainstream. Half a century later, those characters and the world around them was iconic and barely equaled among fiction. James Bond and *Doctor Who* beat the franchise to the punch with half-centennial anniversaries,[56] but the achievement in *Star Trek* reaching fifty years of success remained a huge point of celebration.

Star Trek marked this anniversary with *Star Trek Beyond*, the third and as of writing final of the "reboot" films, in canonical parlance the "Kelvinverse."[57] With 2009's big budget blockbuster, *Star Trek* saw celebrated television producer and burgeoning film director J.J. Abrams revive the franchise by returning, essentially, to the beginning: Kirk, Spock, the *Enterprise*, and *The Original Series* era, except with a time-travel twist involving vengeful future Romulans, Leonard Nimoy's aged Ambassador Spock, and a crafty way of starting anew from the familiar, 1960s-style beginning while not rejecting or invalidating almost five decades of much

4. The 21st Century (So Far)

protected continuity among *Star Trek*'s huge and particularly devoted fandom.

Beyond was the culmination of a seven-year road in which *Star Trek*, following the creative and audience slump of *Nemesis* and the *Enterprise* years, moved forward out of potential oblivion by looking backwards. Ironically, for a movie which celebrated half a century of fandom and futurism, Justin Lin's film[58] is probably the least beholden to existing continuity and particularly nostalgia of all three movies. It is largely about Captain Kirk and his crew learning the dangerous lesson that the "final frontier" is a violent and unexpected place, and the sins of previous explorers who ventured too far too soon being punished for their hubris. *Beyond*'s villain directly tethers back to *Enterprise* Season Three, but to a degree that only fans of the franchise would really notice, and the film contains only one significant paean to the franchise's history.

Underneath the propulsive action of the main story, Spock (here played by reimagined actor Zachary Quinto) learns that his older self from what fans term the "Prime" *Star Trek* universe[59] has died off screen, following the death of Nimoy in the years between production of the films. In honoring Nimoy and the iconic original Spock, "nuSpock" discovers a photograph in his elder self's possessions of *The Original Series* crew on the bridge of the *Enterprise*, middle-aged and at the end of their careers during *The Undiscovered Country*. It is an affecting, emotional beat for any audience member who has a relationship with those characters and the actors (some of whom are no longer with us), working on a "meta"[60] level *beyond* the film itself, no pun intended.

The moment speaks to the power of nostalgia in modern fiction, and how in particular it has driven the *Star Trek* franchise almost entirely since the cancellation of *Enterprise* in the shadow of the trauma of September 11.

The trend began, perhaps pointedly, around the point *Enterprise* sailed into early retirement in 2005.

Doctor Who, by then a kitsch and dated relic of the BBC's archives having not been seen on screen since 1989,[61] returned to screens with a swagger that same year under the auspices of celebrated British screenwriter Russell T. Davies. He appropriated American television show-running sensibilities akin to producers such as Joss Whedon and transformed *Doctor Who* into a fast-moving, exciting, fun barrage of science-fiction, re-cementing the franchise as a key staple of British television, which it remains to this day.

That same year, after years wallowing in the indignity of *Batman &*

Star Trek, History and Us

Robin in 1997, one of the most iconic superheroes ever in Bruce Wayne's Batman returned to screens thanks to filmmaker Christopher Nolan in 2005's *Batman Begins*. The film brings the character down to earth in a thrilling re-imagining of the concept which spawned one of the most critically acclaimed superhero trilogies in cinema history. It also helped lay the foundations for the incumbent Marvel Cinematic Universe with 2008's *Iron Man*, a franchise which itself trades heavily on the nostalgia of Stan Lee & Steve Ditko's colorful 1960s Marvel creations. A year later, while less successful critically or commercially, Bryan Singer revived the "other" iconic superhero in Clark Kent's Superman for *Superman Returns*, pitched as a direct sequel to the first two Richard Donner *Superman* movies from the late 1970s and early 1980s.

Perhaps most successfully, in 2006, James Bond gained a whole new lease of life with Martin Campbell's *Casino Royale*, which moved 007 away from the *Austin Powers*-esque camp of *Die Another Day* and back toward the grit and sleazy glamor of Ian Fleming's 1950's source novel, adapting Fleming's seminal first Bond adventure while simultaneously updating it for a modern audience. It turned unlikely Bond Daniel Craig into an overnight household name. All of these franchises, with perhaps the exception of *Superman*, have one thing in common: they were reborn into an entirely new age, for an audience with fresh expectations, by going back to the beginning.

Batman Begins reconnects Bruce Wayne to his origin story, helping us understand *why* he puts on the suit in the first place. *Doctor Who*, under Davies, transformed the Doctor from a wacky old man on wobbly sets fighting rubber monsters into a tortured warrior, the last of his kind following a devastating war, who … well, fights rubber monsters, but it wouldn't be *Doctor Who* if he didn't. *Casino Royale* wants to investigate the psychology underpinning a Bond who has to earn his status as a 00 in a far deeper manner than any of the films over the last forty plus years to date. It updates Fleming's characters and ideas for the 21st century, utilizing character as an approach to the franchise in a manner the Bond series had never before witnessed. It feels important to understand these other significant examples in popular culture because *Star Trek*, in 2009's reboot, adopts precisely the same approach.

All three of the "Kelvinverse" films are about, at their core, the relationship between Kirk and Spock, and beyond that, the road Kirk travels from washed out Iowa farm boy to the man William Shatner portrayed in 1966. *The Original Series* very clearly told stories which revolved around the Kirk, Spock, McCoy triumvirate but, in some sense, this feels

4. The 21st Century (So Far)

an accidental by-product of the way *Star Trek*'s ideas were written in the 1960s. As television evolved in the 1990s era, greater care was taken (for the most part) in giving an ensemble cast their own specific character stories and showcases in future *Star Trek* series. However, every show ultimately would revolve around a central trio, be it Picard, Data and (to an extent) Riker in *The Next Generation*; Janeway, Seven & the Doctor in *Voyager*; Archer, T'Pol and Trip in *Enterprise*; with *Deep Space Nine* perhaps serving as the one exception to the rule, given its increasingly sprawling ensemble cast of players. Even the eventual *Next Generation* films, almost without exception, craft their narratives around Picard and Data as the two primary characters.

Star Trek 2009 is merely, in that sense, an extension of how the franchise has always been approached, except with a modern focus on the audience's nostalgic attraction to characters we already know, and in some cases know well.

Abrams' film tells the story through the vantage point of Kirk and Spock, from birth all the way through to serving on the *Enterprise*, rattling through key points of internal series mythology that previous series had mentioned: Spock's rejection of the Vulcan Science Academy (and part of his heritage) to attend Starfleet, Kirk's cheating on the Kobayashi Maru test, and both of them attending Starfleet Academy at various points. To some audiences, they are new characters, but for many *Star Trek* fans, this movie shows us aspects of backstory that are legendary within fandom, and have been for decades, thereby expressly mining our nostalgia for them in order to craft the story. This works in the same manner that *Doctor Who* brings back classic monsters from the franchise's history such as the Daleks or the Cybermen, or how *Batman Begins* tells an origin story for our well-known protagonist. *Star Trek* is a Kirk and Spock origin story that may feel intentionally contemporary, but in fact does have its roots in *Star Trek* history and lore, as Glen C. Oliver has stated:

> Regarding this project and its obvious correlation to J.J. Abrams' 2009 film, it should be noted that "recasting" TOS roles ... and exploring the relationship of these characters in different ways ... was actually a notion Gene Roddenberry himself acknowledged early on in Trek's history. Not only did he feel this was possible, he even expressed some level of enthusiasm for the conceit. Meaning: those dismissing such projects on the basis that "this wasn't the creator's intent" don't actually have much of an argument in this regard.[62]

Oliver here refers principally to "The Academy Years," a project that was originally intended to serve as the basis for the 25th anniversary celebrations of the franchise in 1991, before Nicholas Meyer developed

Star Trek, History and Us

The Undiscovered Country as a way to retire the original crew. Written by David Loughery, who co-wrote *The Final Frontier*, and produced by both Harve Bennett and Ralph Winter, "The Academy Years" would have told the story of a youthful Kirk and Spock meeting at Starfleet Academy while William Shatner and Leonard Nimoy would have "bookended" the film with appearances as their older selves, serving as the framing device to flash back and recount their origin story. While the details changed and "The Academy Years" as a film did not particularly factor in to *Star Trek* 2009, the seeds of an Academy-based story for the series' two principal characters had existed for decades before Abrams' film expressly recounted their origin and framed that story through the lens of an intentional reboot of the series.

Following the cancellation of *Enterprise*, *Star Trek* could have travelled in numerous different directions. J. Michael Straczynski and Bryce Zabel developed a pitch for a remake of *The Original Series* before Abrams' film.[63] Erik Jendresen, writer of HBO's successful World War II mini-series *Band of Brothers*, wrote the first script of an intended trilogy called "The Beginning," featuring an ancestor of Kirk on a quest modeled after Homer's *The Odyssey* in order to depict the formative, post–*Enterprise* Earth-Romulan War that directly led to the foundation of the Federation.[64] While both cleave to the franchise's internal history, trading off characters and aspects of the series' past, both would have served as potentially radical new approaches to *Star Trek* following the Berman-era, as would Bryan Singer and Christopher McQuarrie's pitch in the early 2010s, which featured a descendant of Kirk in the early 25th century.[65] None of these projects came to fruition under a changing Paramount guard until Abrams came along with a take that expressly was designed to evoke nostalgic attachment to the 1960s, as the director describes:

> I came late to this particular party, but—with all due respect to the films and the TV spin-offs—the original series, to my mind, is what *Star Trek* was. All of the subsequent series and films felt to me, as they went on, that they were less and less relatable. It felt to me that if you were going to do a version of *Star Trek*, you would have to do it in such a way that it would bring it to life in a way that never had been done before. What I realized was that in my mind Kirk and Spock were the key, the heart, of Trek. Approaching this movie, [screenwriters] Alex Kurtzman and Roberto Orci, [producers] Damon Lindelof and Bryan Burk, and I discovered that's what we wanted to examine and explore: what Kirk and Spock were all about.[66]

Arguably, many *Star Trek* fans would take issue with a statement like this from Abrams, a director who has been accused of attempting

4. The 21st Century (So Far)

to bring a *Star Wars*-approach to the *Star Trek* franchise by delivering pulse-pounding science-fiction spectacle, with dashes of fantasy, as opposed to philosophical exploration and world-building. Yet while Abrams might only see *Star Trek* through the prism of a casual fan attached to the essential building blocks of the concept, his views represent a powerful magnetic force when it comes to fandom and how, broadly across multiple different iconic franchises with long-running fanbases, the 2000s and beyond brought a yearning for a return to comfortable, recognizable and safe surroundings. Although *Casino Royale* engendered itself to fans for a stripped back approach to James Bond, the subsequent Daniel Craig era alienated 007 purists who felt the series had lost touch with its own essence.[67] Whenever *Doctor Who* attempted to introduce new monsters, fans pushed back in frustration.[68] Superman's gritty, Christopher Nolan-inspired 2013 reboot *Man of Steel*, from Zack Snyder, and its sequel *Batman vs. Superman: Dawn of Justice*, were pilloried for serving as 9/11 allegories that stripped away the magic of Superman down to the point he actually executes one of his own kind, with comics legend Mark Waid being particularly withering on the subject.[69] *Star Trek* 2009 divided fans in this regard.

On the one hand, a fresh approach to what had become something of a stagnant franchise running in place was welcomed, particularly by critics who celebrated Abrams' entry as one of the more relatable, inclusive *Star Trek* films in history. *Nemesis* had underwhelmed significantly in box office and critical terms, with Captain Picard and his crew limping off the stage as opposed to experiencing the bravura of the acclaimed goodbye of Kirk and company in *The Undiscovered Country*. On the other, *Star Trek* purists struggled with Abrams' recasting of not just Kirk, Spock etc...., despite how well he filled the shoes of Shatner, Nimoy and so on, but the approach to this new timeline. Philosophical curiosity was replaced by plot-propelling action adventure, a plot some believed at times did not entirely make sense. Vulcan, a bastion of *Star Trek* lore, was completely destroyed, as indeed was Romulus in the "Prime" timeline Ambassador Spock hailed from, unknowingly sowing the seeds for storylines *Star Trek: Picard* would pick up on a decade later. Abrams was unafraid to both capture the spirit of the 1960s in his revival but tear up the rule book when it came to what you could and could not do in the *Star Trek* universe. Destroying the planets and shattering the civilizations of two primary forces within *Star Trek* lore, going right back to the 1960s, echoed this duality between nostalgic appeasement and daring challenge of what was expected from the franchise.

Star Trek, History and Us

In that sense, *Star Trek* 2009 had a foot in both camps, in the slipstream of the aforementioned franchise examples which were pushing forward by looking back and recapturing or recasting key elements of what fans loved about those franchises and why they endured for decades in the popular consciousness. Abrams understood that the magic of *The Original Series* revolved around the Kirk and Spock relationship, particularly in the subsequent movie series primarily across the 1980s. While this, in real terms, was a consequence of how 1960s television wrote primarily for the main stars of their shows and did not really embrace the idea of an ensemble cast, the legacy of that show remains powerful. *Star Trek* 2009 worked hard to give Zoe Saldana or John Cho more action and character for supporting players such as Uhura and Sulu, who were often relegated to bit parts in many *The Original Series* episodes. However, Abrams feeds into audience nostalgia by projecting the entire narrative through Kirk and Spock's prism, even to the extent that Eric Bana's villain Nero, threatening the Federation with a black hole-creating weapon of mass destruction, has a personal connection to both our heroes in being the man responsible for the death of Kirk's father and Spock's mother. Such connections were rarely present in the villains of *Star Trek* films past, barring one or two exceptions.[70]

How ironic, then, that sequel *Star Trek Into Darkness* brings back the character who, to the audience, remains probably the most iconic antagonist in the franchise, yet the new Kirk and Spock begin the story with zero context about who he is. Khan, so memorable as previously discussed in *The Wrath of Khan*, is resurrected and framed less in the vein of a thawed-out, eugenically-crazed pirate prince, but rather a dangerous, Machiavellian one-man terror organization in league with Peter Weller's hawkish, corrupt Starfleet Admiral Marcus. Our audience nostalgia here works on a level that the narrative itself, barring a cameo from Nimoy's elder Spock,[71] is unaware of. Aside from Khan's revival after some thirty years, *Into Darkness* reverses what could be the most iconic moment in *Star Trek* history—Spock's sudden and tragic "death" (albeit temporary) after saving the *Enterprise* from Khan's exploding superweapon, separated by a pane of glass from his best friend Kirk as he dies. *Into Darkness* has Kirk be the one who sacrifices himself, and the scene plays out with near identical dialogue to famous moment in *The Wrath of Khan*. You can practically hear Kurtzman and Orci's glee as they penned these scenes as fans. Yet they are designed to serve the greater purpose of the "Kelvinverse" revival—exploiting our nostalgic understanding of *Star Trek*'s "greatest hits" to affirm, or reaffirm, Kirk and Spock's special bond, as Kurtzman explains:

4. The 21st Century (So Far)

> The mistake we did not want to make was assuming that the result of them coming together is that they're the bridge crew we knew before. It was particularly critical in relation to Kirk and Spock, because at the end of the first movie, they've come together as a means of necessity. It isn't like they joined forces because they're the best of friends. They're not the Kirk and Spock you remember from *The Wrath of Khan*. They still have to earn their friendship; they have trials to go through together before they can get to that place.[72]

One trend of modern nostalgia in *Star Trek* and the long-standing franchises discussed is often the sense that these properties need to earn the right to revel in what we, as fans, enjoy about them. James Bond begins, in *Casino Royale*, as a new 007 in need of seasoning, and arguably it takes three films for Daniel Craig's incarnation to reach the comfortable, established position in the role as his predecessors—indeed there is an argument this version of Bond, deconstructed as he is, never has. The same argument could be leveled at The Doctor, reimagined as a haunted, tortured warrior living his life of adventure to forget the sins of his past. The last fifteen years, and over a dozen seasons, have been characterized by his deconstruction, reconstruction and self-analysis over multiple incarnations. Thus, a nostalgic revival of 1960s *Star Trek*, within this reflexive, post-modern contextualization, cannot simply replicate the position of Kirk, Spock and crew as we knew them fifty years earlier. Spock must grow to respect and value Jim Kirk, who across the first film, *Into Darkness*, and through into *Beyond*, must learn what it takes to be captain of the *Enterprise*. Zachary Quinto has to *become* Leonard Nimoy as Chris Pine has to *become* William Shatner—they cannot just expect to inherit those mantles. Does this necessity among modern properties to force these iconic characters into "trials," as Kurtzman puts it, suggest an innate embarrassment, or perhaps to put it kindlier, an anxiety about obsessively recapturing the past in order to move these franchises forward?

While the "Kelvinverse" films were more financially successful than many previous *Star Trek* big screen adventures, *Beyond* especially failed to turn enough of a profit to, as of writing in 2020, warrant a fourth adventure, despite many reports since 2016 that it is in production.[73] In that time, the franchise made a successful return to the realm many fans long believed *Star Trek* was most at home in—television.

Star Trek: Discovery was originally designed, under the aegis of Bryan Fuller, as an anthology series that, season by season, would focus on a different era of *Star Trek* with new characters, evoking the growing trend for season-long anthological storytelling in the streaming era with shows such as *American Horror Story* or *Fargo*. Due to myriad reasons, not the least of which was Fuller's departure as showrunner after developing the initial concept and first couple of episodes,[74] *Discovery* very quickly settled permanently into the era Fuller had designed the first season to be: the 23rd century. The show responded to fan pleas to return the series to the "Prime" timeline and explored a hitherto under-represented era of *Star Trek* history—roughly a decade before *The Original Series*, placing it roughly analogous to the same time zone the "Kelvinverse" films were exploring. *Discovery* created new characters, with a new ship and mission statement, within a destructive war between the Federation and the Klingon Empire, but where possible it grasped the same threads of nostalgic connection to *The Original Series* as Abrams himself had, not to mention borrowing aesthetically from the modern style and motion of his films. *Discovery* very quickly asserted itself, stylistically, as serialized *Star Trek* for a new era, but it absolutely felt the need to explore a sandbox the audience would be very familiar with.

How else to explain the fact that Michael Burnham, *Discovery*'s troubled mutineer protagonist, is not just a human woman raised by a Vulcan family to detach herself from human emotion, but said family happens to also be Spock's? Burnham, as an adopted daughter of Sarek, serves as a significant problem for *Star Trek* continuity that *Discovery* rather inelegantly has to work hard to resolve by the end of the second season. One wonders if the entire plot line of the second season finale, which results in the Discovery and her crew being thrust almost a thousand years into the future and their existence being decreed top secret by Starfleet and never to be discussed or admitted, was entirely designed to explain why Spock, across the entirety of *The Original Series* or Nimoy's era, never mentions that he had a sister. A continuity point-of-issue to only die-hard "Trekkies" this may be, but it speaks to the lengths the new era of *Star Trek* is willing to go in order to exploit our need for recognizable characters, nostalgic settings, and a feeling of familiarity, even while the stylistics of production might change. *Discovery* also reintroduces the memorable *Original Series* con man Harry Mudd, here played by Rainn Wilson, and the Mirror Universe concept that both *The Original Series* and the *Next Generation*–era of *Star Trek* played with. For every new innovation, two familiar touchstones were around the corner.

Which brings us neatly to *Discovery*'s second season, perhaps the most egregious example of nostalgic storytelling in the modern *Star Trek* era yet.

After concluding many of the narratives of the first season, *Discovery* ends with an enormously enticing cliff-hanger as the original USS

4. The 21st Century (So Far)

Enterprise arrives on screen. Thanks to the failure of "The Cage," *Star Trek* lore held that Kirk was not the first commander of the starship *Enterprise*, and was immediately preceded by Captain Christopher Pike, who would appear in "The Menagerie" and whose fate was a bittersweet and strange point of *Star Trek* continuity. *Discovery*, set during the point of Pike's five year mission commanding the *Enterprise*, utilizes the opportunity to sketch in this "lost" part of *Star Trek* history, thereby allowing them to recast Spock once again—this time played by Ethan Peck—and play out the Sarek family drama involving Burnham, while simultaneously introducing Pike as a main character and directly shading in details between "The Cage" and "The Menagerie" that have for fifty years remained ambiguous. "If Memory Serves" even begins with a recap of "The Cage," which is perhaps the first example of any *Star Trek* series—possibly any series ever—delivering a "previously" style recap of a story produced half a century earlier. Even the primary narrative and antagonism behind the "Red Angel" mystery at the heart of the season calls back (or forward) to the *Next Generation* era, specifically *Deep Space Nine* and, to some degree, *Enterprise*, by reintroducing the morally dubious Starfleet agency Section-31, who are corrupted by a universe-destroying artificial intelligence. Very little about *Discovery*'s second season is not designed, expressly, to fill in gaps within existing *Star Trek* continuity. Had it not been produced as television, it would not be unreasonable to describe it as "fan fiction."

This is not to decry fan fiction as an entity. While the amount of poor writing outweighs the bad in online forums such as FanFiction.Net and Archive of Our Own, there do exist prose stories and indeed television-style scripts which are, occasionally, more worthy of production than what we see on screen. However, fan fiction is designed to service a need on the part of the audience as opposed to what is best for the sandbox it plays in. Putting aside so-called "slash fiction," which takes franchise characters and places them in erotic or sexually explicit scenarios, fan fiction deliberately fills in points of continuity and allows fans to tell the stories they wish they could have seen: the Earth-Romulan War that *Enterprise* never got to make, for example,[75] or the purported "team up" movie of numerous characters from the *Next Generation* era, in the style we would later see *The Avengers* and the Marvel Cinematic Universe deliver.[76] The latter particularly could well have been an indulgence that might have alienated the casual audiences Abrams sought to engage with his rebooted universe, but fans of those series would have delighted at watching characters interact with each other, weighed with the brace of backstory the audience understood. *Discovery's* second season deliberately services those kinds of fan impulses by surrendering, utterly, to the nostalgic temptation of recreating the iconic *Original Series* as closely as possible. Pike, Spock and the first *Enterprise* crew even now have their own spin-off series in development, *Strange New Worlds*, which could be a remake of *The Original Series* in all but name. Fans are, understandably, delighted. Critics are no doubt divided on whether such a project truly allows *Star Trek* to push into new frontiers.

That balance was achieved, to a degree, by what on paper was the most nostalgia-inducing modern *Star Trek* series ever produced—*Star Trek: Picard*.

After many years of being lobbied by numerous teams and creatives, Sir Patrick Stewart finally acquiesced to Alex Kurtzman—now in charge of the CBS/Viacom production house developing the *Star Trek* universe—and the approach from him, Akiva Goldsman and Kirsten Beyer, at how to resurrect Captain Jean-Luc Picard, outside of Brent Spiner's Commander Data, arguably the most iconic representation of *Next Generation*–era *Star Trek*. Everything about *Picard* is as designed to appeal to the familiarity of '90s *Star Trek* as *Discovery's* placement in the *Original Series* era was engineered toward the '60s era *Star Trek* fan. The show has no ambiguity—it is named after the man himself. *Discovery* included elements of *Star Trek's* past, but *Picard* is *about* Picard. It was early on described as more of a meditative character study,[77] designed to explore an aged Picard two decades on from his last appearance in *Nemesis*, no longer in command of the *Enterprise*, no longer even in Starfleet, rediscovering his zest for life in a much darker, late 24th century universe. While the show ultimately served to be more action packed and propulsive than early rhetoric may have suggested, *Picard* ultimately delivered on what it promised. It was darker. Starfleet was not the entity we remembered. Picard himself has changed. The universe around him had suffered major polarizing shifts following, as established in *Star Trek* 2009, the destruction of Romulus from a supernova star. What was also evident, from the get-go, was that *Picard* was just as much about nostalgic connections to previous eras as *Discovery* or the "Kelvinverse" films.

The core motivation for Picard across the entire season was helping the "daughter" (or "daughters") of the man who sacrificed his life to save Picard at the end of *Nemesis*, as a means of assuaging the survivor's guilt he has experienced since that moment. Picard's personal motivation, much like Burnham's in *Discovery*, becomes inextricably linked to another threat to the fate of the galaxy, here from an ancient Romulan

4. The 21st Century (So Far)

cult seeking to awaken an ancient, malevolent artificial intelligence. Data's spirit hovers over everything that takes place in *Picard*'s first season. The series introduces new characters to the *Star Trek* lexicon, but all of them are marked by the consequences of traumatic galactic events that occurred after *Nemesis* which, ultimately, tie directly into Picard's quest and the legacy of Data's death. Even when they don't, the show tethers directly back to '90s era *Star Trek*, with appearances by characters such as Will Riker and Deanna Troi, Hugh of Borg,[78] Icheb[79] and Seven of Nine. The series might explore life on the ragged edges of the Federation, but *Picard*'s chief motivation as a first season is to resolve what many fans considered to be an unsatisfying death for the beloved Data. The denouement of season finale "In Et Arcadia Ego pt 2," a long conversation between Picard and the "essence" of Data within a machine matrix, feels as much about the series attempting to resolve and let go of the *Next Generation* era as it does conclude the season. Whether the second season will explore further hanging threads from that era is open to debate, but *Picard*'s flirtation with dynamic new frontiers is quelled by the apparent need to appease the long-held wishes in *Star Trek* fandom to explore more of the post–*Nemesis* era of the 24th century. This will soon, as of this writing, happen again with the animated comedy series, *Star Trek: Lower Decks*, which is rumored to contain many *Next Generation*–era references and possible cameo appearances from well-known characters.

Where does, ultimately, *Star Trek*'s inability to let go of its own internal history end? *Discovery* has the potential with the upcoming third season, as of writing, which thrusts the series into an entirely unexplored *Star Trek* future. *Picard*, too, for its second season, can tell stories in a closer but still entirely canonically open era. *Lower Decks*, while constrained by one or two points of canon, also has an open field to sketch in new stories. These are the series we know about. CBS is believed to want to reach a point where a new series of *Star Trek* is on air every week of the year, across a range of different shows with a wide variety of concepts. This is an exciting prospect, but one which brings significant levels of expectation and uncertainty.

Star Trek's modern era, thus far, has been preoccupied with exploring the fallout of the post–9/11 world through clear allegory and liberal symbolism, yet at the same time a determined fondness to remain, on some level, within the borders of its own history in a manner *Star Trek* series of earlier eras avoided. This is as much a response to broader cultural trends in entertainment whereby looking back to the safety of what we knew is more appealing than treading the murky, uncertain waters of what might come in our less than opaque century.

Star Trek does, internally, point ahead to where we might go as a society across the 21st century, and it is at periods a disturbing picture. The biggest question is whether *Star Trek*'s "future history" will end up prophetic, and whether we as a race will survive the trials yet to come that makes the universe of *Star Trek* a realistic possibility for us to continue striving for.

Epilogue:
Getting from Here to There

April 5, 2063, is perhaps the signature date in all of what we might term *Star Trek*'s "future history." It is the distant past for the Starfleet crews and heroes we follow, yet the near future for us as their audience.

On that date, as witnessed at the end of *First Contact*, humanity has their first official interaction with an extra-terrestrial species, as a Vulcan scout ship lands in Montana having detected Zefram Cochrane's first, successful warp drive test beyond Earth's solar system.[1] This is the moment the Vulcans choose to make contact, believing humanity to have reached a point of technological and social evolution whereby they can make their first, tentative steps toward being part of a galactic community. Cochrane's test forms the basis of a century of human development in *Star Trek* history, as humans eradicate hunger, war and nation states, and come together, steadily, as a unified world, building on technological innovation until, in 2151, the first *Enterprise* starship under Jonathan Archer launches and begins to explore the final frontier.

The very premise of *First Contact* as a movie is that, had the villainous Borg Queen succeeded in changing history and preventing Cochrane's flight from ever happening, the *Star Trek* universe as we know it would never have existed. No Starfleet. No Federation. No *Enterprise*. No boldly going where no man, and subsequently no one, had gone before. The date of April 5, 2063, is as pivotal to *Star Trek*'s future as March 15, 44 BCE was to Ancient Rome,[2] or October 14, 1066, for the nascent English people,[3] or May 8, 1945, for the entirety of Western Europe.[4] These are epochal days and moments in human history which shape decades or centuries to come, and *Star Trek*'s date rests in, as of writing, our near future.

April 5, 2063, is now closer to us than we are to 1966, the year *Star Trek* first began, within a decade filled with ideas about what the next century would be.

The end of the 20th century imagined the 21st century as a metropo-

Epilogue

lis of technological wonders. We would all be using hoverboards to travel around by 2015 as Marty McFly would in *Back to the Future Part II*. The space-age world of flying cars and super cities in *The Jetsons* would move from '60s science-fiction cartoonish fancy to eventual reality. Having overcome world wars and transitioning from feudal autocracies or totalitarian regimes locked in centuries upon centuries of perpetual war to progressive, unified global democracies, humanity would begin edging ever closer to a world of warp drive engines, transporter systems capable of moving us vast distances in the blink of an eye, or replicators able to eradicate the need for an economic society as they produced food, water and beyond out of nothing. These are modern miracles via scientific progress which, in the future of *Star Trek*, unlocked humanity's untapped potential.

Yet the future history of *Star Trek* is marked by a troubling reality. The world of Starfleet and the United Federation of Planets, of a united humanity creating an intergalactic organization of peace and scientific discovery, was forged from near-apocalyptic adversity in the years that preceded April 5, 2063. In the decades before the arrival of the Vulcans, and Cochrane's scientific discovery which forever changes the history of humanity, the world of *Star Trek* was plunged into the terrifying possibility in whose shadow *The Original Series* was born: World War Three.

We have seen that *Star Trek* has been haunted by the legacy of World War II from the moment Gene Roddenberry devised his "Wagon Train to the Stars," forged in no small part from his own, scarring wartime experiences, but *The Original Series* was born amid the existential threat of a very real, all-destructive nuclear conflict.

A Third World War fought by towering geopolitical superpowers feels more science-fiction than genuine possibility in the early 21st century, despite continued nuclear saber rattling,[5] but in the 1960s the anxiety of such a conflict was all too potent. The Cuban Missile Crisis heightened tensions. Vietnam fuelled the ongoing Cold War between American and Soviet forces. Nuclear arsenals and weapons tests continued, after their apex during a particularly tension-filled 1950s of powerful rhetoric on both sides, building up the maxim of Mutually Assured Destruction. *Star Trek* imagined a future where an American and a Russian could work together on the bridge of a starship exploring the galaxy when the leaders of those countries remained one button push away from killing millions of the other's civilians and razing their cities to the ground in nuclear fire. Even while such anxiety lessened as the 1980s brought *glasnost, perestroika*, and the collapse of the Berlin Wall to usher in the end of the Cold War, *Star Trek* continued reflecting the specter of a planet-destroying conflict by establishing that, before Starfleet and the Federation, such a war had happened in *Star Trek*'s otherwise utopian future.

The details of such a conflict have always remained vague across the fifty-year history of the franchise, but the war supposedly began in the year 2026 and lasted for twenty-seven long years until a cease-fire in 2056. It has never been entirely revealed which nation states were involved in the conflict or any specific details about what might have led to the outbreak of a war which, while involving nuclear weapons, was not entirely fought by drones, munitions and stealth aircraft. Troops were involved, led by a legendary figure in *Star Trek*'s future history known as Colonel Phillip Green.

"The Savage Curtain," which depicts a version of Green re-created by the alien Excalbians alongside other key figures from Earth's history, sees Spock describe him as having "led a genocidal war in the early 21st century."[6] There are strong suggestions Green might have been a key instigating figure in a war described as revolving around genetic manipulation and human genome enhancement, which in itself ties back to the destructive Eugenics Wars of the 1990s which led to the exile of Khan. In the future history of *Star Trek*, Green serves as a functional version of a historical Adolf Hitler, a genocidal leader at the head of an army of "eco-terrorists" whose actions resulted in thirty-six million deaths. Even following a cease-fire in 2056, he still advocated for a racial purity, as we see him describe on a video recording in "Demons": "In the shadow of this incalculable devastation, we find ourselves facing a colossal challenge. There's an entire world to rebuild. Not only our cities and homes, but mankind itself! Now is not the time for timidity and second guessing. We cannot afford to doubt ourselves."[7] He would go on, as described by xenophobic follower John Frederick Paxton a century later, to "euthanize" hundreds of thousands of people inflicted with radiation sickness due to the after-effects of the war. Conventional history of the Federation remembers him as a zealot who sought a eugenic, human superiority, and he suggests that the 21st century would not be rid of such despotic, militaristic populists who use propaganda and rhetoric for their own aims.

By any stretch of the imagination, *Star Trek*'s World War Three is the most destructive conflict to that point in human history. Will Riker describes the landscape of 2063 in *First Contact* in grim terms: "Most of the major cities have been destroyed. There are few governments left. Six hundred million dead."[8] This is a loss of life dwarfing any of the conflicts *Star Trek* as a series was born out of. World Wars I and II saw the collapse of empires and governments but not on a global scale. Civilization survived

Epilogue

and endured, if at great cost. World War Three suggests few functional nation states in the aftermath of what Picard describes in "Encounter at Farpoint" as the "post-atomic horror" as he defends humanity's progress from Q's charge of being a "grievously savage race,"[9] one he adds during the war used narcotics to control their military forces. It is not clear if the United States of America even still functionally exists, though one suspects it might, given Starfleet's central positioning in San Francisco and the heavy American influence, at least initially, on the post-first contact development of humanity.

"Encounter at Farpoint" proves that no official, aligned World War III chronology in *Star Trek* exists, citing the post-atomic court Picard is thrown into created by Q as existing in 2079 *after* a United Earth system was abolished, when in reality it was likely just getting started in the wake of Cochrane's warp flight. Picard also adds that in 2036, "the new United Nations declared that no Earth citizen could be made to answer for the crimes of his race or forbears,"[10] but given that this would have been in the middle of a global conflict fought between presumed eugenically-enhanced warriors with atomic weapons, the chances of the UN declaring any such progressive law sounds unlikely. What these examples serve to show, ultimately, is that the 21st century faced the kind of total war, fuelled by technological advances, that filled the creators of *Star Trek* series and their audiences across the latter half of the 20th century, and the beginning of the 21st, with abject terror.

The vague nature of the conflict, with Green's actions, references to such entities as the Eastern Coalition,[11] or "New Eden" cementing that nuclear weapons were indeed detonated on U.S. soil, Indiana specifically, only serves to increase the horror of the entire conflict. It is the equivalent of a Trojan War to our modern day, a historical war of which we know pieces, more mythologized, but the scale and indeed reality of which we will likely never truly understand. Unless *Star Trek* one day definitively, and canonically tells the story of World War III, it lies in the Federation's past as a decisive turning point in history, and an ever-approaching warning for our future.

Yet it remains a future history filled with contradictions. Despite the innovations in technology we saw in *The Original Series*, with Kirk's communicator analogous to a flip phone, or Picard's PADD in *The Next Generation* resembling the iPad, at the same time *Star Trek* never truly seems to anticipate the rise of the internet in 21st century human society, and fails to predict the insidious reach of communication technology in our lives. While on the one hand, the early 21st century suggests decades of global strife which wipe out a large proportion of the human population, "The Royale" suggests that a space shuttle called the Charybdis launched in 2037, described by Picard as the "third manned attempt to travel beyond the confines of the Earth's solar system."[12] "One Small Step" suggests that only five years earlier, in 2032, the shuttle Ares Four was lost on a manned mission to Mars that, as Tom Paris describes, "almost derailed the Mars programme,"[13] suggesting the United States continued to fly manned missions into space and advance scientific discovery years after the supposed beginning of the war.

There are also the visible, if unspoken, links between eugenic advancement and growing anxieties over artificial intelligence within the franchise. While AI does not seem to feature in the issues that cause a third global conflict, eugenics and their use certainly do, and the "Borderland" trilogy in *Enterprise* establishes that a major player in eugenic science and manipulation into the 22nd century was Arik Soong,[14] as played by Brent Spiner. His descendants would include 24th century genius Noonien Soong, who goes on to create, among other androids, Data, and whose biological son Altan Inigo Soong later that century helps devise androids Daaj, Soji, Sutra and more. They work to fulfill an ancient Romulan prophecy and unleash a dark, Lovecraftian artificial intelligence upon the universe, following an AI "revolt" which kills thousands on Mars and directly affects Federation policy and the geopolitical map for years, ostensibly for the worst. If the troubled history of *Star Trek* does not include anxieties about AI, its future certainly does, and draws direct connective tissue back to manipulations over the advancement of human genes, and human existence, that fostered the conflict that almost destroyed the human race.

The specious facts of World War III conflict, then, with the advancement of humanity, led to April 5, 2063. The much-pilloried *Enterprise* theme tune starts with the line, "It's been a long road, getting from there to here..." and *Star Trek* struggles, across its own future history, to provide a roadmap which shows us how we get from *here* to *there*.

As the new era of *Star Trek* continues and shows no signs of abating into the creative slump that characterized the immediate post–9/11 years, it nevertheless works hard to reflect the world we are currently living in back to us.

Climate change denial is on the rise as *Picard* suggests such ignorance partly led to the destruction of Romulus. Democracies continue to erode under the weight of fragmented, divisive partisan politics and the election of dangerous, totalitarian "strong men," as *Discovery* plunges the

Epilogue

crew into the repressive Mirror Universe and revives the merciless, xenophobic Terran Empire.

Yet what perhaps the franchise should do, in a different way to simply exploiting nostalgia in order to satiate cultural trends and fan expectations, is to look back at what combined to make *Star Trek* the popular cultural force it was in the 1960s and across the decades it has survived, evolved and become a key fixture in the Western public consciousness. Not in terms of bringing back fan favorites or replicating age old storylines, but by focusing on a symbolic, core idea that the franchise has extolled since 1966.

Hope.

First contact day is a symbolic, representative future date which suggests we, as a collective and unified species, can survive the trauma a new century can bring. This acceptance of a difficult road to first contact, and eventually the Federation, feels in tune with *Star Trek*'s obsession, across every single one of its series, with coming to terms with the scars and legacies of World War II, and the paradigm that sprang from it. *The Original Series* is divided between the necessary conservatism of the Vietnam conflict and the liberal progression of civil rights and anti-war protest brewing at home. *The Next Generation* reconciles Reaganite, neoliberal progress with a steady world view at the end of the Cold War, a calm assuredness that Federation history would extend on beyond the horizon, before *Deep Space Nine*—in plunging that secure world into devastating conflict—anxiously wonders at the turn of the century if history might not repeat itself. *Voyager* remains blissfully ignorant, divorced from trauma serving as a unipolar representation of human prosperity stretching from the 21st to the 29th century, before *Enterprise* has to face the cold, hard reality of a post–9/11 paradigm, thrust into an uncertain future of unseen enemies and rapidly altering geopolitical landscapes.

Yet all of these shows believe in the same thing: we, as a species, will endure.

History may end, and begin again, and then end once more, but *Star Trek* believes another beginning is always just around the corner. Even if we might never embrace the Federation future in the utopian manner *Star Trek* proscribes, the stories this franchise tells believes we will, eventually, find our way from here to there.

It is a bold message and perhaps one we need now more than ever before.

Chapter Notes

Preface

1. *Wagon Train* was a highly successful Western of the period on television, as the genre dominated American cinema during a similar period. According to Wikipedia, "The series chronicles the adventures of a wagon train as it makes its way from St. Joseph, Missouri across the mid-Western plains and the Rocky Mountains to California and the trials and tribulations of the series regulars who conducted the train through the American West." You can understand the tangential comparisons to *Star Trek*, the idea of a journey across a dangerous and unknown frontier at a time of high adventure, though Roddenberry was as influenced by Jonathan Swift's classic *Gulliver's Travels* and the *Hornblower* novels of C.S. Forrester. *Wagon Train* was by no means the sole inspiration for this franchise.

2. According to one of William Shatner's autobiographies, NBC reported that "The Cage" was "too cerebral," "too intellectual" and "too slow" with "not enough action." Roddenberry subsequently delivered them "Where No One Has Gone Before," featuring the psychic, destructive Gary Mitchell and a voyage to the center of the galaxy—much more of a traditional, pulp science-fiction story of the kind that, ironically, *Star Trek* would not become beloved for producing. "The Cage" over the decades has subsequently been heavily re-appreciated by fans and critics.

3. Though it was not actually "Where No Man Has Gone Before" that aired first, rather "The Man Trap," which in hindsight seems like an odd choice as an introductory story compared to either of the other options.

4. Johnson-Smith, Jan. *American Science Fiction TV: Star Trek, Stargate and Beyond*. Wesleyan University Press, January 10, 2005.

5. Abrams was only a producer on *Beyond*, it should be noted, having vacated the director's chair for Justin Lin—best known for several *Fast & Furious* films—in order to work on *Star Wars: The Force Awakens*.

Chapter 1

1. Not to mention their disbelief that Majel Barrett's female first officer Number One was qualified to be in that role, although Roddenberry seemed to suggest that this was as much down to negative female reactions as much as inevitable, ingrained masculine prejudice. "There were no female leads then—women in those days were just set dressing. So, another thing they felt was wrong with our film was that we had Majel as a female second-in-command of the vessel. It's nice now, I'm sure, for the ladies to say, 'Well, the men did it,' but in the test reports, the women in the audience were saying, 'Who does she think she is?' They hated her. It is hard to believe that we have gone from a totally sexist society to where we are today—where all intelligent people certainly accept sexual equality. We've made progress." Gross, Edward. *The Fifty-Year Mission: The Complete, Uncensored, Unauthorized Oral History of Star Trek: The First 25 Years* (p. 87).

2. Gross, Edward. *The Fifty-Year Mis-

Notes—Chapter 1

sion: *The Complete, Uncensored, Unauthorized Oral History of Star Trek: The First 25 Years* (p. 140).

3. Gross, Edward. *The Fifty-Year Mission: The Complete, Uncensored, Unauthorized Oral History of Star Trek: The First 25 Years* (p. 66–67).

4. Though his physical features were subtly altered into the more measured, Vulcan design that he immortalised after concerns the original ears and facial features were too explicitly Satanic!

5. Gross, Edward. *The Fifty-Year Mission: The Complete, Uncensored, Unauthorized Oral History of Star Trek: The First 25 Years* (p. 33).

6. Gross, Edward. *The Fifty-Year Mission: The Complete, Uncensored, Unauthorized Oral History of Star Trek: The First 25 Years* (pp. 33–34).

7. Roddenberry extemporises on the creation of the name *Enterprise* in greater detail. "With the name *Enterprise*, I'd been an army bomber pilot in World War II. I'd been fascinated by the navy and particularly fascinated by the story of the *Enterprise* in World War II, which at Midway really turned the tide in the whole war in our favor. I'd always been proud of that ship and wanted to use the name." Gross, Edward. *The Fifty-Year Mission: The Complete, Uncensored, Unauthorized Oral History of Star Trek: The First 25 Years* (p. 69).

8. A Japanese Zero fighter plane would eventually make its way into the Season One episode "Shore Leave," strafing and firing at *Enterprise* crewmen, perhaps as a reflection of the Japanese attack that marked Roddenberry and indeed the broader American psyche.

9. Rothschild, Matthew. "George Takei, Mr. Sulu of Star Trek, Comes Out and Speaks Out." *The Progressive*. May 8, 2006.

10. A colloquialism for the rank of first lieutenant, which would have made Roddenberry a junior commissioned officer at this point, slightly under the rank of captain.

11. The brake systems on B-17's were notoriously bad and would often fail, according to David Alexander. "For a plane that was loved by its crews—a plane that was extremely difficult to shoot out of the sky, a plane that was remarkably, even miraculously, forgiving in flight—it had absolutely awful brakes. The brakes were operated by a sensitive hydraulic system engaged by pressing the toes forward against the tops of the rudder pedals." Alexander, David. *Star Trek Creator: The Authorized Biography of Gene Roddenberry* (p. 75).

12. Alexander, David. *Star Trek Creator: The Authorized Biography of Gene Roddenberry* (p. 85–86).

13. Roddenberry said of this: "I don't think it possible to capture the feeling of the survivors as they experienced the sunrise on that morning so many years ago. There was a small group of us who were alive and thankful that we had survived what was an unsurvivable crash. I could never display the impact surviving had on me and the others. I knew, for all my skills, I could not capture that moment." Alexander, David. *Star Trek Creator: The Authorized Biography of Gene Roddenberry* (p. 97–98).

14. *Star Trek: The Original Series*, 1x20.
15. *Ibid.*
16. *Ibid.*
17. *Ibid.*
18. *Ibid.*

19. Every other member of the main cast was jettisoned, with Majel Barrett—being Roddenberry's paramour—repurposed into the recurring role of Nurse Christine Chapel, demoted essentially from the main cast. Spock's features were softened and around him steadily arrived the iconic ensemble, chiefly William Shatner's James T. Kirk, who would pass into legend. Not until 2019 and the arrival of Anson Mount in the role on *Star Trek: Discovery* would Christopher Pike again truly get his due.

20. *Star Trek: The Original Series*, 1x13.

21. In the Season Two episode, "Through the Valley of Shadows," on the Klingon planet Boreth, Pike receives visions thanks to a 'time crystal' of the events leading up to "The Menagerie" and his life before the events of that episode. Whether the awareness of his disturbing fate will factor into the Pike-led series *Strange New Worlds* remains, as of writing, to be seen, but it would seem strange

Notes—Chapter 1

if Pike is not somewhat weighed down and tortured by such knowledge.

22. *Star Trek III: The Search for Spock.*
23. *Star Trek IV: The Voyage Home.*
24. Admittedly, this one is not exactly on Picard's watch, given Riker was in charge and Deanna Troi gets most of the blame, being the one forced to take the helm at the time!
25. *Star Trek: The Next Generation*, 1x08.
26. This turns out to be a ruse by the revenge-seeking Daimon Bok, whose own son was lost in the battle.
27. *Star Trek: The Next Generation*, 1x18.
28. Alexander, David. *Star Trek Creator: The Authorized Biography of Gene Roddenberry.* (p. 85–86).
29. In *Star Trek* parlance, a "pre-warp" civilization essentially refers to a species who have not yet reached a level of technological sophistication, by nature of mastering faster than light travel, that warrants Starfleet making first contact. A comparison historically would be the reluctance of advanced democracies interfering with protected tribes, such as the Brazilian government's non-contact policy with indigenous Amazonian peoples.
30. Shatner, William, and Kreski, Chris. *Star Trek Movie Memories.* 2009.
31. Nimoy spoke Yiddish and talked about how important it was to him: "And my grandmother never learned English. So my brother and I needed to speak to her in Yiddish. But my brother was born in Boston and his first language was Yiddish because my parents only spoke Yiddish when he was a little child. When I was born… they were better with English. So my first language was English, but I needed Yiddish to speak with my grandparents." Whitney, Christa (February 6, 2014). Yiddish Book Center. Archive.org.
32. Ashton, Bodie. "The Myth of Nazi Efficiency." *Coffee Cup History*, May 6, 2013.
33. *Star Trek: The Original Series*, 1x22.
34. Wolf, David. "Who Was Nietzsche?" Salon.com, October 1, 2012.
35. Greven, David. *Gender and Sexuality in* Star Trek: *Allegories of Desire in the Television Series and Films.* 2009.
36. *Star Trek: The Original Series*, 1x22.
37. *Ibid.*
38. *Ibid.* The story of Khan's "descent" into "Hell" would later be chronicled by tie-in novelist Greg Cox in a series of novels which both tell the story of Khan's birth and the Eugenics Wars, plus what happened between "Space Seed" and *The Wrath of Khan*. Though non-canonical, and thus cannot be entered as "historical" fact within the *Star Trek* universe, these novels are impressive expansions of what we see on screen and are well worth considering, if unofficially, a deeper part of the same story.
39. Horakova, Erin. K. "From 'Shalom Aleichem' to 'Live Long and Prosper': Engaging with post-war Jewish identity via Star Trek: The Original Series." *Set Phasers to Teach!: Star Trek in Research and Teaching*, 2018.
40. Horakova goes further on this thesis: "There are a range of recognisable American Jewish performance styles, most of which are rooted in the legacy of the Askenazi community" (from which Shatner hailed). "If cultural affiliations are performative, then Shatner at times brings his own to Kirk—perhaps unwittingly, perhaps slyly. Shatner's at times vehement physical performances and 'titled' line deliveries strike me not only as strongly rooted in his Olivier-era Shakespearean background but also as somewhat reliant on the emphatic gestures and 'stilted' speech patterns of the community to which he belongs." Erin K. Horakova. "From 'Shalom Aleichem' to 'Live Long and Prosper': Engaging with post-war Jewish identity via Star Trek: The Original Series." *Set Phasers to Teach!: Star Trek in Research and Teaching*, 2018.
41. Horakova, Erin. K. "From 'Shalom Aleichem' to 'Live Long and Prosper': Engaging with post-war Jewish identity via Star Trek: The Original Series." *Set Phasers to Teach!: Star Trek in Research and Teaching*, 2018.
42. *Star Trek: The Original Series*, 1x13.
43. The title of the episode refers to Shakespeare's *Hamlet*, and the conclusion of a major speech from the titular character, from Act 2; Scene 2, in which he utters: "The play's the thing wherein I'll catch the conscience of the King."
44. *Star Trek: The Original Series*, 1x13.

Notes—Chapter 1

45. *Ibid.*
46. *Ibid.*
47. John F. Kennedy Moon Speech—Rice Stadium, September 12, 1962.
48. O'Connor, Mike. *Liberals in Space: The 1960s Politics of Star Trek.* December 2012.
49. This remains a debated topic amongst TV historians. While *Star Trek's* kiss has passed into the cultural lexicon as ground-breaking, there are other contenders for this crown, including amongst others the British soap opera *Emergency—Ward 10* in 1964, and possibly a Granada Play of the Week, "You in Your Small Corner," from 1962, the discovery of which led to the rediscovery of a play from 1959 televised in the UK and featuring the same Jamaican actor. The place of the Kirk and Uhura kiss nonetheless remains a signature interracial moment on one of television's biggest and most iconic properties.
50. *Star Trek: The Original Series*, 3x10.
51. Nichols, Nichelle. *Beyond Uhura: Star Trek and Other Memories*. 1996 (p. 164–5).
52. *Star Trek: The Original Series*, 3x10.
53. Braunstein, Peter. "Forever Young: Insurgent youth and the Sixties Culture of Rejuvenation." *Imagine Nation: The American Counterculture of the 1960's and 70's.* 2001.
54. *Star Trek: The Original Series*, 3x20.
55. *Ibid.*
56. *Ibid.*
57. Otherwise known as Mary Mallon, an Irish-born cook who was believed to have infected 53 people, of whom three died, with typhoid fever in 1907. She was the first person in the U.S. classified as being asymptomatic while carrying the disease and spent almost thirty years in quarantine until her death. Her nickname has passed into the cultural lexicon to denote anyone who serves as an asymptomatic carrier of a disease which spreads into the population.
58. *Star Trek: The Original Series*, 3x20.
59. Munger, Sean. "Hippies in Space: A Star Trek episode in 1960's Historical Context." SeanMunger.com, May 11, 2015.
60. *Star Trek: The Original Series*, 3x20.
61. *Star Trek: The Original Series*, 1x24.
62. Lundeen, Jan, and Wagner, Jon. *Deep Space and Sacred Time: "Star Trek" in the American Mythos.* 1998.
63. *Star Trek: The Original Series*, 1x24.
64. Sohl, Jerry. *The History of Star Trek—Trek Classic.*
65. Vettel-Becker, Patricia. "Space and the Single Girl: Star Trek, Aesthetics, and 1960s Femininity." *Frontiers – A Journal of Women's Studies.* October 2014.
66. Nichols, Nichelle. *Beyond Uhura: Star Trek and Other Memories.* 1996 (p. 169).
67. Coined by feminist film theorist Laura Mulvey, the "male gaze" is an idea built around the depiction of women in the world, in literature and across art, from a masculine and resolutely heterosexual perspective. Particularly, this approach represents women as sexual objects principally built around the pleasure of a male viewer, either from behind the camera, the characters within the story, or the audience watching the drama.
68. Who would much later be re-cast in 2019 in the form of Rebecca Romijn for Season Two of *Discovery*, and as a regular on the forthcoming *Strange New Worlds*.
69. O'Connor, Mike. *Liberals in Space: The 1960s Politics of Star Trek.* December 2012.
70. Franklin, H. Bruce. "Star Trek in the Vietnam Era." *Science Fiction Studies.* March 1994.
71. *South Park* would produce an episode of the same name, with numerous *Star Trek* references, in its second season. *Men Behaving Badly* frames an entire episode in its sixth season, "Watching TV," around watching "City on the Edge of Forever" and riffing off the narrative and tropes of the series.
72. Ellison's original draft was much more militaristic and involved the Enterprise crew taking a crew member convicted of being part of an illegal drug trade to be executed by firing squad on the planet with the titular "city." Roddenberry was never entirely happy with the concept and was relieved when, after multiple drafts, he passed the script on to another writer. Ellison disliked the eventual product, declaring it "precisely the kind of dopey Utopian bullshit that Roddenberry loved."

Ellison, Harlan (1996). *Harlan Ellison's The City on the Edge of Forever*.

73. Franklin, "Star Trek in the Vietnam Era."

74. *Star Trek: The Original Series*, 1x28.

75. Ibid.

76. Isaacs, Bruce. "A Vision of Time and Place: Spiritual Humanism and the Utopian Impulse." *Star Trek as Myth*. 2010.

77. Powis, Neville. "The Human Be-In and The Hippy Revolution." *Radio Netherlands*, January 11, 2003.

78. Harrison, Scott. "From the Archives: 1967 Antiwar Protest turns Violent." *Los Angeles Times*. June 22, 2017.

79. *Star Trek: The Original Series*, 1x28.

80. Ibid.

81. From a story by his lifelong friend Don Ingalls, using the pseudonym Jud Crucis.

82. Doherty, Thomas. *Vietnam in Film*.

83. *Star Trek: The Original Series*, 2x19.

84. *Star Trek: The Original Series*, 1x28.

85. *Star Trek: The Original Series*, 2x19.

86. Ibid.

87. *Star Trek: The Original Series*, 1x28.

88. Ibid.

89. *Star Trek: The Original Series*, 2x23.

90. *Star Trek: The Original Series*, 1x28.

91. Ibid.

92. Played memorably by a rasping, venomous Morgan Woodward, one of American cinema and television's finest character actors.

93. *Star Trek: The Original Series*, 2x23.

94. Austin, Allan. A. "The Limits of Star Trek's Final Frontier: 'The Omega Glory' and 1960s American Liberalism." *Space and Time: Essays on Visions of History in Science Fiction and Fantasy Television*. 2010.

95. This pledge came from Nixon's "Peace and Honor" speech in January 1973 to describe the Paris Peace Accords as signifying an end to the Vietnam War.

96. Maycock, James. "War Within war." *The Guardian*, September 15, 2001.

97. *Star Trek: The Original Series*, 1x28.

Chapter 2

1. Typically, final episodes of television series conclude with some level of closure for both the concept and the characters. This does not always happen for cancelled series, many of which end inconclusively, though networks have over time worked harder to allow producers the means to conclude storylines with advance warning of cancellation. *Enterprise*'s "These Are the Voyages" is an example (if not a "good" one, as such) of a show ending before its time but being allowed the space to end the show in some fashion. "Turnabout Intruder," by contrast, could have been placed at any point in the three-year run of *The Original Series*.

2. Though given limited time to pen a finale having learned of *The Prisoner*'s cancellation, McGoohan nevertheless wanted to develop a conclusion that was deliberately open-ended, as befitted the often-baffling nature of the series itself: "There are numbers here, there are no names, so you can't expect it to end like James Bond, so you have to have an allegorical ending. Now (...) what is the most evil thing on earth? Is it jealousy? Is it hate? Is it revenge? Is it the bomb? What is it? When one really searches, it's only one thing, it's the evil part of oneself that one is constantly fighting until the moment of our demise. The Jekyll and Hyde if you like, but on a much larger scale." Postma, Laurens C. (director), Rodley, Chris (writer) (1984), *Six into One: The Prisoner File* (documentary).

3. The One-Armed Man was the principal villain of *The Fugitive*, in which respected Dr. Richard Kimble—played by David Janssen—was framed for the murder of his wife and went on the run, hunted by police while he sought to expose the identity of the real killer and prove his innocence. One of the most popular TV series of the 1960s, it spawned an equally successful big screen revival in 1993 starring Harrison Ford in the Kimble role.

4. "These Are the Voyages" was deemed a finale for the entirety of the "Rick Berman era" of *Star Trek*, from 1987 through to 2005, focusing as it did on *Next Generation*-characters Will Riker and Deanna Troi. It was derided by fans and remains intensely disliked by many to this day. Berman explains in more depth: "We have Riker come on board, go into the

Notes—Chapter 2

holodeck to study the famous day ninety years earlier when something happened to Jonathan Archer which eventually led to the formation of the Federation. He's watching Archer at a very critical moment with a group of aliens and a friend who's in danger, and it was a very moving story. We thought that, in a sense, we would be honoring our characters by seeing them through the eyes of future generations. But a lot of people took it as being disrespectful to the cast and felt that we had turned the final episode into an episode of *The Next Generation*, which was very far from the truth. But you can't control how people feel about it. Both Brannon and I have wondered in the years since that perhaps it was a mistake. There were those who thought the episode was terrific and there's a lot more who thought that it was sort of a disrespectful way to end the series." Gross, Edward. *The Fifty-Year Mission: The Next 25 Years: From* The Next Generation *to J. J. Abrams* (p. 729).

5. Nichols, Nichelle. *Beyond Uhura: Star Trek and Other Memories*. 1996 (p. 189).

6. Mooney, Darren. "Star Trek: The Original Series (Reviews)." TheM0vieBlog.com.

7. Joan Didion sums up this feeling in her 1979 book of essays, *The White Album*: "There were rumors. There were stories. Everything was unmentionable but nothing was unimaginable. This mystical flirtation with the idea of 'sin'—this sense that it was possible to go 'too far,' and that many people were doing it—was very much with us in Los Angeles in 1968 and 1969. A demented and seductive vortical tension was building in the community. The jitters were setting in. I recall a time when the dogs barked every night and the moon was always full. On August 9, 1969, I was sitting in the shallow end of my sister-in-law's swimming pool in Beverly Hills when she received a telephone call from a friend who had just heard about the murders at Sharon Tate Polanksi's house on Cielo Drive. The phone rang many times during the next hour. These early reports were garbled and contradictory. One caller would say hoods, the next would say chains. There were twenty dead, no, twelve, ten, eighteen. Black masses were imagined, and bad trips blamed. I remember all of the day's misinformation very clearly, and I also remember this, and I wish I did not: *I remember that no one was surprised*."

8. The earliest being in September 1966 at the "Tricon World Science Fiction Convention" in Cleveland, Ohio, in which Roddenberry was in attendance promoting *Star Trek*, which would debut the week after, so this cannot be considered in the truest sense the first "*Star Trek* Convention" as nobody knew the series at that point.

9. Gross, Edward. *The Fifty-Year Mission: The Complete, Uncensored, Unauthorized Oral History of Star Trek: The First 25 Years* (p. 33).

10. Buck, Jerry. "'Star Trek' Engenders Cult in U.S., England." *Youngstown Vindicator*. Mar 14, 1972.

11. Which came to an end, of course, in 1991, the same year as *The Undiscovered Country* arrived. But more on that later...

12. So named for the mythical sword in the stone from Arthurian legend, and which would later be appropriated by novelist Peter David for the name of his Starfleet ship in the non-canonical tie-in series, *New Frontier*.

13. The series, *Excalibur*, would have been expressly designed to focus on story and teaching aspects within the narrative of *Star Trek*, eschewing the simple replication of *The Original Series* esthetic we later got in *The Animated Series*. The well-known *Star Trek* characters would have had youthful counterparts including Sulu's Stick, McCoy's Bob and—this is perhaps the best—Spock and his particularly Vulcan-named protégé ... Steve.

14. Gross, Edward. *The Fifty-Year Mission: The Complete, Uncensored, Unauthorized Oral History of Star Trek: The First 25 Years* (p. 265).

15. With the exception of Walter Koenig, whom it appears the budget did not stretch to hiring, hence Chekov being absent from the series. As succour for this rebuke, Koenig was hired to pen the episode that would become "The Slaver Weapon."

16. In the late 1980s, Roddenberry

Notes—Chapter 2

requested *The Animated Series* be removed from "official" canon, but CBS has not confirmed an official position on whether it exists in the history of the show. Nevertheless, both *Picard* and *Lower Decks* have included references to *Animated Series* aspects, such as species like the Kzinti or a Caitian officer in *Lower Decks*, which suggest the current (as of this writing) era of writers consider *The Animated Series* canonical.

17. Gene Roddenberry told *Circus* magazine: "Right after the show was canceled by the network in America, Paramount, who owned the show fifty-fifty with me, decided they needed the studio space. So they tore down and broke up the sets. The costumes were sold or broken up! All that was left was seventy-nine cans of film ... and memories ... and fans ... hundreds of thousands of them. There were rounds and rounds of meetings about reviving *Star Trek*. You would think that after laying an egg the size of Jupiter, the network would accept any offer ... No! They wanted another pilot show. Paramount refused because the sets would cost seven hundred fifty thousand dollars to replace, too much of an investment for anything short of a whole season's worth of new episodes. That was the stalemate."

18. Shatner, William. *Star Trek: Movie Memories*. 1993.

19. Gross, Edward. *The Fifty-Year Mission: The Complete, Uncensored, Unauthorized Oral History of Star Trek: The First 25 Years* (p. 272).

20. Gross, Edward. *The Fifty-Year Mission: The Complete, Uncensored, Unauthorized Oral History of Star Trek: The First 25 Years* (pp. 281–282).

21. Gross, Edward. *The Fifty-Year Mission: The Complete, Uncensored, Unauthorized Oral History of Star Trek: The First 25 Years* (pp. 271–272).

22. In particular, Judith and Garfield Reeves-Stevens' excellent history of the production, *Star Trek Phase II: The Making of the Lost Series*.

23. Gross, Edward. *The Fifty-Year Mission: The Complete, Uncensored, Unauthorized Oral History of Star Trek: The First 25 Years* (p. 321).

24. A film now slightly lost to history, despite being repeated more readily on television in the wake of Kirk Douglas's passing, *The Final Countdown* is an alternate history science-fiction tale in which a nuclear-powered aircraft carrier enters a storm which transports them back to the day before Pearl Harbor, where they struggle not to change this pivotal moment in American history.

25. One of two scripts written for *Phase II* that was repurposed for *The Next Generation*, the other being the Season Four episode "Devil's Due."

26. Gross, Edward. *The Fifty-Year Mission: The Complete, Uncensored, Unauthorized Oral History of Star Trek: The First 25 Years* (p. 320).

27. A forerunner of what we recognize as the holodeck appears in *The Animated Series* episode "The Practical Joker," where it is referred to as the "recreation room," inside which the ship's computer traps McCoy, Sulu and Uhura.

28. The son of Captain Matt Decker, the ill-fated commander of the USS *Constitution*, whom we see in *The Original Series* episode "The Doomsday Machine."

29. Bach, Richard. "Practice in Waking." *Star Trek: Phase II*.

30. Itself a remake, essentially, of *The Manchurian Candidate*.

31. The script does see *The Original Series* characters spread apart and somewhat disaffected, prefiguring how some of *The Motion Picture* would begin, but "The God Thing" perhaps better resembles *The Final Frontier*, the later fifth movie in the series, with a plot that sees an alien entity more directly tied into Christian mythology threaten the ship and crew.

32. "Planet of the Titans" is arguably the most fascinating unrealized *Star Trek* cinematic project. As described by Mark A. Altman and Edward Gross: "In the script, the crew searches for Kirk and discovers him stranded on a planet where they must face off with both the Klingons and an alien race called the Cygnans, eventually being thrust back in time through a black hole to the dawn of humanity on Earth where the crew members themselves are revealed as the Titans of Greek mythology." Kaufman himself expanded on some

Notes—Chapter 2

of his wishes for the film: "I had loved the power of those Kurosawa movies and The Seven Samurai. If any country other than America had a sense of science fiction, it was Japan. Toshiro Mifune up against Spock would have been a great piece of casting. There would have been a couple of scenes between the two of them, emotion versus Spock's logical mind shield, trying to close things off, and having humor play between them. Leonard is a funny guy and the idea was not to break the mold of *Star Trek*, but to introduce it to a bigger audience around the world." Gross, Edward. *The Fifty-Year Mission: The Complete, Uncensored, Unauthorized Oral History of Star Trek: The First 25 Years* (p. 310).

33. Which co-starred none other than Leonard Nimoy.

34. Bryan Fuller, co-creator of *Star Trek: Discovery* among other *Star Trek* accolades, defends the film: "It's a really interesting, very rich film. Most people dismiss it as dull, but I think they're not paying attention. Khan is much more rock and roll. It is much more of a cowboy picture. It has such drive and momentum. There's no chance to stop and pontificate, which *Star Trek: The Motion Picture* allowed the audience to do. But I think during that time a lot of them had their eyes roll in boredom, but not me. I understand it's a colder, more intellectual film, particularly when you compare it to *The Wrath of Khan*, which was 'let's Moby Dick this son of a bitch.' Whereas *The Motion Picture* was filled with a lot of ideas and the notion of bringing *Star Trek* into a Kubrickian universe where we can explore intellectual ideas." Gross, Edward. *The Fifty-Year Mission: The Complete, Uncensored, Unauthorized Oral History of Star Trek: The First 25 Years* (pp. 380–381).

35. Barrett, Michele, and Barrett, Duncan. *Star Trek: The Human Frontier* (p. 184–185).

36. Gross, Edward. *The Fifty-Year Mission: The Complete, Uncensored, Unauthorized Oral History of Star Trek: The First 25 Years* (p. 297).

37. *Star Trek: The Motion Picture*.

38. Thompson, Derek. "Three Decades Ago, America Lost Its Religion. Why?" *The Atlantic*. September 2019.

39. *Star Trek: The Motion Picture*.

40. The story has strong similarities, in fact, with The Original Series episode "The Apple."

41. Gross, Edward. *The Fifty-Year Mission: The Complete, Uncensored, Unauthorized Oral History of Star Trek: The First 25 Years* (p. 380).

42. This turned Roddenberry into something of an irritant to all involved during the production of subsequent feature films. Harve Bennett explains how this was perceived: "Gene is frequently a historical revisionist, and he uses a phrase that is difficult for anybody else to refute: 'That is not Star Trek.' When a man of his eminence and his position says that, especially in my early days, I didn't want to go against the church. But the fact of the matter is he uses that phrase whenever he chooses to. It makes no sense. He fought the character of Saavik savagely, saying you couldn't intermarry Vulcans and Romulans, that it was not possible. It had never been done, and he would cite everybody from Arthur C. Clarke to Isaac Asimov, who he would always run to and they would always say, 'Yes, Gene, you're right.' I am not a science-fiction writer. I just tell good yarns. You get into a situation where you say, 'I'm not Heinlein, I'm not Clarke.' I'm just a pop artist trying to tell a story here." Gross, Edward. *The Fifty-Year Mission: The Complete, Uncensored, Unauthorized Oral History of Star Trek: The First 25 Years* (p. 391).

43. Gross, Edward. *The Fifty-Year Mission: The Complete, Uncensored, Unauthorized Oral History of Star Trek: The First 25 Years* (pp. 370–371).

44. Over the course of the subsequent films, few characters outside of the central trio get much in the way of screen time, particularly in *The Final Frontier*, where characters such as Chekov and Sulu are reduced to the odd line here and there.

45. Gross, Edward. *The Fifty-Year Mission: The Complete, Uncensored, Unauthorized Oral History of Star Trek: The First 25 Years* (p. 410).

46. *Star Trek II: The Wrath of Khan*.

47. We should put aside for a second

just how Khan thinks he is going to accomplish this with one starship and a solitary superweapon. Granted, he and his crew are Eugenic supermen, but even I wouldn't bet on Khan against the entire Klingon army, for example!

48. *Star Trek II: The Wrath of Khan.*
49. *Ibid.*
50. *Star Trek III: The Search for Spock.*
51. Ananth, Mahesh. "Spock's Vulcan Mind Meld." *Star Trek and Philosophy.* 2008.
52. *Star Trek III: The Search for Spock.*
53. Gross, Edward. *The Fifty-Year Mission: The Complete, Uncensored, Unauthorized Oral History of Star Trek: The First 25 Years* (p. 477).
54. The mid-section, 1986-set portion of *The Voyage Home* was written in no small part by Nicholas Meyer, writer of *The Wrath of Khan* and *The Undiscovered Country* respectively, and his comedic take on a time-travel romp has echoes of his earlier, somewhat darker thriller *Time After Time* from 1979, wherein H. G. Wells pursues Jack the Ripper through to disco-era San Francisco in a time machine he has built.
55. A cameo from internationally renowned Indian tennis star Vijay Amitraj, who just three years earlier appeared in James Bond movie *Octopussy* as an equally ill-fated Indian secret agent.
56. *Star Trek IV: The Voyage Home.*
57. *Ibid.*
58. *Ibid.*
59. Clarke, Arthur. C. "Hazards of Prophecy: The Failure of Imagination" in the collection *Profiles of the Future: An Enquiry into the Limits of the Possible* (1962, rev. 1973).
60. They also break what is known as the "Temporal Prime Directive" here by doing so, actively changing history. Although, there is no evidence that it *wasn't* that manufacturer who didn't "invent" transparent aluminium in the *Star Trek* universe, so maybe they didn't! Time-travel...
61. *Star Trek IV: The Voyage Home.*
62. *Ibid.*
63. Remarkably, the genesis of this character began with attempts to cast none other than American comedy legend Eddie Murphy, who would have played a, well ... nutty professor, as Peter Krikes explains: "He would play whale songs, and it was the whale songs he played in the classroom that the ship locked on to. That was in the first draft we wrote, but the second draft was different. After you write a first draft of anything, once the director, the cast, and the producers come aboard, everything changes, and not necessarily for the better. But the tone was pretty much a reflection of what was in the movie. For example, there was a scene where the Eddie Murphy character was trying to convince the Catherine Hicks character that aliens do exist on Earth. In the first draft, Hicks was a newswoman and there was a marine biologist as well. Gillian Taylor was ultimately a marriage of about three characters. Murphy believed in aliens and saw them beam into his classroom." Gross, Edward. *The Fifty-Year Mission: The Complete, Uncensored, Unauthorized Oral History of Star Trek: The First 25 Years* (p. 481).
64. Named after beloved 20th century American comedy pairing George Burns and Gracie Allen.
65. *Star Trek IV: The Voyage Home.*
66. *Ibid.*
67. Asa, Robert. "Classic Star Trek and the Death of God." *Star Trek and Sacred Ground: Explorations of Star Trek, Religion, and American Culture.* 1999.
68. *Star Trek V: The Final Frontier.*
69. Gross, Edward. *The Fifty-Year Mission: The Complete, Uncensored, Unauthorized Oral History of Star Trek: The First 25 Years* (pp. 497–498).
70. Merk, Frederick, and Merk, Lois Bannister. *Manifest Destiny and Mission in American History: A Reinterpretation.* 1963.
71. Hine, Robert V., and Faragher, John Mack. *The American West: A New Interpretive History.* 2000.
72. Indeed, Greg Cox's "Q-Space" non-canonical book trilogy explicitly ties the events of *The Final Frontier* into the broader mythology of Q, in ways which explain and contextualize the being encountered by Kirk and crew in the film.
73. Gross, Edward. *The Fifty-Year Mission: The Next 25 Years: From* The Next Generation *to J. J. Abrams* (pp. 114–115).

Notes—Chapter 2

74. Michael Piller cites an example of how this forced a level of creativity from the staff. "Somebody gave me a script called 'The Bonding,' by a guy named Ron Moore who was about to go into the Marines, and it was a very interesting story about a kid whose mother goes down on an away mission and gets killed. The kid is obviously torn apart by the death of his mother, and seeing how much he's suffering, aliens provide him with a mother substitute. The writing was rough and amateurish in some ways, but I thought it had real potential to tell an interesting story. I went to Gene and pitched him the story, and he said it didn't work. I asked him why, and he said, 'Because in the twenty-fourth century, death is accepted as a part of life, so this child would not be mourning the death of his mother. He would be perfectly accepting of the fact that she had lived a good life, and he would move on with his life.' I went back to the writing staff and told them what Gene had said, and they sort of smirked and said, 'Ah-ha, you see? Now you know what we've been going through.' I said, 'Wait a minute, let's think about it. Is there any way we can satisfy Gene's twenty-fourth-century rules and at the same time not lose the story that we have to shoot on Tuesday?' I finally said, 'Look, what if this kid has in fact been taught all of his life not to mourn the death of his loved ones, because that's what society expects of him? He's taught that death is a part of life, so he loses his mother and doesn't have any reaction at all. That's what Gene is telling us has to happen. Well, that is freaky, that is weird, and that's going to feel far more interesting on film than if he's crying for two acts. What if the aliens who feel guilty about killing his mother provide him with a mother substitute and the kid bonds with this mother substitute, and it's Troi who goes to Picard and says, "We have a problem? The kid is not going to give up this mother substitute until he really accepts and mourns the death of his real mother, and we're going to have to penetrate centuries of civilization to get to the emotional core of this kid in order to wake up his emotional life.' So the show becomes a quest for emotional release and the privilege of mourning." Gross, Edward. *The Fifty-Year Mission: The Next 25 Years: From* The Next Generation *to J. J. Abrams* (pp. 175–176).

75. Or as More subtitled it: "*Libellus vere aureus, nec minus salutaris quam festivus, de optimo rei publicae statu deque nova insula Utopia,*" A little, true book, not less beneficial than enjoyable, about how things should be in the new island Utopia". Baker-Smith, Dominic. *More's Utopia*. 2000.

76. Which ended up serving as the title of a *Next Generation* Season Five episode all about a colony of genetically engineered people living in what they term a "perfect" society.

77. A term coined in the era of British imperialism, whereby the pursuit of foreign policy comes at the end of displays of naval power against other nations, threatening warfare unless agreeable terms are met by the force displaying bravado. Examples of this are considered to be Woodrow Wilson's actions during the Mexican Revolution, Roosevelt's economic approaches, and Clinton's involvement in the Balkans.

78. Although this may not be canonical fact, McCoy being a father, given his daughter Joanna was mentioned only in *The Animated Series.*

79. *Star Trek V: The Final Frontier.*

80. *Star Trek: First Contact.*

81. *Star Trek: The Next Generation* 1x26.

82. *Ibid.*

83. *Ibid.*

84. *Ibid..*

85. *Ibid.*

86. Burston-Chorowicz, Alex. "Engage! Captain Picard, Federationism and U.S. Foreign Policy in the Emerging Post–Cold War World." In Lee, Peter W., ed., *Exploring Picard's Galaxy: Essays on* Star Trek: The Next Generation, pg. 11. 2018.

87. The Romulans in *The Next Generation* tend to operate as the kind of pre–WWII isolationists, fearful of being corrupted by outside interests, that marked American foreign policy before Pearl Harbor.

88. *Star Trek: The Next Generation* 1x26.

89. *Star Trek: First Contact.*

90. Burston-Chorowicz, Alex. "Engage! Captain Picard, Federationism and U.S. Foreign Policy in the Emerging Post–Cold War World." In Lee, Peter W., ed., *Exploring Picard's Galaxy: Essays on* Star Trek: The Next Generation, pg. 11. 2018.

91. A phrase revived in 2016, of course, by Donald Trump's successful election campaign, marking him as a "next generation" Reaganite president, in essence, his rise in no small measure emerged from the wreckage of the global recession caused by the 2007–2008 financial crash.

92. Rowland, Robert C., and Jones, John. M. *Reagan at Westminster: Foreshadowing the End of the Cold War.* 2010.

93. Luce, H. R. "The American Century". *TIME Magazine.* 1941.

94. Roughly a means of transforming 19th century economic liberalism into benefiting the private sector by radicalizing laissez-faire theory and free-market capitalism through deregulation, privatization, globalization, austerity, free trade and the reduction of tariffs. Economic governance designed to stimulate the market in direct opposition to Keynesian economic theory, which drove initial post-war thinking until the beginning of the 1980s.

95. Reagan, Ronald. 'Evil Empire Speech.' NationalCenter.org. 1983.

96. *Star Trek: The Next Generation* 1x01.

97. Not to mention appear more than once on *Voyager*, and briefly on *Deep Space Nine*—long enough for the writers to realize his whimsy was incompatible with the tone of that series.

98. The Season One episode "Conspiracy" flirted with the idea that Starfleet had been infiltrated and corrupted by a sinister alien race of parasites who infected human bodies, but the idea failed to recur beyond an initial episode, except in non-canonical novels.

99. *Star Trek: The Next Generation* 1x26.

100. Or as *Voyager* later establishes, around seventy years from Earth at maximum warp.

101. *Star Trek: The Next Generation* 2x16.

102. *Star Trek: First Contact.*

103. *Star Trek: The Next Generation* 1x26.

104. *Star Trek: First Contact.*

105. Cranny-Francis. Anne. *Technology and Touch: The Biopolitics of Emerging Technologies.* 2013.

106. This turns out to be thanks, retroactively, to a pre-destination paradox. When the Borg attack Earth in *First Contact*, and the Queen travels back to the mid-21st century to change history, the *Enterprise* destroys her sphere, wreckage of which crashes in the Arctic and is later found by scientists who in the 22nd century, in the *Enterprise* episode "Regeneration," accidentally awaken Borg genes and send a communication to the Borg Collective through space, which is later picked up by the same Cube which the *Enterprise* encounters in "Q Who?," which was already on the way to Earth. A classic "chicken and egg" scenario…

107. Translated roughly into "openness" and "restructuring," displaying Soviet efforts to reform in partnership with the United States after years of geopolitical tension.

108. *Star Trek: The Next Generation* 3x10.

109. Russell, Lynette, and Wolski, Nathan. "Beyond the Final Frontier: Star Trek, the Borg and the Post-Colonial." 2001.

110. *Ibid.*

Chapter 3

1. The '90s being a decade in which *Star Trek* was on air, with a new series, every single year, a feat as yet unmatched by any other decade. Time will tell if the 2020s yield such results.

2. Haviland, Aaron. "Star Trek and Realism." *E-International Relations.* November 2014.

3. *Star Trek VI: The Undiscovered Country.*

4. Douthat, Ross. "The Return of the Paranoid Style." *The Atlantic.* 2008.

5. *Star Trek: Deep Space Nine* 6x18.

6. *Star Trek VI: The Undiscovered Country.*

7. Fukuyama, Francis. *The End of History and the Last Man.* 1992.

Notes—Chapter 3

8. Worland, Rick. "Captain Kirk: Cold Warrior." *Journal of Popular Film and Television*. Vol. 16. 1989.
9. *Star Trek: The Original Series* 1x26.
10. *Revelations from the Russian Archives*. Library of Congress.
11. The non-physical boundary which divided Europe into two distinct geopolitical areas following the end of World War II from 1945 through until 1991, an attempt by the Soviet Union to prevent open contact with the West for itself and its satellite states.
12. Played by actor Mark Lenard, who would later portray Spock's father Sarek in "Journey to Babel," several big screen adventures, and several episodes of *The Next Generation*.
13. *Star Trek: The Original Series* 1x14.
14. *Ibid*.
15. O'Connor, Mike. "Liberals in Space: The 1960s Politics of Star Trek." *The Sixties: A Journal of History, Politics and Culture*. 2012.
16. The foundation stone for Starfleet's interaction with other cultures. The Prime Directive is to only make contact with a culture if it is safe to do so and will not adversely affect the natural development of their species' evolution.
17. *Star Trek IV: The Voyage Home*.
18. Orilk, Peter. B. *Media Criticism in a Digital Age: Professional and Consumer Considerations*. 2016.
19. *Star Trek VI: The Undiscovered Country*.
20. *Ibid*.
21. *Ibid*.
22. Burston-Chorowicz, Alex. "Engage! Captain Picard, Federationism and U.S. Foreign Policy in the Emerging Post–Cold War World." In Peter W. Lee, ed., *Exploring Picard's Galaxy: Essays on* Star Trek: The Next Generation. p. 14. 2018.
23. Memory Alpha:AOL chats/ Ronald D. Moore/ron012.txt.
24. The Bajoran experience as seen in *Star Trek* has also been compared to that of the Palestinians, and arguably it depends on one's personal point of view as to whether the Bajoran experience best represents modern Israeli or Palestinian. Rick Berman certainly acknowledges the issue, discussing how they are influenced by: "the Palestinians, [...] the boat people from Haiti—unfortunately, the homeless and terrorism are problems [of every age]." Nemecek, Larry. *Star Trek: The Next Generation Companion*. p. 178. 1995.
25. Memory Alpha:AOL chats/ Ronald D. Moore/ron012.txt.
26. *Star Trek: Deep Space Nine* 1x18.
27. *Star Trek: Deep Space Nine* 2x20.
28. *Star Trek: Deep Space Nine* 2x21.
29. Erdmann, Terry J., and Block, Paula M. *Star Trek: Deep Space Nine Companion*. 2000.
30. *Star Trek: Deep Space Nine* 4x21.
31. *Star Trek: Deep Space Nine* 5x13.
32. *Ibid*.
33. Memory Alpha:AOL chats/ Ronald D. Moore/ron012.txt.
34. *Cinefantastique*, Vol. 30, No. 9/10, p. 87.
35. *Star Trek: Deep Space Nine* 7x25.
36. Roswell has developed into an entire cottage industry, certainly for the small New Mexico town on the outskirts of which the defining event in UFOlogy happened. The town has a small but detailed museum devoted to the subject, and a myriad set of TV shows, movies and books have been written about the supposed alien contact near Roswell. Fascination and conspiracy theory swirls around it to this day, after reaching something of an apogee in the 1990s.
37. The fact they were also a mixed-race couple during the 1960s, a time as described earlier in this book of heightened racial tensions *Star Trek* shone a lens upon, certainly amplified their celebrity.
38. In which 18-year-old hitchhiker Norman Muscarello was followed while hitchhiking at 2 a.m. near Exeter by a UFO with red pulsating lights, later witnessed by two police officers who came to investigate the scene.
39. One of the more infamous UFO sightings reported by police officer Lonnie Zamora in Socorro (again in New Mexico) which left behind trace evidence such as burned vegetation and metallic fragments.
40. An enduring piece of folklore from Point Pleasant, Virginia, which skirts UFOlogy—the strange case of a "winged

Notes—Chapter 3

man" referred to as the "Mothman" in the 1960s which corresponded with UFO activity. A film was even produced in 2002, *The Mothman Prophecies* starring Richard Gere, from John Keel's 1975 investigation book of the same name, that fuelled continued interest in the legend.

41. *Star Trek: The Original Series* 1x19.
42. Ibid.
43. Ibid.
44. Krauss, Lawrence. *The Physics of Star Trek*. 1995.
45. A reimagining of which, titled *Roswell, New Mexico*, is now entering a third season as of writing and has served as quite a hit for network The CW, which has built its profile on series geared toward the teenage market.
46. As of the recent 2016 revival seasons, the answer appears to be that, in the lore of *The X-Files*, Roswell was the foundation stone for a 70+ year conspiracy against the American people, and the world, to collude with extra-terrestrial life in the extinction of the human race—one of the darker portrayals of the Roswell mythology in fiction!
47. A key aspect of UFO legend in being the supposed Nevada hangar, clouded in secrecy, where alien technology is stored and tested by the U.S. military, even to this day. Though one suspects if they are involved in such business, a venue as publicly known as Area 51 would long ago no longer have been the place that business was conducted!
48. This sequence is not as macabre, or disturbing, as it might sound.
49. Which served as more of a serious, thrilling adventure, combining Spielbergian wonder with 1970s conspiracy drama undertones, arriving at the tail end of the 1990s boom in conspiracy theory.
50. Though the Ferengi started out in *The Next Generation* as the potential new era bad guys to rival Klingons or Romulans, their garrulous temperament and diminutive stature quickly lent them more adept for comedy, which Ira Steven Behr amped up for *Deep Space Nine*. "The Nagus" in Season One kickstarted a tradition that was cemented by "Little Green Men" in multiple episodes in a season that would approach Ferengi culture and society from a comedic perspective—at times with, to be charitable, mixed results!
51. Lambourne, R.J., Shallis, M., and Shortland, M. *Close Encounters?: Science and Science Fiction*. 1990.
52. Most apparent when he was replaced for half of Season Five, unbeknownst to both his fellow characters and the audience, by a Dominion Changeling.
53. Erdmann, Terry J., with Block, Paula M. *Star Trek: Deep Space Nine Companion*. 2000. Pg. 551.
54. *Star Trek: Deep Space Nine* 4x11.
55. *Star Trek: Deep Space Nine* 6x18.
56. *Cinefantastique*, Vol. 30, No. 9/10, p. 56.
57. Pakula was one of the signature filmmakers of the 1970s who portrayed the American institution of government as corrupt and resolutely sinister, in films such as *Klute*, *The Parallax View* and most famously *All the President's Men*, which told the story of Watergate.
58. Simons, Marlene. "Clinton Apologizes for Radiation Tests: Experiments: Cabinet will study compensation for some victims and their families. About 4,000 secret studies through 1974 were disclosed." *Los Angeles Times*, Oct. 4, 1995.
59. *Star Trek: Insurrection*.
60. Ibid.
61. *Star Trek: The Original Series* 1x22.
62. *Star Trek: Deep Space Nine* 5x16.
63. *Star Trek: Deep Space Nine* 6x18.
64. Alex Burston-Chorowicz describes him as such: "Picard's liberalism underscores the many attributes he shares with President Woodrow Wilson, the American president during World War I. Their scholarly passion for history, deeply moralistic outlooks, and desire to project their liberal views are among their defining characteristics. Wilson's 'Fourteen Points'—his plan to remodel the world system after the Great War—articulated the sanctity of self-determination, guided and regulated by an international body composed of nation-states. This came to define liberal internationalism (Ambrosius 54–64; Knock 25–52; Layne 54–62). Picard, an ardent supporter of such values, defends them in the show time and time again. When the *Enterprise* responds to various threats and challenges

to Federation power, Picard consistently chooses solutions that emphasize individual rights." In Peter W. Lee, ed., *Exploring Picard's Galaxy* (p. 12).
65. *Star Trek: Deep Space Nine* 6x19.
66. Fukuyama, Francis. *The End of History and the Last Man*. 1992.

Chapter 4

1. Mooney, Darren. "Star Trek Voyager (Reviews)." TheM0vieBlog.com.
2. As most schoolchildren grow up understanding from a young age, certainly in the West, the assassination of Franz Ferdinand served as the tipping point for a continent already preparing for long-brewing conflict, and initiated hostilities that directly started World War I, the first significant turning point in 20th century history.
3. "Year of Hell" was a strong two-part episode of *Voyager* in which the ship and crew were brought almost to destruction across a year battling the Krenim Imperium and Annorax, a villain using technology that allowed him to re-write time, causing untold destruction as he went. Bryan Fuller has described how the writing time initially hoped to develop the entire fourth season of *Voyager* to encompass that story: "We wanted to see *Voyager* get its ass kicked every episode and through that season was going to be marbled the story of Annorax and the time ship that was changing things. So, we would go back to it every once in a while, to remind the audience that is the larger story. We are really going to be on the outskirts of the galaxy, and we are going to be fighting enemies that are kicking us when we are down. The crew is going to have to separate and we are going to be following episodes that are going to deal with people on shuttlecrafts with escape pods that are electrically buoyed together. There would be an episode where you never saw Janeway and never saw *Voyager* because you are with the people who are on the escape pods trying to find a new source of power or safety. It was like creative crack for the writers' room, because all of a sudden there were so many opportunities. But [it was rejected] because *Deep Space Nine* made Rick Berman allergic to serialized storytelling, violently so." Inglorious Treksperts podcast. "Voyager's 25th Anniversary Party w/Bryan Fuller." May 23, 2020.
4. Mooney, Darren. "Star Trek: Enterprise (Reviews)." TheM0vieBlog.com.
5. The true reasons for this were down to production design, and efforts in the 1970s in *The Motion Picture* to establish a definitive new look for the Klingons, but *Enterprise* was forced to ascribe an in-world narrative reason for such differences due to fan frustration and pressure.
6. Sims, David. "Star Wars: The Nostalgia Awakens." *The Atlantic*. April 2015.
7. *Nemesis* made $67.3 million whereas *Star Trek* 2009 came out with $385.7 million. With just seven years between them, such a gap between earnings and audience response was enormous.
8. This is the reputed ambition of CBS, who now own and produce the franchise, according to CBS Studios TV President David Stapf: "My goal is that there should be a *Star Trek* something on all the time on All Access. We know it draws an audience, and *Discovery* has done quite well." Andreeva, Nellie, and Patten, Dominic. "CBS All Access Bosses On More 'Star Trek' Series, 'The Twilight Zone' Status, Stephen King & More—TCA." *Deadline*, Aug. 6, 2018.
9. Gross, Edward. *The Fifty-Year Mission: The Next 25 Years: From The Next Generation to J. J. Abrams* (p. 604).
10. As seen in the Borg invasion in *First Contact*, and the Dominion War which raged across *Deep Space Nine*.
11. With the exception of *Nemesis*, which arrived around a year after *Voyager* came to an end, but in truth it could have been set around the same point. The only acknowledgment it took place later was a brief cameo by Kate Mulgrew as a newly promoted Admiral Janeway.
12. Mooney, Darren. "Star Trek Voyager (Reviews)." TheM0vieBlog.com.
13. Though as writer Kenneth Biller reports, the original name of the fledgling network was originally intended as something different. "They were going to call it the Paramount United Network until they

Notes—Chapter 4

discovered PUN would be the acronym." Gross, Edward. *The Fifty-Year Mission: The Next 25 Years: From* The Next Generation *to J. J. Abrams* (p. 553).

14. Michael Piller expands on this: "Rick really felt that *Deep Space Nine* deserved an opportunity to be on the air by itself and that the franchise could use a little breathing room. He wanted the studio to hold off on *Voyager* for a year at least. The studio came back and more or less said, 'Well, Rick, we're going to do this with or without you. We'd rather do it with you, but we're not going to give up the station groups' and things like that. With that edict, Rick came to me and said, 'Okay, they want to do another one.'" Gross, Edward. *The Fifty-Year Mission: The Next 25 Years: From* The Next Generation *to J. J. Abrams* (p. 552).

15. Though crucially not the first female captain ever seen in *Star Trek*, Madge Sinclair briefly appeared in *The Voyage Home* as commander of the ill-fated USS *Saratoga*, while even the captain of the USS *Enterprise-C* was female, Rachel Garrett, seen in *The Next Generation* episode "Yesterday's Enterprise." She is lesser known for the fact she was killed, and her ship destroyed in a temporal anomaly some twenty years or more before the start of *The Next Generation*, but subsequent non-canonical material has fleshed the character out. Janeway, however, is the first female lead in a *Star Trek* series.

16. Coupland, Douglas. "1990s: The Good Decade." History.com. April 23, 2019.

17. Palahniuk, Chuck. *Fight Club*. 1996.

18. *Voyager* is, perhaps surprisingly, the highest-watched *Star Trek* series on streaming service Netflix, with six out of the ten most watched episodes belonging to *Voyager*. Only *The Next Generation* also places in the list, with four episodes. "Netflix's Top-10 Most Re-Watched Trek Episodes." StarTrek.com. September 2017.

19. Gross, Edward. *The Fifty-Year Mission: The Next 25 Years: From* The Next Generation *to J. J. Abrams* (p. 589).

20. Rick Berman was, ultimately, unable to control the whims of Ira Steven Behr as a producer, as Ronald D. Moore suggests: "Ira's very smart and cunning. He knows when not to run straight at people to get what he wants. He knew how to deal with Rick. He knew how to deal with Mike. He knew how to make his arguments and to make incremental progress and then make breakthroughs every once in a while. When he would fight with Rick, he knew how to fight with him. He knew when to give and when not to. When he could get Rick to back down a little bit by throwing him something else … well, he was just very clever about it." Gross, Edward. *The Fifty-Year Mission: The Next 25 Years: From* The Next Generation *to J. J. Abrams* (p. 484).

21. Mooney, Darren. "Star Trek: Enterprise (Reviews)." TheM0vieBlog.com.

22. *Ibid*.

23. Lovecraftian referring to horror writer H. P. Lovecraft, who between the 1910s and the late 1930s penned a collection of short stories that became known as "cosmic horror," blending science-fiction, horror and fantasy in a concoction that influenced almost a century of writers, including Stephen King. Lovecraft's stories differed from *Star Trek* in that his characters frequently were sent mad by the unknowable power of the universe, unlike our Starfleet crews who seek to understand the unknown through scientific discovery. Gene Roddenberry was excited about the frontier of space. Lovecraft was terrified by it.

24. Gross, Edward. *The Fifty-Year Mission: The Next 25 Years: From* The Next Generation *to J. J. Abrams* (p. 625).

25. Which has a lot of similarities to *The Voyage Home*, with the *Voyager* crew going incognito in mid-'90s Los Angeles, in a similar style to the *Enterprise* crew infiltrating mid-'80s San Francisco.

26. An episode that also features Jonathan Frakes in a brief cameo as Will Riker, spirited by Q to tell the story of one of his ancestors on *Voyager* in an encounter he will never go on and remember.

27. Who, as of writing, remains the only *Voyager* character to be revisited in the later era of *Star Trek*, appearing as a major character on *Picard*.

28. "To Paris, U.S. Looks Like a 'Hyperpower.'" *The New York Times*, February 5, 1999.

Notes—Chapter 4

29. Gross, Edward. *The Fifty-Year Mission: The Next 25 Years: From* The Next Generation *to J. J. Abrams* (p. 556).

30. *Star Trek: Voyager* 4x15.

31. Gross, Edward. *The Fifty-Year Mission: The Next 25 Years: From* The Next Generation *to J. J. Abrams* (p. 556).

32. Darren Mooney expands on this: "Despite the fact that *Voyager* never embraced serialised or long-form storytelling, it was fascinated with idea of memory and manipulation. Perhaps tapping into the fear that the trauma of the Holocaust was slipping from living memory, *Voyager* touched time and again on the horror of revisionist history and importance of preserving memory. Remember and Memorial were explicitly about memorialising genocide. Distant Origin and Living Witness were more broadly about the dangers of erasing history to suit political narratives."

33. A Hindu scripture dated roughly to the 2nd century BCE which forms part of the epic Mahabharata. Oppenheimer had this particular line on his mind during the atomic test: "We knew the world would not be the same. A few people laughed, a few people cried. Most people were silent. I remembered the line from the Hindu scripture, the Bhagavad Gita; Vishnu is trying to persuade the Prince that he should do his duty and, to impress him, takes on his multi-armed form and says, 'Now I am become Death, the destroyer of worlds.' I suppose we all thought that, one way or another." "J. Robert Oppenheimer on the Trinity test (1965)". *Atomic Archive*. Retrieved 23 May 2008.

34. Gross, Edward. *The Fifty-Year Mission: The Next 25 Years: From* The Next Generation *to J. J. Abrams* (pp. 646–647).

35. In 2001, it was promoted simply as "Enterprise," with producers believing both that audiences would have enough cultural awareness of the ship name to make the connection, and further the show's aims of being more contemporary by losing the *Star Trek* branding. In retrospect, while clearly recognising that the franchise had lost something of the allure it once had—and certainly was not "cool" to younger audiences—it also removed the signature name of the franchise's IP. The decision was reversed for Season Three onwards.

36. Russell Watson's ballad "Faith of the Heart," written along with celebrated musician Diane Warren, which was roundly despised by many viewers despite applause for the show's actual credit sequence itself. Braga has admitted as much himself: "Rick and I felt that a song would set the slightly more contemporary feeling we were going after with Enterprise. For the longest time, we had a temporary song we cut the main titles to, U2's "Beautiful Day." If we had used that—or could have afforded it—that would have been a great song. Those main titles with U2 are amazing. It's hip and cool, whereas the song we ended up with is awful. I'm a big fan of Diane Warren, she's a great songwriter, but this particular song and the way it was sung was tacky. I still cringe when I hear it and, by the way, I think the song had a lot to do with people's adverse reaction to the show. If you look at the main titles themselves, it's a really cool sequence. But the song is awful, just awful." Gross, Edward. *The Fifty-Year Mission: The Next 25 Years: From* The Next Generation *to J. J. Abrams* (p. 668).

37. The lesser-known spin-off series from *The X-Files*, though it did not begin as such, revolving around a criminal profiler with a near-psychic ability who hunts human monsters and becomes involved in apocalyptic mystery cults.

38. Feder, Barnaby. J. "Fear of the Year 2000 Bug Is a Problem, Too." *The New York Times*. February 9, 1999.

39. Douglas Kellner argues that Bush's subsequent language was designed to evoke a decidedly patriotic tone amidst the promises of swift military action, which only stoked the flames: "Disturbingly, in outlining the goals of the war, Bush never mentioned democracy, and the new name for the war on terrorism became 'Operation Enduring Freedom.' The Bush administration mantra repeated constantly that the war against terrorism was being fought for 'freedom.' But the history of political theory suggests that freedom must be paired with equality, or concepts like justice, rights, or democracy, to provide adequate political theory and legitimation for political action. It is precisely the

contempt for democracy and national self-determination that has characterized U.S. foreign policy in the Middle East for the past decades, which is a prime reason why groups and individuals in the area passionately hate the U.S." "9/11, spectacles of terror, and media manipulation: A critique of Jihadist and Bush media politics." *Critical Discourse Studies*, 1:1 (2004).

40. "Enterprise Sets New Course." *SciFiWire*, May 20, 2003.

41. This was initially the case, as reported by Philip Bump in *The Washington Post*: "We can track the unity of the country after 9/11 in the approval ratings of President George W. Bush. No president in the history of Gallup's approval ratings has seen a higher rating than Bush did right after the attacks. Two weeks afterward, nearly 9 in 10 Democrats and independents approved of the Republican president, with Democratic approval trailing Republicans by 10 percentage points. Right after the 2001 terrorist attacks, The Washington Post and ABC News polled Americans to get a sense of their attitudes about Bush and the attacks. ... Americans were broadly supportive of engaging in military conflict, though those attitudes waned as the possible side effects of conflict were raised. By the following September, though? Democratic approval of Bush was under 50 percent, 42 points lower than the approval of Republicans." Bump, Philip. "Americans united after 9/11. When did we rip back apart?" *The Washington Post*, September 11, 2017.

42. "Democrats slam 'go-it-alone' Bush." *BBC News*, January 21, 2004.

43. Mooney, Darren. "Star Trek: Enterprise—Stratagem (Review)." TheM0vieBlog.com, August 20, 2015.

44. *Star Trek: Enterprise* 3x14.

45. Here played by British thespian Benedict Cumberbatch, as opposed to the Latin Ricardo Montalban, which only further confuses the supposedly Indian origins of the character. It's telling that the only person who uses his full name, including the Noonien Singh, in *Into Darkness*, is the elder Spock. That almost feels like a call back to a point where the casting of the character at least had some connective tissue to his ethnic origin.

46. It was, tellingly, devised to coincide with the 50th anniversary of the franchise, and as a result *Beyond* was expressly designed to lean into aspects that evoked *The Original Series*.

47. Gross, Edward. *The Fifty-Year Mission: The Next 25 Years: From* The Next Generation *to J. J. Abrams* (p. 802).

48. *Star Trek Into Darkness*.

49. *Ibid*.

50. *Ibid*.

51. Demarcated roughly with the arrival of *Star Trek: Discovery* in 2017, and the franchise's long-awaited return to television screens.

52. *Star Trek: Discovery* 1x01.

53. *Star Trek Beyond*.

54. Spock's beard certainly grew to become something of a cultural reference point for an "evil" alternate version of a character. The comedy series *Community* plays on this with the Evil Abed character from the so-called "Darkest Timeline."

55. *Star Trek: Discovery* 1x09.

56. They both celebrated five decades in 2012 for James Bond and 2013 for *Doctor Who* respectively, and with their own major high points in *Skyfall* and "The Day of the Doctor," both of which were arguably more celebrated and popular than *Star Trek Beyond*.

57. So named for the alternate timeline in which the films take place, created in *Star Trek* 2009 when the USS *Kelvin* is destroyed by the *Narada* when it appears from the future.

58. Abrams having departed as director to helm *Star Wars: The Force Awakens*, though he remained a producer.

59. The name for the original series timeline encompassing everything up to *Star Trek* 2009. The only project that remains exactly the same in both timelines is *Enterprise*, having taken place earlier than when the *Kelvin* was destroyed.

60. Metafiction, coined by William H. Gass in his work, *Fiction and the Figures of Life*, is described as, according to Wikipedia, "a form of fiction that emphasizes its own constructedness in a way that continually reminds the reader to be aware that they are reading or viewing a fictional work." In relation to *Beyond* in this instance, the audience has a deeper aware-

Notes—Chapter 4

ness of the characters nuSpock observes in the photograph that transcends both the story and how the photo emotionally resonates for the character himself.

61. Aside from an American co-production TV movie in 1996 which featured Paul McGann as a half-human Doctor, a film considered non-canonical for decades before Steven Moffat's tenure re-introduced his 8th Doctor in minisode "The Night of the Doctor" in 2013 as part of the buildup to "The Day of the Doctor."

62. Gross, Edward. *The Fifty-Year Mission: The Next 25 Years: From* The Next Generation *to J. J. Abrams* (pp. 752–753).

63. MZP.tv. "Star Trek: Reboot the Universe." *Movie Scripts*. PDF.

64. Merrick. "Remember That STAR TREK: THE BEGINNING Movie Which Went Missing?? Merrick Found It...." *Ain't It Cool News*, June 10, 2008.

65. Pascale, Anthony. "Exclusive: The True Story Behind the Bryan Singer 'Pitch' of 'Star Trek: Federation.'" April 14, 2011.

66. Gross, Edward. *The Fifty-Year Mission: The Next 25 Years: From* The Next Generation *to J. J. Abrams* (p. 755).

67. Moore, Charles. "James Bond today is a security guard, not a gentleman." *The Telegraph*, October 25, 2015

68. Jefferies, Lewis. "Old Enemies Likely to Return in Series 12 of 'Doctor Who'—Who Will Make a Comeback?" *Futurism*. 2018.

69. Waid, Mark. "Man of Steel, since you asked." *Thrillbent*. June 14, 2013.

70. Khan, of course, had a history with Admiral Kirk, and *The Final Frontier* introduces Sybok, Spock's semi-canonical half-brother, as the primary antagonist. *First Contact* and *Nemesis* provide villains with a personal connection to Picard but these are retroactive in terms of continuity, with the Borg Queen having been influencing events as far back as "The Best of Both Worlds"—when she had not been imagined at the time—and Shinzon part of an off-screen Romulan plot to clone and replace Picard. As a result, neither example equates with both the previous villains and those to come in the same regard.

71. In what would be Leonard Nimoy's final appearance as the character before his death in 2014.

72. Gross, Edward. *The Fifty-Year Mission: The Next 25 Years: From* The Next Generation *to J. J. Abrams* (p. 798).

73. At this writing, the production appears to have been completely stalled, despite initial reports following *Beyond* that a fourth film would star Chris Hemsworth, returning as Kirk's deceased father George Kirk, in a time-travel story. Subsequent reports that Quentin Tarantino and Noah Hawley are working on scripts have, to date, yielded no announcements as to any sequel on the immediate horizon.

74. Fuller later commented briefly on the experience after leaving: "I got to dream big. I was sad for a week and then I salute the ship and compartmentalize my experience." Hibberd, James. "Bryan Fuller on his *Star Trek: Discovery* exit: 'I got to dream big'." *EW*, July 28, 2017.

75. Which is explored in the non-canonical novel universe around the on-screen *Star Trek* series and would have sketched in the events that led directly to the formation of the United Federation of Planets.

76. Berman and Braga discussed this tantalizing prospect further while recording a Blu-ray commentary for *Enterprise*: "We were gonna get Picard, Data, Odo, the holographic Doctor ... all the *Star Trek* characters on one ship, like a think tank," "In Conversation: Rick Berman and Brannon Braga" ENT Season 1 Blu-ray special features.

77. Ordona, Michael. "Star Trek' was canceled 50 years ago. Now, the franchise is flying warp speed ahead." *Los Angeles Times*, May 9, 2019.

78. A former member of the Borg Collective who, in *The Next Generation* Season Five episode "I, Borg" is found by Picard and his crew who help him achieve individuality. This story arguably was a forerunner for the creation of Seven of Nine on *Voyager*.

79. A former Borg rescued by *Voyager* in Season Six, who falls under Seven's wing and eventually, once *Voyager* returns home, joins Starfleet until he is brutally murdered, as seen in "Stardust City Rag."

Epilogue

1. Achieved with the help of the crew of the USS *Enterprise-E* from the 24th century, something left out of the official history of Cochrane's warp flight.
2. Otherwise known as "the Ides of March," in which Roman emperor Julius Caesar was murdered at the heart of the Senate after being stabbed in the back.
3. The date of the Battle of Hastings, in which William the Conqueror established the foundation of the Anglo-Saxon kingdom that would become the England known to history today.
4. AKA V.E. Day, on which World War II was declared over in Western Europe after the collapse of Nazi Germany following the Allied invasion of Berlin.
5. Principally between the United States and a resurgent North Korea, following the accession of Donald Trump to the American presidency.
6. *Star Trek: The Original Series* 3x22.
7. *Star Trek: Enterprise* 4x20.
8. *Star Trek: First Contact.*
9. *Star Trek: The Next Generation* 1x01.
10. *Ibid.*
11. *First Contact* leaves specifics about this group ambiguous, but the *Star Trek* Encyclopedia describes them as "a loose alliance of eastern powers" which "was often adversarial towards the powers controlling North America." Brannon Braga has also stated that the script originally referred simply to "China," but this was deemed too politically incorrect.
12. *Star Trek: The Next Generation* 2x12.
13. *Star Trek: Voyager* 6x08.
14. A character originally devised to be the aforementioned Colonel Green, though one wonders quite how that would have worked practically.

Bibliography

Alexander, David. *Star Trek Creator: The Authorized Biography of Gene Roddenberry*. Roc, 1994.
Ananth, Mahesh. "Spock's Vulcan Mind Meld: A Primer for the Philosophy of Mind." In Jason T. Eberl and Kevin S. Decker, eds., *Star Trek and Philosophy: The Wrath of Kant*. Carus, 2008.
Andreeva, Nellie, and Dominic Patten. "CBS All Access Bosses on More 'Star Trek' Series, 'The Twilight Zone' Status, Stephen King & More—TCA." *Deadline*. Aug. 6, 2018.
Asa, Robert. "Classic Star Trek and the Death of God." In Jennifer E. Porter and Darcee L. McLaren, eds., *Star Trek and Sacred Ground: Explorations of Star Trek, Religion, and American Culture*. Suny Press, 1999.
Ashton, Bodie. "The Myth of Nazi Efficiency." *Coffee Cup History*. May 6, 2013.
Atomic Archive. "J. Robert Oppenheimer on the Trinity test (1965)." Retrieved May 23, 2008.
Austin, Allan W. "The Limits of Star Trek's Final Frontier: 'The Omega Glory' and 1960s American Liberalism." In David C. Wright, Jr., and Allan W. Austin, eds., *Space and Time: Essays on Visions of History in Science Fiction and Fantasy Television*. McFarland, 2010.
Baker-Smith, Dominic. *More's Utopia*. University of Toronto Press, 2000.
Barrett, Michele, and Duncan Barrett. *Star Trek: The Human Frontier*. Routledge, 2001.
BBC News. "Democrats Slam 'Go-It-Alone' Bush." Jan. 21, 2004.
Braunstein, Peter. "Forever Young: Insurgent Youth and the Sixties Culture of Rejuvenation." In Peter Braunstein and Michael William Doyle, *Imagine Nation: The American Counterculture of the 1960's and '70s*. Taylor & Francis Group, 2001.
Buck, Jerry. "'Star Trek' Engenders Cult in U.S., England." *Youngstown Vindicator*. March 14, 1972.
Bump, Philip. "Americans United After 9/11. When Did We Rip Back Apart?" *The Washington Post*. September 11, 2017.
Burston-Chorowicz, Alex. "Engage! Captain Picard, Federationism and U.S. Foreign Policy in the Emerging Post–Cold War World." In Peter W. Lee, ed., *Exploring Picard's Galaxy: Essays on Star Trek: The Next Generation*. p. 11. McFarland, 2018.
Clarke, Arthur. C. "Hazards of Prophecy: The Failure of Imagination." *Profiles of the Future: An Enquiry into the Limits of the Possible*. 1962, rev. 1973.
Coupland, Douglas. "1990s: The Good Decade." History.com. April 23, 2019.
Cranny-Francis, Anne. *Technology and Touch: The Biopolitics of Emerging Technologies*. Palgrave Macmillan, 2013.
Didion, Joan. *The White Album*. Simon & Schuster, 1979.

Bibliography

Douthat, Ross. "The Return of the Paranoid Style." *The Atlantic*. 2008.
Erdmann, Terry J., and Paula M. Block. *Star Trek: Deep Space Nine Companion*. 2000.
Feder, Barnaby. J. "Fear of the Year 2000 Bug Is a Problem, Too." *New York Times*. Feb. 9, 1999.
Franklin, H. Bruce. "Star Trek in the Vietnam Era." *Science Fiction Studies*. March 1994.
Fukuyama, Francis. *The End of History and the Last Man*. Free Press, 1992.
Greven, David. *Gender and Sexuality in Star Trek: Allegories of Desire in the Television Series and Films*. McFarland, 2009.
Gross, Edward, and Mark A. Altman. *The Fifty-Year Mission: The Complete, Uncensored, Unauthorized Oral History of Star Trek: The First 25 Years*. Thomas Dunne Books, 2016.
Gross, Edward, and Mark A. Altman. *The Fifty-Year Mission: The Next 25 Years: From The Next Generation to J. J. Abrams*. Thomas Dunne Books, 2016.
Harrison, Scott. "From the Archives: 1967 Antiwar Protest Turns Violent." *Los Angeles Times*. June 22, 2017.
Haviland, Aaron. "Star Trek and Realism." *E-International Relations*. November 2014.
Hibberd, James. "Bryan Fuller on his *Star Trek: Discovery* Exit: 'I got to dream big.'" *EW*. July 28, 2017.
Hine, Robert V., and John Mack Faragher. *The American West: A New Interpretive History*. Yale University Press, 2000.
Horakova, Erin. K. "From 'Shalom Aleichem' to 'Live Long and Prosper': Engaging with post-war Jewish identity via *Star Trek: The Original Series*." *Set Phasers to Teach!: Star Trek in Research and Teaching*. Springer, 2018.
Inglorious Treksperts podcast. "Voyager's 25th Anniversary Party w/Bryan Fuller." May 23, 2020.
Isaacs, Bruce. "A Vision of Time and Place: Spiritual Humanism and the Utopian Impulse." In Matthew Wilhelm Kapell, ed., *Star Trek as Myth: Essays on Symbol and Archetype at the Final Frontier*. McFarland, 2010.
Jefferies, Lewis. "Old Enemies Likely to Return in Series 12 of 'Doctor Who'—Who Will Make a Comeback?" *Futurism*. 2018.
Johnson-Smith, Jan. *American Science Fiction TV: Star Trek, Stargate and Beyond*. Wesleyan University Press. January 10, 2005.
Kellner, Douglas. "9/11, spectacles of terror, and media manipulation: A critique of Jihadist and Bush media politics." *Critical Discourse Studies*. Aug. 15, 2006.
Krauss, Lawrence. *The Physics of Star Trek*. Flamingo, 1995.
Lambourne, R.J., M. J. Shallis, and M. Shortland. *Close Encounters? Science and Science Fiction*. CRC Press, 1990.
Luce, Henry R. "The American Century." *Life*, February 17, 1941, pp. 61-65.
Lundeen, Jan, and Jon Wagner. *Deep Space and Sacred Time: "Star Trek" in the American Mythos*. Praeger, 1998.
Maycock, James. "War within War." *The Guardian*. Sept. 15, 2001.
Merk, Frederick, and Lois Bannister Merk. *Manifest Destiny and Mission in American History: A Reinterpretation*. Harvard University Press, 1995.
Merrick. "Remember That STAR TREK: THE BEGINNING Movie Which Went Missing?? Merrick Found It..." *Ain't It Cool News*. June 10, 2008.
Mooney, Darren. "Star Trek: The Original Series (Reviews)." TheM0vieBlog.com.
Moore, Charles. "James Bond Today Is a Security Guard, not a Gentleman." *The Telegraph*. Oct. 25, 2015.

Bibliography

Munger, Sean. "Hippies in Space: A Star Trek Episode in 1960's Historical Context." SeanMunger.com. May 11, 2015.
MZP.tv. "Star Trek: Reboot the Universe." Movie Scripts. PDF.
Nemecek, Larry. *Star Trek: The Next Generation Companion*. 1995.
Nichols, Nichelle. *Beyond Uhura: Star Trek and Other Memories*. Putnam, 1996.
O'Connor, Mike. "Liberals in Space: The 1960s Politics of *Star Trek*." *The Sixties: A Journal of History, Politics and Culture*. December 2012.
Ordona, Michael. "'Star Trek' was Canceled 50 Years Ago. Now, the Franchise is Flying Warp Speed Ahead." *Los Angeles Times*. May 9, 2019.
Orilk, Peter. B. *Media Criticism in a Digital Age: Professional and Consumer Considerations*. Routledge, 2016.
Palahniuk, Chuck. *Fight Club*. Vintage, 1996.
Pascale, Anthony. "Exclusive: The True Story Behind the Bryan Singer 'Pitch' of 'Star Trek: Federation.'" April 14, 2011.
Powis, Neville. "The Human Be-In and The Hippy Revolution." *Radio Netherlands*. January 11, 2003.
Rothschild, Matthew. "George Takei, Mr. Sulu of Star Trek, Comes Out and Speaks Out." *The Progressive*. May 8, 2006.
Rowland, Robert C., and John Jones. *M. Reagan at Westminster: Foreshadowing the End of the Cold War*. Texas A&M University Press, 2010.
Russell, Lynette, and Nathan Wolski. "Beyond the Final Frontier: Star Trek, the Borg and the Post-colonial." Unpublished paper, 2001.
Shatner, William, and Chris Kreski. *Star Trek Memories*. It Books, 2009.
Simons, Marlene. "Clinton Apologizes for Radiation Tests." *Los Angeles Times*. October 4, 1995.
Sims, David. "Star Wars: The Nostalgia Awakens." *The Atlantic*. April 2015.
Sohl, Jerry. *The History of Star Trek*. Trek Classic.
StarTrek.com. "Netflix's Top-10 Most Re-Watched Trek Episodes." StarTrek.com. September 2017.
Thompson, Derek. "Three Decades Ago, America Lost Its Religion. Why?" *The Atlantic*. September 2019.
"To Paris, U.S. Looks Like a 'Hyperpower.'" *New York Times*, February 5, 1999.
Vettel-Becker, Patricia. "Space and the Single Girl: Star Trek, Aesthetics, and 1960s Femininity." *Frontiers—A Journal of Women's Studies*. October 2014.
Waid, Mark. "Man of Steel, Since you Asked." *Thrillbent*. June 14, 2013.
Wolf, David. "Who Was Nietzsche?" Salon.com. Oct. 1, 2012.
Worland, Rick. "Captain Kirk: Cold Warrior." *Journal of Popular Film and Television*. Vol. 16. 1989.

Index

A-bomb 32
Abrams, J.J. 4, 117–118, 136–138, 142, 145–148, 150
Abu Ghrayib 134
Adam (character) 25
Afghanistan 91
AIDS 75
Alexander (character) 23
Alexander, David 14
Alexander, Larry 50–51
All the President's Men 52
Alpha Quadrant 81, 100, 113, 123, 125–127, 129
Al-Qaeda 92, 130, 132, 140
Ambrose, David 52
"American Century" 72, 77
American Constitution 38, 45
American Horror Story 149
"American New Wave" 30
Ananth, Mahesh 61
Andorians (race) 123
The Andromeda Strain 54
Anij (character) 111
Annorax (character) 124
Apella (character) 36
Apollo 11 mission 84
Archer, Jonathan (character) 101, 105, 116–117, 131–136, 139, 145, 155
Archive of Our Own 151
Area-51 107, 110
Ares Four (vessel) 159
Ariannus (planet) 40
artificial intelligence 159
Aryan 17
Ashton, Bodie 16
Asia 16
Austin, Allan 40
Austin Powers (franchise) *144*
Austro-Hungarian Empire 15
The Avengers (2012 film) 151
Axis 7
Azetbur, Chancellor (character) 82

"B-movie" 7, 80
Bach, Richard 52
Back to the Future Part II 156
Bad Robot 136
"The Badlands" 99, 121
Bajorans (race) 80, 92–96, 101–102, 141
Bak'u (race) 110–111
Bakula, Scott 131
Ball, Lucille 7
Bana, Eric 148
Band of Brothers 146
Barclay, Reg (character) 126
Barrett, Duncan 54
Barrett, Majel 28–29
Barrett, Michele 54
Bashir, Dr. Julian (character) 81, 108, 111–112
Batman (1960s series) 2, 7
Batman & Robin (film) 144
Batman Begins 144–145
Batman vs Superman: Dawn of Justice 147
Battle of Maxia 13
Battlestar Galactica (2004 series) 100, 122
Bauer, Jack (character) 132, 134–135
The Beatles 22
Behr, Ira Steven 96–97, 106, 109
Beimler, Hans 67
Bele (character) 41
Bennett, Harve 57, 59, 146
Bennett, Rear-Admiral (character) 111
Berlin Wall 75, 82, 88–90, 156
Berman, Rick 82, 119–120, 122, 130–133, 136, 146
Berthold rays 27
Beta Quadrant 123
Betazoid (race) 51, 100
Beyer, Kirsten 152
Beyond Uhura (book) 23
Bhagavad-Gita 130
bin Laden, Osama 135

185

Index

Bird of Prey (vessel) 62–63, 87
Black, John F.W. 44
Boeing B-17 Flying Fortress 9
Bond, James (character) 142, 144
Bonnie & Clyde (1967 film) 30
Borg (race) 46, 69, 74–77, 79, 101, 119, 125–127, 133
Borg Cube (vessel) 74
Borg Queen (character) 74–75, 125, 155
Boston 15
Botany Bay, S.S. (vessel) 16, 138
"The Boy Wonder" (character) 7
Braga, Brannon 122, 124–125, 130, 132
Braunstein, Peter 25
Breen (race) 127, 133
Brezhnev, Leonid 86
Burnham, Michael (character) 139–140, 150, 153
Burroughs, Edgar Rice 9
Burston-Chorowicz, Alex 70–71, 91
Burton, Tim 107
Bush, George. W. 132, 135
"The Butcher of Gallitep" (character) 94
Butler, Nathan 28

Campbell, Martin 144
"The Caped Crusader" (character) 7
capitalism 69–70, 107
Cardassians (race) 80–81, 91–102, 108–109, 123, 127, 141
Casino Royale (2006 film) 144, 147, 149
Catulla (planet) 24-25
CBS (network) 4, 152–153
Ceti Alpha V (planet) 16, 18
Ceti Alpha VI (planet) 59
Chakotay (character) 99–100, 122, 127
Chamberlain, Neville 90
Chang, General (character) 82, 90
Changelings (race) 101–102, 109
Chapel, Dr. Christine (character) 28, 30
Charon (planet) 41
Charybdis (vessel) 159
Chekov, Pavel (character) 1, 25, 63, 88
Chernobyl 89
Cho, John 148
Christopher, Captain John (character) 104–105
Churchill, Winston 89, 98
Civil Rights movement 8, 20–24, 41, 71, 160
Clarke, Arthur. C. 63
Clee, Mona 69
Clemonds, L. Q. "Sonny" (character) 70
Clinton, Bill 110, 120

Clinton, Hillary 112
Clipper America 10
Cochrane, Zefram (character) 155–156, 158
Cogley, Samuel (character) 11
Cold War 3, 7–8, 31, 37, 40, 42, 45–46, 51–52, 59, 63, 72, 74–75, 78, 80, 82, 86–88, 90–91, 108, 110, 121, 123, 156, 160
Colla, Richard 54–55
Collins, Stephen 52
communism 37–38, 51–52, 68, 70, 72, 87, 124
Communist China 83, 85
conservatism 21, 25, 72, 81, 118, 135
conventions 3
Coon, Gene. L. 6, 16, 44
Cosmopolitan 29
counter-culture 2, 8, 71
Coupland, Douglas 121
Courage, Alexander 49
Craig, Daniel 144, 147, 159
Crawford, Oliver 41
Crusher, Dr. Beverly (character) 70
Crusher, Wesley (character) 73
Cuban Missile Crisis 8, 31, 84, 156
Cukurs, Herbert 19
Cybermen (race) 145

Daaj (character) 159
Daleks (race) 145
Daniels, Marc 47
Darhe'el, Gul (character) 94–95
Dark City 123
Data (character) 110, 145, 152–153, 159
Davies, Russell. T. 143–144
The Day the Earth Stood Still 54
DC Universe (comics) 7
D-day 96
Decius, Commander (character) 85–86
Decker, Will (character) 52–53, 55
de Gaulle, Charles 96, 98
Degra (character) 135–136
de Lancie, John 73
Delphic Expanse 132
Delta Flyer (vessel) 126
Delta Quadrant 100, 115, 121, 123–124, 126–128
Deltan (race) 5
Demilitarized Zone 95–99
Department of Internal Affairs 108
Department of Temporal Investigations 106
Descartian 61

Index

Desilu Studios 5
détente 8, 37, 66, 84, 86–87
The Devil 18, 49
Die Another Day 144
Dinh Diem, Ngo 31
"directed dreaming" 52
Discovery, U.S.S. (vessel) 139, 150
Ditko, Steve 144
The Doctor (character) 2, 144–145, 149
The Doctor (*Voyager* character) 145
Doctor Who 2, 142–145, 147
Doherty, Thomas 6, 35
The Dominion (organization) 80, 91, 98, 100, 102, 108–110, 112, 127, 129, 133
Dominion War (event) 97, 99, 108, 127
Donner, Richard 144
Doohan, James 1, 6
Dougherty, Admiral (character) 39, 111, 138
Douglas, Kirk 50
Douthat, Ross 81
Dorn, Michael 74
Dukat, Gul (character) 94–96

"Earth-Romulan War" (event) 85, 146
"Eastern Coalition" 158
Easy Rider 21
Ebola virus 75
Eddington, Michael (character) 97–99
"Eden" 24–27, 60, 64
Eichmann, Adolf 19
Ekos (planet) 14
Ekosian (race) 15
El Paso 9
Ellis, Ray 49
Ellison, Harlan 6, 32, 50, 105
Emergency Medical Hologram (character) 124
"end of history" 86, 88, 113
"The End of History" (essay) 82
The End of History and the Last Man (book) 82
Enterprise, U.S.S. (vessel) 1, 3, 5, 8–9, 11–13, 16, 18, 20, 23–24, 27–28, 30, 32, 35, 38, 40–41, 45, 47–54, 60, 62, 69, 85, 88, 103–106, 137–138, 143, 148, 150–151
Enterprise-A, U.S.S. (vessel) 13, 61, 64, 82
Enterprise-D, U.S.S. (vessel) 3–4, 46, 67, 69, 74, 76
Enterprise-E, U.S.S. (vessel) 69, 98, 152, 155
Enterprise, NX-01 (vessel) 134
eugenics 16–17, 111–112

Eugenics Wars 16, 20, 111–112, 157
Euhemerus 68
Excalbians (race) 157
Excalibur, U.S.S. (vessel) 47
Excelsior, U.S.S. (vessel) 82
eXistenZ 123
Exodus (book) 18
Exodus (film) 18

"fan fiction" 151
FanFiction.Net 151
Faragher, John Mack 66
Fargo (TV series) 149
fascism 93–96, 102
Feder, Barnaby. J. 131
Ferdinand, Archduke 116
Ferengi (race) 13, 103, 107
"Ferengi comedy" 107
Fields, Peter Allan 112
Fight Club (book) 121
Fight Club (film) 121
The Final *Countdown* 51
Fincher, David 121
Finney, Benjamin (character) 11–12
"first louie" 10
Fleming, Ian 144
Fontana, D.C. 28, 47, 48, 103–105
"foo fighter" 103
Foster, Alan Dean 50–51, 53
Founders (race) 109
Frakes, Jonathan 77
Francis, Anne Cranny 75
Frankenheimer, John 52
Franklin, H. Bruce 31–42
Freiberger, Fred 44
French resistance 93–98, 100–101
"Friday night death-slot" 44
"the frontier" 6, 65
The Fugitive (1960s series) 7, 43
Fukuyama, Francis 79, 82, 88, 113–114
Fuller, Bryan 125, 149–150
"future history" 154–160

Gagarin, Yuri 20
Galileo II (vessel) 25
Gallunin, Irina (character) 25–27
Garak (character) 99, 112–113
Genesis (planet) 13, 59–60, 87
Genesis Device 137
George and Gracie (characters) 64
Georgiou, Phillipa (character) 139, 141
Gerrold, David 47, 56
Gill, John (character) 14–15
glasnost 75–76, 87, 90, 156

Index

God 54–55, 65
"God" (character) 10, 64–66
"The God Thing" (script) 53–55
Gogol, General (character) 88
"Golden Age of Star Trek" 78, 118
"The Golden Age of Television" 7
Goldman, Akiva 152
Goldsmith, Jerry 56, 66
Goodman, David. A. 45–46
Gorbachev, Mikhail 75, 79, 87–88
Gorkon, Chancellor (character) 90
Gotham City 7
The Graduate 30
Great Barrier 64
"The Great Bird of the Galaxy" 66
Great Britain 7
Great Depression 15, 32–33, 72
"Great Leap Forward" 83
"Great Satan" 92, 135
Greeks (civilization) 23, 68
Green, Colonel Philip (character) 157–158
Greven, David 17
"Greys" 107
Guadalcanal 9–10
Guantanamo Bay 134
Guardian of Forever (character) 32, 35, 48
Gulliver's Travels 5
"gunboat diplomacy" 69
Gurley-Brown, Helen 29

Haight-Ashbury 25
Hamlet 18
Harrison, John (character) 138
Harsh Realm 123
Haviland, Aaron 79
HBO 122, 131, 146
Heaven 55
Hicks, Catherine 64
Hill, Barney 104
Hill, Betty 104
Hine, Robert. V. 66
"hippie" 21, 24–25
Hirogen (race) 100–101, 124
Hiroshima 103, 130
Hitler, Adolf 7, 90, 157
Holocaust 15, 18–20, 80, 127, 135
"holodeck episode" 52, 126
Homer 146
Horakova, Erin K. 18–19
Hornblower, Horatio (character) 58
Hudson, Captain Cal (character) 95, 97
Hugh of Borg (character) 153
Hugo, Victor 98
"Human Be-In" 34

Hunter, Jeffrey 5, 12
Huntington, Samuel 79
Hurley, Maurice 69, 74
"hyper power" 126

I Love Lucy 7
Icheb (character) 153
Ilia, Lieutenant (character) 51
Independence Day 80, 107
Indiana Jones (character) 60
Indiana Jones and the Temple of Doom 60
Invasion of the Body Snatchers (1978 movie) 53
iPad 158
"Iron Curtain" 30, 74, 76, 78, 85, 89
Iron Man (film) 144
Isaacs, Bruce 33
Isil 92, 140
It Came from Outer Space 107

James Bond (character) 88, 142, 147, 149
Janeway, Kathryn (character) 99–101, 106, 112, 116, 121–122, 124–125, 129, 132, 145
Jarok, Admiral (character) 76
Javert, Inspector (character) 98
Jem'Hadar (race) 102
Jendresen, Erik 146
Jetrel (character) 135
The Jetsons 156
Jewish 15, 18, 80, 92
JFK (film) 110
John Carter of Mars (book) 9
Johnson, Lyndon B. 31, 34–35, 71
Jones, Tommy Lee 107

Kahless (character) 1490
Kalomi, Leila (character) 27–28
Kang (character) 85
Karidian, Anton (character) 18–20
"katra" 60–61
Katrine (character) 101
Kaufman, Philip 53
Kazon (race) 125
Keeler, Edith (character) 32–34, 51, 104
Kelley, DeForest 57
Kelly, Elsa (character) 51
Kelly, Richard (character) 51
"Kelvinverse" 118, 142, 144, 147–148, 150, 152
Kennedy, John. F. 20, 30–31, 90; assassination 110
Kent, Clark (character) 144

Index

Keynesian economics 72
KGB 81, 89, 108
Khambatta, Persis 51
Khitomer Accords 90
Kimble, Dr. Richard (character) 7
King, Dr. Martin Luther, Jr. 20, 23, 34, 41
Kirk, James. T (character) 1, 3, 6, 9–20, 22–29, 32–40, 42–43, 46–53, 55, 57–65, 69, 73, 78, 82, 84–88, 90–91, 104–106, 112, 117–118, 136, 138–139, 141, 143–150
Klaa, Captain (character) 88
Klingon Ambassador (character) 13
Klingons (race) 8, 13, 35–36, 50, 53, 60, 62, 65, 74, 79–80, 82–92, 98, 102, 108, 117, 123, 125, 127, 138–142, 150
Kobayashi Maru 145
Kodos the Executioner (character) 18–20
Koenig, Walter 1
Kohms (people) 38, 40
Koloth (character) 85
Kor, Commander (character) 83
Koresh, David 113
Kosovo 113
Krall (character) 137, 141
Krauss, Lawrence. M. 105
Kremlin 89
Krenim Imperium (race) 114
Kruge, Commander (character) 13, 60, 87
Kubrickian 53
Kurtzman, Alex 136, 148–149, 152

La Forge, Geordi (character) 53, 76, 126
Lambourne, R.J. 107
Laren, Ensign Ro (character) 95, 97
Lawrence of Arabia 21
Lecter, Hannibal (character) 94
Lee, Stan 144
Leighton, Dr. Thomas (character) 18–20
Leiter, Brian 17
Lenore (character) 20
Lester, Dr. Janice (character) 43
Lewinsky, Monica 110
Leyton, Admiral (character) 109
Li, Nalas (character) 94
liberalism 21
Lichtenberg, Jacqueline 5
Lin, Justin 136, 143
"little green men" 107
Livingston, David 50, 53
Lloyd, Christopher 60
Lockheed Constellation 10
Locutus (character) 75, 77
Lokai (character) 41

Loki 41
"Lone Gunman" 110
The Long Chance (vessel) 52
Lorca, Gabriel (character) 141–142
Los Alamos 130
Los Angeles 106
Lost in Space (1960s series) 2, 7, 80
Loughery, David 65, 146
Lovecraftian 49, 124, 159
Lucas, George 56
Lucas, John Meredyth 14–15, 44
Luce, Henry 72
Lundeen, Jan 27

MacLachlan, Kyle 106
"make America great again" 72
Malcolm X 20, 41
"male gaze" 29
Man of Steel 147
The Manchurian Candidate 53
"manifest destiny" 34, 65–66, 69
Mankiewicz, Don. M. 11
Manson family murders 44
Maoism 74, 83
The Maquis (fictitious organization) 95, 97–101, 122, 127
The Maquis (real organization) 96, 99
Marcus, Admiral (character) 138–140, 148
Marritza, Aamin (character) 95
Mars 129, 159
Mars Attacks! 107
Martok, Chancellor (character) 140
Marxism 70, 72
"masterpiece society" 69
The Matrix 123
Marvel Cinematic Universe 144, 151
Maxwell, Benjamin (character) 138
Maycock, James 41
McCarthy, Joseph 52
McClintock, Deborah 52
McCoy, Dr. Leonard "Bones" (character) 6, 13, 22, 25, 32–33, 35–36, 38, 57–58, 60–61, 63, 69, 136, 142, 144
McFly, Marty (character) 156
McGivers, Marla (character) 16, 18
McGoohan, Patrick 43
McIntrye, Deborah 69
McQuarrie, Christopher 146
McVeigh, Timothy 113
Men Behaving Badly 32
Men in Black (film) 107
Mengele, Dr. Josef 94
Menosky, Joe 101
Merk, Lawrence 65–66

Index

Merry, Robert. W. 79
Meyer, Nicholas 13, 53, 57–59, 63–64, 83, 137, 145
The Middle East 10, 16, 92, 113, 136, 139
Millennium (TV series) 131
"Millennium Eve" 115, 129
Millennium Gate 129
Milton, John 18
Ministry of State Security 108
"Mirror Universe" 118, 141–142, 150, 160
Les Miserables 98
MK-Ultra 110
A Modern Utopia (book) 68
Monroe, Marilyn 110
Mooney, Darren 44, 115–116, 120, 123–124, 135
Moore, Ronald. D. 93–94, 99–100, 122
More, Sir Thomas 68
Mossad 19, 108
"Mothman" 104
Mudd, Harry (character) 53, 150
Munger, Sean 25
mutually assured destruction 156

Nagasaki 130
Na'khul (race) 101
Native American 99, 125
Nazism 14–20, 32, 34, 89, 93–98, 100–101, 127, 135
NBC (network) 2, 5–6, 43–44, 49
Nechayev, Admiral (character) 96
Neelix (character) 101
neoliberalism 59, 72, 80
Nero (character) 136–137, 148
Nerys, Kira (character) 93–96, 109
Neural (planet) 35
The Neutral Zone 25, 74, 85, 89–90
New Deal 72
New Hampshire 104
New Mexico 103, 130
New York City 130, 134
New York Times 131
Nichols, Nichelle 1, 23, 28, 44
Nietzsche, Friedrich 17
Nietzschian 17
Nimbus III (planet) 64, 66
Nimoy, Leonard 6, 12, 15, 18, 43, 50, 59, 62, 64, 136, 142, 146–147, 149
9/11 4, 80, 91, 110, 116–117, 130–134, 136–137, 139, 141–143, 147, 153, 160
Nixon (film) 110
Nixon, Richard 20, 41, 45, 79, 87, 110, 112
Nog (character) 103
Nolan, Christopher 144, 147

Nona (character) 35
North Vietnam 31, 34, 36–37, 40
"nuclear family" 7
Number One (character) 29
Number 6 (character) 7
Nuremberg 19

Obama, Barack 118
Obsidian Order (organization) 81, 108–109, 112
Ocampa (race) 99
"The Occupation" 93, 135
O'Connor, Mike 22–24, 30, 86
Odo (character) 103, 112
O'Donnell, Shannon 129
The Odyssey 146
Offenhouse, Ralph (character) 70–71
O'Herlihy, Michael 105
Old Testament 65
Oliver, Glen. C. 145
Omega IV (planet) 38, 40
Omicron Ceti III (planet) 27–28
Oosarian (race) 134
Operation Junction City 34
Operation Market Garden 34
Oppenheimer, Robert 130, 135
Orci, Roberto 136–137, 148
Organians (race) 84
Orlik, Peter. B. 87–88
The Outer Limits 2

Pakula, Alan. J. 52, 110
Palahniuk, Chuck 121
Pan Am 10
Pandora's Box 130
"Paradise Lost" 18
The Parallax View 52
Paramount 53, 56, 59, 67, 118, 120, 146
Paris, Tom (character) 99–100, 159
Parker, Sarah Jessica 107
Parmen (character) 24
Paxton, John Frederick (character) 157
Pearl Harbor 9, 50–51, 133
Peck, Ethan 151
Pentagon 130
perestroika 75, 90, 156
Pevney, Joseph 33
"phage" 124
Picard, Jean-Luc (character) 10, 13–14, 46, 67–71, 73–75, 77, 91, 95–97, 99, 110–112, 123, 125, 132–133, 137, 139, 145, 147, 152–153, 158–159
Pike, Christopher (character) 5, 12–13, 29, 138, 151–152

Index

Piller, Michael 73, 75–77, 110, 119–120, 122, 128
Pine, Chris 137, 149
Pinter, Harold 96
"Planet of the Titans" (script) 53
Planet Q (planet) 18, 20
Plato 23, 68
"post-atomic horror" 158
Povill, Jon 51
Praxis (planet) 89, 98
Predator (movie) 100
"Prime Directive" 38, 40, 58, 69, 86, 104–105
Pripyat 89
The Prisoner 7, 43; "Fall Out" 43
"Prophets" 94
Puritans 6

Q (character) 66, 73–74, 79, 125, 158
The Q (race) 10, 125
Quark (character) 73, 103
Quinto, Zachary 143, 149

Ransom, Captain (character) 138
Reagan, Ronald 8, 46, 55, 59, 67, 71–72, 75, 77, 79–80, 87, 112, 160
"Red Angel" (character) 151
Reliant, U.S.S. (vessel) 59
Remick, Commander (character) 13
Renoir, Jean 97
The Republic (book) 68
Republican 20
Riker, William (character) 77, 99, 145, 153, 157
Riley (character) 20
rock 'n' roll 8
Roddenberry, Gene 1–18, 20–24, 29, 34–36, 38, 40, 43, 45–47, 51, 53–58, 63–69, 72, 75, 80–81, 82, 86–88, 92, 96, 109–110, 115, 117–119, 122, 128, 133–134, 156
Roddenberry, Rod 49
"Roddenberry's Box" 67
The Rolling Stones 21
Rom (character) 103
Roman Empire 15, 85, 155
Romulans (race) 8, 15, 25, 65, 71, 74–76, 80–81, 83, 85–86, 91, 98–99, 102, 108–109, 112, 123, 127, 136, 142, 152–153, 159
Roosevelt, Franklin Delano 72
Roswell 103
Roswell High 106
Roswell incident 103–104, 106–107
Russell, Lynette 76–77

Sacred History (book) 68
The Saint 80
Sainte-Claire 101
Saldana, Zoe 148
Sandoval, Elias (character) 27
Sarek (character) 60–61, 150–151
Saru (character) 139
Satanism 40
Schneider, Paul 85
Scott, Montgomery "Scotty" (character), 1, 6, 17, 52, 69
"Second Dark Age of Star Trek" 136
Section-31 (organization) 81, 108–110, 112, 137, 151
Sela (character) 108
Serling, Rod 2, 7
Seven of Nine (character) 101, 125, 145, 153
Sevrin (character) 24–25
Sex and the Office 29
Sex and the Single Girl 29
Sha'ka'ree (planet) 64
Shakespeare, William 18–19, 67
Shallis, M. J. 107
Shatner, William 1, 12, 15, 18, 20, 43, 47, 64–66, 144, 146–147, 149
Shaw, Areel (character) 11
Shenzhou, U.S.S. (vessel) 139
Shinzon (character) 137
"shock and awe" 132
Shortland, M. 107
sightings 106
Sims, David 118
Singer, Bryan 144, 146
Singh, Khan Noonien 16–17, 20, 57–59, 111–112, 137–138, 141, 157
Sisko, Benjamin (character) 93, 95–99, 108, 112–113, 134, 138–139
Skylark (series) 9
"slash fiction" 151
Sloan, Luther (character) 81, 108–109
Sloane, Lily (character) 69, 71
Smith, E.E. 9
Smith, Will 107
The Smith family (characters) 7
Snyder, Zack 147
Sohl, Jerry 28
Soji (character) 159
Son'a (race) 111
Soong, Altan Inigo (character) 159
Soong, Arik (character) 11
Soong, Noonien (character) 159
The Sopranos 122, 131
South Park 32
South Vietnam 31, 36–37

191

Index

Soviet Union 7, 20, 34, 36–38, 40, 46, 51, 72, 75, 79, 81–83, 86–90, 108, 140, 156
"space race" 20
Sphere Builders (race) 132
Spock (character) 2–3, 6, 12, 14–19, 22, 25–28, 32–34, 35, 38, 46, 48, 50, 53, 55, 57, 59–61, 63–64, 66, 77–78, 85, 87, 89–90, 104–105, 108, 111, 117, 136, 142, 144–152
Sputnik 20
Spiner, Brent 152
Stalinism 86
Stangl, Franz 19
Star Trek (2009 film) 4, 117–118, 136–137, 142, 146–148, 152
Star Trek II: The Wrath of Khan 16, 18, 46, 56–59, 64, 77, 111, 137, 148
Star Trek III: The Search for Spock 13, 59–61, 86–88
Star Trek IV: The Voyage Home 3, 13, 61–64, 87, 133
Star Trek V: The Final Frontier 3, 10, 58, 64–66, 69, 88, 146
Star Trek VI: The Undiscovered Country 3, 13, 53, 63, 78–79, 82–83, 88–91, 127, 134, 143, 146–147
Star Trek: "The Academy Years" 145–146
Star Trek: *The Animated Series* 46–51, 53–54, 59; "The Ambergris Experiment" 48; "The Lorelai Signal" 53; "The Magicks of Megas-Tu" 49; "Yesteryear" 48
Star Trek: "The Beginning" 146
Star Trek: Beyond 4, 118, 136–137, 142–143, 149
Star Trek: Deep Space Nine 3, 13, 20, 74, 78, 80–82, 91–98, 100–104, 106–113, 115–117, 119–121, 123, 126–129, 133–134, 140–141, 145, 151, 160; "The Changing Face of Evil" 127; "The Darkness and the Light" 93; "The Die Is Cast" 109; "Dr. Bashir, I Presume?" 111–112; "Duet" 94; "For the Cause" 97; "For the Uniform" 98; "Homefront" 109, 134; "In the Pale Moonlight" 99, 108, 112–113; "Inquisition" 81, 108, 112; "Little Green Men" 103–104, 106–107; "The Maquis" 95, 97, 109; "Paradise Lost" 109, 134; "Second Skin" 109; "The Siege" 94; "Trials and Tribble-ations" 106; "What You Leave Behind" 102
Star Trek: Discovery 2, 4, 12–13, 84, 92, 117–118, 122, 128, 137, 139–142, 149–153, 158, 159–160; "If Memory Serves" 151; "New Eden" 158
Star Trek: Enterprise 3, 43, 45, 80, 92, 101, 115–117, 119–120, 124, 128, 130–137, 139, 143, 145–146, 151, 157, 159, 160; "Anomaly" 134; "Borderland" 111, 159; "The Council" 136; "Demons" 134, 157; "The Expanse" 116, 132–134; "Precious Cargo" 132; "Shockwave" 132; "Storm Front" 101; "Terra Prime" 134; "These Are the Voyages" 43
Star Trek: First Contact 4, 69, 71, 74–75, 115, 133, 155, 157
Star Trek: Generations 13
Star Trek: Insurrection 39, 98, 110–111, 138
Star Trek: Into Darkness 4, 118, 136–137, 139–140, 148–149
Star Trek: Lower Decks 153
Star Trek: The Motion Picture 3, 46, 49–61, 64–65, 84–85, 133
Star Trek: Nemesis 118, 137, 147, 152
Star Trek: The Next Generation 3–4, 10, 13, 24, 46, 50–53, 56–58, 66–80, 82, 85, 87–88, 90–92, 95, 97–98, 102, 108–109, 115, 117, 119–120, 123, 125–128, 132–133, 136, 138–140, 145, 150–151, 153, 158, 160; "The Battle" 13; "The Best of Both Worlds" 75–77, 127, 133; "The Child" 52; "Coming of Age" 13–14; "The Defector" 76, 91; "Deja-Q" 73; "The Drumhead" 138; "The Emissary" 74; "Encounter at Farpoint" 73; "The Enemy" 76, 91; "Heart of Glory" 74; "Hide and Q" 73; "The Mind's Eye" 53; "The Naked Now" 73; "The Naked Time" 73; "The Neutral Zone" 69–70, 74, 127; "Pre-emptive Strike" 95; "Q-Pid" 73; "Q-Who?" 74; "Redemption" 91, 108; "The Royale" 159; "Unification" 108–109, 136; "Where No One Has Gone Before" 73; "Who Watches the Watchers?" 77
Star Trek: The Original Series 1, 3–20, 22–28, 30–45, 47–55, 57–58, 60, 62, 65–69, 71, 73, 77–78, 80, 83, 85, 88, 92, 100, 103–106, 111, 115, 117, 121, 128, 132, 136–142, 146, 148, 150–151, 156–158, 160; "Amok Time" 60; "Assignment: Earth" 62; "Balance of Terror" 8, 85–86; "Bread and Circuses" 15; "The Cage" 1, 5–6, 12, 29, 31, 53, 151; "City on the Edge of Forever" 8, 32–35, 39, 48, 50–51, 62, 104; "The Conscience of

192

Index

the King" 18–20; "Court Martial" 11–12, 14; "Curtain, the Savage" 157; "Errand of Mercy" 8, 83, 86, 92; "Journey to Babel" 60; "Let That Be Your Last Battlefield" 23, 32, 41–43; "The Man Trap" 142; "The Menagerie" 12–13, 151; "Mirror, Mirror" 141; "The Omega Glory" 32, 38–40, 42, 138; "Patterns of Force" 14–16, 18–19, 38, 92, 100; "A Piece of the Action" 15; "Plato's Stepchildren" 22–25; "A Private Little War" 8, 32, 35–38; "The Return of the Archons" 27; "Space Seed" 16, 57, 69, 111, 138; "The Squire of Gothos" 53; "A Taste of Armageddon" 8; "This Side of Paradise" 27–28; "Tomorrow Is Yesterday" 53, 62, 103–106; "Turnabout Intruder" 43, 45; "The Way to Eden" 24–27; "Where No Man Has Gone Before" 6, 73
Star Trek: "Phase II" 46, 49–53, 56; "Are Unheard Melodies Sweet?" 53; "The Child" 51; "Deadlock" 52; "In Thy Image" 53; "Lord Bobby's Obsession" 53; "Practice in Waking" 52; "Tomorrow and the Stars" 50–51
Star Trek: Picard 4, 77, 96, 98, 118, 120, 122, 147, 152–153; "In Et Arcadia Ego Pt. 2" 153
Star Trek: Strange New Worlds 152
Star Trek: Voyager 3, 78, 82, 93, 96, 99–101, 106, 115–116, 119–129, 132–133, 136, 138, 145, 159; "Caretaker" 99, 121; "Death Wish" 125; "11:59" 128; "Equinox" 126, 138; "Endgame" 126, 128; "Extreme Risk" 127; "False Profits" 125; "Future's End" 106, 125, 128; "In the Flesh" 125; "Jetrel" 136; "The Killing Game" 100–101; "Message in a Bottle" 125; "One Small Step" 159; "The Q and the Grey" 125; "Relativity" 128; "Worst Case Scenario" 100; "Year of Hell" 116, 124–125
Star Wars (franchise) 56, 60, 118
Star Wars Episode III: Return of the Jedi 60
Star Wars Episode VII: The Force Awakens 118
Starfleet (organization) 4, 11, 13–14, 25, 30, 32, 38–39, 41, 52, 57, 59, 62, 64, 69, 73–74, 81–83, 85, 87–88, 90–91, 93, 95–96, 98–101, 104, 108, 110–112, 120, 124, 127, 134–135, 137–140, 145, 148, 150, 152, 155, 157
Starfleet Academy 53, 125, 145

Starfleet Command 96
Starfleet Headquarters 34, 63, 133
Stargazer, U.S.S. (vessel) 13
Starling, Henry (character) 106
Stasi 108
Stewart, Patrick 4, 67, 77, 118, 152
Stone, Commodore (character) 11–12
Stone, Oliver 110
Sturgeon, Theodore 6
Straczynski, J. Michael 146
Suder, Lon (character) 100
Suliban (race) 132
Sulu, Hikaru (character) 1, 6, 9, 52, 148
"Summer of Love '67" 25
Summers, Jaron 51
Superman (character) 144, 147
Superman (1978 film) 144
Superman Returns 144
Superman III 60
Sutra (character) 159
Swift, Jonathan 5
"Sword of Damocles" 7
Sybok (character) 64
Syria 10, 139

Takei, George 1, 9
Taliban 132
Talos IV (planet) 12
Tal'Shiar (organization) 81, 108–109, 112
Tarsus IV (planet) 19–20
Tarzan (character) 9
Taylor, Don 51
Taylor, Dr. Gillian (character) 64
Taylor, Jeri 119, 122, 124
Taylor, Michael 112
Tebok, Commander (character) 74
Temporal Cold War 101, 128, 132
"Terok Nor" 92, 95
Terran Empire 141, 160
Tet Offensive 35
Texas 9
Third Reich 17
The Thirteenth Floor 123
Thompson, Bradley 108
Thompson, Derek 55
Thorne, Wesley 53
Time (magazine) 72
The Time Machine 68
T'Kuvma (character) 139–141
Torres, B'Elanna (character) 99–101, 127
T'Pol (character) 145
Tracey, Ron (character) 38–40, 138
"Trekker" 45
"Trekkie" 45, 150

193

Index

Trelane (character) 10, 53
Trivers, Barry 18
Troi, Deanna (character) 4, 51, 126, 153
Trojan War 158
Truman, Harry. S. 130
The Truman Show 123
Trump, Donald 118, 139–140
Tucker, Trip (character) 132, 145
Tuvok (character) 99–101
24 (series) 116, 131, 134–135
The Twilight Zone (1950s series) 2, 7, 43
Twin Peaks 110
2001: A Space Odyssey 57
"Typhoid Mary" 25
Tyree (character) 35–36
Tzenkethi (race) 127

Ubermensch 17
UFO culture 53, 103–108, 110
Uhura, Nyota (character) 1, 6, 22–24, 28, 30, 148
Ukraine 89
United Federation of Planets 4, 8, 13–14, 18, 24–26, 41, 58, 62–63, 69, 71, 73–74, 76–77, 82, 86–91, 95–100, 102, 105, 108–109, 111–112, 115, 118, 120, 123, 127–128, 132, 138–140, 148, 150, 153, 155–157, 160
United Nations 7, 80, 158
United Paramount Network 120
United States 7, 31–32, 46, 59, 67, 75, 82, 86, 90, 104, 110, 126, 130, 159
United States Air Force 104–105
United States Army 103
United States Army Air Corps 9
Unsolved Mysteries 106
Utopia (book) 68
utopia 68, 86, 137

V2 rocket 34
Valjean, Jean (character) 98
Vedrine, Hubert 126
Vengeance, U.S.S. (vessel) 138
Veridian III (planet) 13
Vettel-Becker, Patricia 29
V'Ger 53, 55, 61
Viacom 152
Vidiians (race) 124
Vietnam War 2, 5, 8, 21, 30–42, 45, 71, 86–87, 136, 156, 160
"The Village" 7
Vina (character) 12
Voyager, U.S.S. (vessel) 99, 101, 121–129

Vulcan Science Academy 145
Vulcans (race) 2, 12, 17, 28, 48, 60–62, 65, 85, 104, 109, 123, 132, 136, 145, 147, 55

Wagner, Jon 27
"Wagon Train to the Stars" 1, 69, 128, 156
Waid, Mark 147
Wall Street crash 72
War of the Worlds (book) 107
"War on Terror" 80, 117, 132, 135–136
Watergate 45, 79, 87, 110, 112
Wayne, Bruce (character) 144
Weddle, David 108–109
Weisenthal, Simon 19–20
Weller, Peter 138, 148
Wells, H.G. 68, 107
Weyoun (character) 102
Whedon, Joss 143
The White House 20
Wilber, Carey 16
Winter, Ralph 146
Wilson, Edward. O. 62
Wilson, Rainn 150
Wilson, Woodrow 112
Wincelberg, Shimon 53
Wise, Robert 54, 65
Wolfe, Robert Hewitt 106
Wolski, Nathan 76–77
Worf (character) 74, 87–88
Worland, Rick 83
World Trade Center 130
World War I 157
World War II 4, 7–10, 14, 17, 20, 31–32, 34–35, 51, 72, 78, 89–91, 93–94, 100–104, 106, 111, 113–114, 127, 130, 156–157, 160
"World War III" 31, 69, 134, 146, 156–159

The X-Files 80, 106–108, 110, 131, 134
The X-Files: Fight the Future 107
Xindi (race) 132–136

Y2K bug 131
Yangs (people) 38–40
Yates, Kasidy (character) 97
Yorktown, U.S.S. (vessel) 63

Zabel, Bryce 146
Zamora, Lonnie 104
Zeon (planet) 15
Zerbe, Anthony 110
Zion 15